"Bion's contributions to psychoanalytic technique are complex, innovative, profound and deserve intense and repeated studies. His formulations represent the most radical paradigm shift in psychoanalysis"

—*James Grotstein*

Bion's Legacy in São Paulo

This collection illuminates the legacy of Wilfred R. Bion in Brazil, illustrating Bion's continued influence on the work of the São Paulo Psychoanalytic Society (SBPSP), how Bionian ideas are applied in contemporary psychoanalysis, and how current practice has evolved over time.

Evelise de Souza Marra and Cecil José Rezze bring together theoretical and clinical approaches to provide a thorough perspective on Bionian work in Brazil. The book includes chapters by senior analysts, well-respected teachers and analytic clinicians in contemporary Brazilian psychoanalysis, each of which explores a topic central to Bion's formulations. With discussion of key themes including turbulence, emotional experience, transference, caesura and mental pain, this book demonstrates how Wilfred R. Bion's thought has been developed, transformed and applied in Brazil since his visits there in the 1970s.

Bion's Legacy in São Paulo will be of great interest to psychoanalysts in practice and in training, particularly those looking to understand Bion's influence in more depth, and for anyone interested in the practice of psychoanalysis in Latin America.

Evelise de Souza Marra is a psychologist and couples and family therapist based in Brazil. A former teacher at Pontificia Universidade Católica, she is a training analyst at the Sociedade Brasileira de Psicanálise de São Paulo (SBPSP) and is a coordinator of their annual Bion Meeting.

Cecil José Rezze is former president and training analyst of the Sociedade Brasileira de Psicanálise de São Paulo (SBPSP), where he regularly presents at congresses, events and clinical and theoretical seminars. He is former Superintendent and Editor-in-Chief of *Revista Brasileira de Psicanálise* and was co-chair of the SBPSP's annual Bion Meeting from 2008 to 2021. His work has been widely published.

The Routledge Wilfred R. Bion Studies Book Series
Series Editor
Howard B. Levine, MD

Editorial Advisory Board
Nicola Abel-Hirsch, Joseph Aguayo, Avner Bergstein, Lawrence J. Brown, Judith Eekhoff, Claudio Laks Eizerik, Robert D. Hinshelwood, Chris Mawson, James Ogilvie, Elias M. da Rocha Barros, Jani Santamaria, Rudi Vermote

The contributions of Wilfred Bion are among the most cited in the analytic literature. Their appeal lies not only in their content and explanatory value, but in their generative potential. Although Bion's training and many of his clinical instincts were deeply rooted in the classical tradition of Melanie Klein, his ideas have a potentially universal appeal. Rather than emphasizing a particular psychic content (e.g., Oedipal conflicts in need of resolution; splits that needed to be healed; preconceived transferences that must be allowed to form and flourish, etc.), he tried to help open and prepare the mind of the analyst (without memory, desire or theoretical preconception) for the encounter with the patient.

Bion's formulations of group mentality and the psychotic and non-psychotic portions of the mind, his theory of thinking and emphasis on facing and articulating the truth of one's existence so that one might truly learn first hand from one's own experience, his description of psychic development (alpha function and container/contained) and his exploration of **O** are "non-denominational" concepts that defy relegation to a particular school or orientation of psychoanalysis. Consequently, his ideas have taken root in many places…. and those ideas continue to inform many different branches of psychoanalytic inquiry and interest.[1]

It is with this heritage and its promise for the future developments of psychoanalysis in mind that we present *The Routledge Wilfred Bion Studies Book Series*. This series gathers together under newly emerging and continually evolving contributions to psychoanalytic thinking that rest upon Bion's foundational texts and explore and extend the implications of his thought. For a full list of titles in the series, please visit the Routledge website at: https://www.routledge.com/The-Routledge-Wilfred-Bion-Studies-Book-Series/book-series/RWBSBS

Howard B. Levine, MD
Series Editor

---

[1] Levine, H.B. and Civitarese, G. (2016). Editors' Preface, *The W.R. Bion Tradition*, Levine and Civitarese, eds., London: Karnac 2016, p. xxi.

Bion's Legacy in São Paulo

Theoretical Applications from the São Paulo Psychoanalytic Society (SBPSP)

Edited by
Evelise de Souza Marra and
Cecil José Rezze

Translated by Carlos Malferrari

LONDON AND NEW YORK

Cover image: Pierell, Getty images

First published in English 2022
by Routledge
4 Park Square, Milton Park, Abingdon, Oxon OX14 4RN

and by Routledge
605 Third Avenue, New York, NY 10158

Routledge is an imprint of the Taylor & Francis Group, an informa business

© 2022 selection and editorial matter, Evelise de Souza Marra and Cecil José Rezze; individual chapters, the contributors

The right of Evelise de Souza Marra and Cecil José Rezze to be identified as the authors of the editorial material, and of the authors for their individual chapters, has been asserted in accordance with sections 77 and 78 of the Copyright, Designs and Patents Act 1988.

All rights reserved. No part of this book may be reprinted or reproduced or utilised in any form or by any electronic, mechanical, or other means, now known or hereafter invented, including photocopying and recording, or in any information storage or retrieval system, without permission in writing from the publishers.

Trademark notice: Product or corporate names may be trademarks or registered trademarks, and are used only for identification and explanation without intent to infringe.

Published in Portuguese by Editora Edgard Blucher Ltda, 2020

British Library Cataloguing in Publication Data
A catalogue record for this book is available from the British Library

Library of Congress Cataloging-in-Publication Data
Names: Marra, Evelise de Souza, editor. | Rezze, Cecil José, editor.
Title: Bion's legacy in São Paulo : theoretical applications from the São Paulo Psychoanalytic Society (SBPSP) / edited by Evelise de Souza Marra and Cecil José Rezze ; translated by Carlos Malferrari (except chapter 6, 12, 14, 17).
Description: Abingdon, Oxon ; New York, NY : Routledge, 2022. | Series: The Routledge Wilfred R. Bion studies book series | Includes bibliographical references and index. |
Summary: "This collection illuminates the legacy of Wilfred R. Bion in Brazil, illustrating Bion's continued influence on the work of the São Paulo Psychoanalytic Society (SBPSP), how Bionian ideas are applied in contemporary psychoanalysis, and how current practice has evolved over time. Bion's Legacy in São Paulo will be of great interest to psychoanalysts in practice and in training, particularly those looking to understand Bion's influence in more depth, and for anyone interested in the practice of psychoanalysis in Latin America"-- Provided by publisher.
Identifiers: LCCN 2021041980 (print) | LCCN 2021041981 (ebook) | ISBN 9780367774752 (hardback) | ISBN 9780367774745 (paperback) | ISBN 9781003171584 (ebook)
Subjects: LCSH: Bion, Wilfred R. (Wilfred Ruprecht), 1897-1979. | Sociedade Brasileira de Psicanálise de São Paulo. | Psychoanalysis--Brazil.
Classification: LCC BF109.B54 B56 2022 (print) | LCC BF109.B54 (ebook) | DDC 150.19/5098161--dc23
LC record available at https://lccn.loc.gov/2021041980
LC ebook record available at https://lccn.loc.gov/2021041981

ISBN: 978-0-367-77475-2 (hbk)
ISBN: 978-0-367-77474-5 (pbk)
ISBN: 978-1-003-17158-4 (ebk)

DOI: 10.4324/9781003171584

Typeset in Times New Roman
by Taylor & Francis Books

Contents

List of figures	ix
Introduction	x
Preface to the first edition	xii
Preface to the second edition	xvi
Acknowledgments	xvii

1 From learning from emotional experience to wild thoughts: Turbulence!   1
CECIL JOSÉ REZZE

2 Me and the other in the analysis room   14
ANTONIO CARLOS EVA

3 Contributions of Bion's thought to the theory and techniques of contemporary psychoanalysis   17
ALICIA BEATRIZ DORADO DE LISONDO

4 α-function: Catastrophic anxiety – panic – container with reverie   27
ANTONIO SAPIENZA

5 Learning from emotional experience and the Grid: Theory and practice   33
CECIL JOSÉ REZZE

6 Emotion, non-emotion and analyst language   46
CELIA FIX KORBIVCHER

7 Clinical use of myths in psychoanalysis: Myth, psychoanalysis and psychic reality   56
CELSO ANTONIO VIEIRA DE CAMARGO

8	Issues related to "cure," "improvement," "normality" and "abnormality": Psychoanalysis and psychotherapies CLAUDIO CASTELO FILHO	70
9	α-function ↔ psychoanalysis: An investigation process (on the *quality of presence* in analytical session models) CÍCERO JOSÉ CAMPOS BRASILIANO	84
10	Transference–transformations EVELISE DE SOUZA MARRA	91
11	Complementarity and clinical practice ISAIAS KIRSCHBAUM	96
12	Empowered by failure – vicissitudes of *Transformations* JOÃO CARLOS BRAGA	103
13	Interpretation: Limits and ruptures of a concept and a practice JÚLIO FROCHTENGARTEN	112
14	The "squabble" (*prise de bec*) between Beckett and Bion: The "experimental" insight in the glaring darkness LUIZ CARLOS U. JUNQUEIRA FILHO	121
15	Caesura and mental pain LUIZ TENÓRIO OLIVEIRA LIMA	135
16	Apprehending psychoanalysis with Bion ODILON DE MELLO FRANCO FILHO	139
17	Extensions into the realm of minus PAULO CESAR SANDLER	144
18	From transference and countertransference to emotional experience in *Transformations* STELA MARIS GARCIA LOUREIRO	171
	Appendix: The Grid	182
	Index	183

Figures

3.1 The place of the real external object in the construction of the psyche 19
9.1 *Auto-Falante* (2007) 86
A.1 The Grid 182

Introduction

Wilfred R. Bion (1897–1979) is certainly one of the most important psychoanalysts of the twentieth century, especially for his creativity. He revolutionized how we conceive of psychoanalysis both in theory and in clinical practice, offering new approach after new approach to psychoanalysts, beginning with the book *Learning from Experience* (1962) and up to *Trilogy*,[1] the final work of his life.

Bion was in São Paulo, Brazil, for conferences and clinical seminars in 1973, 1974 and 1978. His vigorous presence left a deep impression on everyone, leading to endless transformations and offshoots. To crystallize and consolidate these influences, an international meeting – "Bion 2004" – was held in the premises of Santa Cruz School, providing an opportunity to establish profound and emotional connections with psychoanalysts from around the world interested in Bion's work.

Four years later, in 2008, the Brazilian Society of Psychoanalysis of São Paulo (SBPSP), under the coordination of Evelise de Souza Marra and collaborators, organized a weekend symposium focused on the contributions of psychoanalysts from São Paulo. The encounter was a unique opportunity to appreciate and discuss a broad range of papers, and relied on stimulus-driven presentations, a methodology we have been refining and improving since the "Bion 2004" São Paulo conference. Given the high quality of the papers, we proposed they be compiled in a publication, which you now hold in your hands. The articles address a new conception of thought and thinking, which is the result of emotional life. Forms of thought and thinking that simulate symbolic or representative activity are presented here in line with these psychoanalytical insights, and the various studies of these forms are essential tools for understanding and providing clinical treatment for modes of suffering that mask themselves as rational and objective activities.

We cannot recommend strongly enough this compendium for every psychoanalyst and psychotherapist, as well as for those who, in their work and in their lives, deal with people. The volume opens with a lecture by Cecil José Rezze, followed by a stimulus on psychoanalytic clinical practice by Antonio Carlos Eva, which were worked through by small groups during that encounter. Theoretical-clinical essays follow, as offshoots and repercussions of Bion's work here in São Paulo. In short, this is an extremely useful compilation to fathom the Bionian vertex in understanding the human mind.

This publication, thus, is one of the results of Bion's influence among us since 1973–74, one of the many offshoots and transformations that the group of psychoanalysts of São Paulo has been producing and now presents to the public.

Antonio Carlos Eva

Note

1 As is well known, towards the end of his life, Bion brought together three of his books – *The Dream, The Past Presented* and *The Dawn of Oblivion* – into a trilogy, which he named *A Memoir of the Future*.

Preface to the first edition

In April 1973, Wilfred Bion, at the invitation of Frank Philips and Laertes Moura Ferrão, made his first visit to the Brazilian Society of Psychoanalysis of São Paulo (SBPSP). It is a common practice for us to invite visitors who, time and again, have galvanized local societies. This specific visitor, however, with his striking originality and unsaturated communicability, who employed a language that was more poetic than conceptual, led many psychoanalysts to lose sleep. He returned in 1974 and 1978, shoring up the *turbulence* he had incited, unsettling and astonishing us, rousing our enchantment and curiosity. Bion was also in Rio de Janeiro and Brasília on other occasions.

This *turbulence*, experienced intrapsychically at first by those who had the privilege of being there at the time, would be reflected in the life of the Society in various ways over the following years.

Formally, Bion's seminars had been part of our training curriculum since 1972, alongside those of Freud and Melanie Klein.

This gave rise to several study groups, ranging from the mandatory seminars of the official syllabus to independent working groups within the program. These groups are generally long-lasting and have offshoots in universities and research centers outside the Society, a movement that can also be seen in other societies (Rio de Janeiro, Porto Alegre, Brasília), albeit less intensely.

Consequently, in 1996, that is, more than twenty years after the first contacts, the SBPSP held the symposium "Bion in São Paulo – Resonances," organized by Leopold Nosek, Luiz Carlos Junqueira Filho and Maria Olympia Ferreira França, with the presence of several foreign guests, including Parthenope Bion. Maria Olympia was also the editor of the eponymous publication.

In 1999, in preparation for the 2000 international conference in Buenos Aires, we organized the cycle of lectures "São Paulo Seminars: Transformations–Invariances," also published by organizers Maria Olympia Ferreira França, Magaly da Costa Ignácio Thomé and Marta Petricciani.

Paulo Sandler, who took active part in all the international seminars, organized the preparatory discussions, and, in 2004, we held in São Paulo the "Bion 2004" international conference, widely attended by Brazilian psychoanalysts.

In the life of the Society, turbulence had become unremitting, sometimes painfully so, at the relational level. In psychoanalysis, theory, method and personality form an indissoluble precipitate, with far-reaching consequences for the institutional wedlock. I also think that differences in practice and in action preceded the possibility of a more elaborate theorization, at least in my experience. In other words, theories, although underlying the practice, take much longer to be thought out, conceptualized and related.

At a certain point, the "differences" in our practices, albeit foggily perceived, were named by means of antithetical pairings: *real psychoanalysis* (focused on the actuality of the experience) × *classical psychoanalysis* (identifying unconscious structures); or, at other times, *unrooted psychoanalysis* (focused on the immediacy of the experience) × *rooted psychoanalysis* (grounded on the organizational strength of histories); or even *intuitive psychoanalysis* × *theory-based psychoanalysis*; and so forth. In an institution, polarizations easily acquire the connotation of superiority–inferiority, novel–outmoded, evolved–retrograde – in short, resonances that are more value-driven than descriptive and which, despite their speciousness, generate much confusion and misunderstanding.

In this book, we present some developments of our contact with, and *transformations* of, Bion's studies. These include ideas and issues with which we have been involved and that I deem to be a kind of snapshot or scientific X-ray of the SBPSP. Unfortunately, we could not do justice to all the colleagues who had important contributions to make, and that is why I call this publication a snapshot. Nevertheless, what is presented here is undoubtedly the result of their conviviality and participation: of the aficionados and the critics, the devotees and the unbelievers, the ones who speak out and those that remain silent. These are our transformations and offshoots of an enduring contact that has a lot of work and much *turbulence* as a backdrop.

Today, almost forty years later, issues that were presented stepwise in a partial and disorganized manner are beginning to be identified and can be theoretically thought out by us. Thus, we have moved from intrapsychic and relational turbulence to the identification of *turbulence in theories*, the overriding theme we have chosen and which Dr. Cecil Rezze addresses in the initial conference. Antonio Carlos Eva establishes a counterpart in clinical practice by addressing, in almost colloquial language, the foundations of the psychoanalytic encounter. These are two comprehensive texts with regard to theory and quite condensed in their expression. Theoretical-clinical *turbulence* is something we have long considered on the basis of frameworks laid down by Freud, Klein and Bion.

The other essays are personal portrayals that evolved from the experience, interest and style of each author. We have approaches that are more clinical, as well as more theoretical ones, shorter and more inquisitive essays that provoke discussion, others more expository, but all of them by practicing psychoanalysts highly familiar with Bion's work.

Psychoanalysis is a discipline exercised basically through words, even as it acknowledges how limited they are to express what goes on both in the inward emotional experiences of the individual and with someone other than him- or herself.

Verbal language is also the main asset in the communication among psychoanalysts in the pursuit of scientific development.

Still, how can one express the unspeakable, the ineffable, that which is always in transit and originates from private, particular life experiences?

Psychoanalysts are forever immersed in the clinic–theory polarization, that is, they study theories (abstract systems) that will be brought to bear on clinical events (concrete experiences). We have some very sophisticated theories – projective identification, Oedipus and its correlates, transference, countertransference, transformations, recommendations regarding the setting … And then an analysand that comes in and greets you – "How ya doin'? Did you cut your hair?" – and begins to talk (or not) about what emerges in the encounter.

Thus, a "language of success" is necessary, namely, a language of "achievement" to express the "psychoanalytic facts." For Bion, the language of achievement includes the language that is not only a prelude to action, but an action in itself, of which the analytical encounter is an example.

We attend a proliferation of congresses, symposia, conferences, seminars, endless publications, but what is really useful to us? What is there that not only informs, but also nurtures, develops, instructs? How can we learn from these experiences? What is essential and invariant, and what is peripheral and incidental?

In addition to the difficulties in conveying our ideas, achievements or clinical experiences, we also run into ethical issues. How to lay bare to colleagues, or in publications, the intimacy of our clinical practice and, thus, of ourselves?

We have been striving to create forms of encounter that minimize such difficulties. For instance, we have worked with small expository units and, in the groups, we have fostered conversation and discussion among participants in a state of symmetry, aiming for an encounter conducive to "learning from experience." This was the form employed in the encounter of which this publication is the offshoot.

I wish to thank Maria Olympia Ferreira França, Plínio Montagna and Luis Carlos Menezes, who, each in their own time and from their own place, provided the conditions for the encounter to occur. Particularly, I also wish to thank, in my own name and in that of the organizing committee, all those who participated by responding to our individual invitation, and, from their own place and experience, contributed to this unending journey which we all undertake as we strive to practice psychoanalysis and, even more, to *become* psychoanalysts.

With regard to this publication, I wish to thank my colleagues Célia Maria Blini de Lima for her support and Marta Petricciani for her encouragement and also for her extremely efficient and dedicated work in the organization. We are especially grateful to the Casa do Psicólogo for its prompt receptivity.

And we are grateful to the Brazilian Society of Psychoanalysis of São Paulo, with its scientific and administrative structure, for providing the conditions for our achievements.

We pursue a discipline of which, no matter how hard we strive, we only scratch the surface. We are fully aware of that. Perhaps therein lays the need for interlocution. I hope that the reader will benefit from this offshoot-publication to the same extent that we, participants in the encounter, have.

Evelise de Souza Marra
November 30, 2008

Preface to the second edition

Twelve years after the first edition that launched the "Psychoanalysis: Bion" seminars, now held annually at the Brazilian Society of Psychoanalysis of São Paulo (SBPSP), we wish to celebrate and thank everyone who has participated in these working groups. Over the evolution of all these years, we have overseen four other publications: *Psychoanalysis: Bion – Clinical Practice ↔ Theory; Ultimately, What Is Emotional Experience in Psychoanalysis?; Bion: Transference, Transformations, Aesthetic Encounter*; and *Bion: The Tenth Face: New Offshoots*.[1]

Our inquiries have expanded, likewise, the interest in and passion for the open work of Wilfred R. Bion. We wish to thank everyone who has sustained the interest in, and reflection on, what we have proposed, namely, studying and combining our theories and our clinical practice. We are especially grateful to the various boards of the SBPSP that have given full support and provided the physical and administrative structure to make all this happen.

The articles remain current and relevant, and the issues they raise are still ongoing. Thus, we hope readers will benefit from what we have published here in their (and our) constant exercise of becoming psychoanalysts.

Evelise de Souza Marra

Note

1 Original Portuguese titles: *Psicanálise: Bion clínica ↔ teoria; Afinal o que é experiência emocional em psicanálise?; Bion: transferência, transformações, encontro estético*; and *Bion: a décima face: novos desdobramentos*.

Acknowledgments

We are indebted to many people for making this book's gestation possible and we are grateful to them all, but we feel the need to thank some of them in particular.

First, the authors who contributed their precious articles and made themselves available to meet our requests during this journey.

Carlos Malferrari, who not only did the translation but committed himself with his vast knowledge of editorial criteria.

Routledge have enabled us to disseminate in English the work we have been developing in São Paulo, offering us the opportunity to share with Bion scholars part of what we have produced in recent years.

Howard Levine, who accepted our contributions, made a judicious examination of what we presented to him, giving precious time, attention and guidance to improving the texts, thus allowing us to be part of the valuable collection the Routledge Wilfred R. Bion Studies Book Series.

Cecil José Rezze and Evelise de Souza Marra

Chapter 1

From learning from emotional experience to wild thoughts

Turbulence!

Cecil José Rezze

Is the impact of psychoanalytic ideas on our minds negligible?

Bion offers us a new model to identify the experiences of the psyche:

> It includes, besides the *sensorial* and *knowing* dimensions (already present in the models of Freud and Klein), the acknowledgement of the *hallucinatory* dimensions, of *being* or *becoming* reality ("O"), and of thoughts with autonomous existence beyond the worlds of things and ideas (thoughts without a thinker).
>
> (Braga, 2003)

I think it is instructive to contemplate a switchover from a psychoanalysis that uses the structural model to a psychoanalysis that uses the multidimensional model; however, do we realize how much disturbance this determines in our mind? Do we, in the name of the progress of our ideas, realize the disruptive power of the ideas we are trying to develop? Have we assessed the requisite reaction of our personal mental establishment to this impact?

Turbulence!

My goal, over the course of this chapter, is to attempt to track the evolution of certain emerging concepts and appraise the turbulence this may cause in an inquiring analyst. The subheadings that follow are self-explanatory.

1. Throwing light on some concepts associated with emotional experience.
2. Transition from the concept of learning from emotional experience to the concept of transformations.
3. Beyond transformations.

1. Throwing light on some concepts associated with emotional experience

Elements from a session

The door is ajar.

The patient knocks and asks, "May I come in?"

DOI: 10.4324/9781003171584-1

I introduce myself and say, "Yes."
He walks in and asks, "Should I lock the door with the key?"
I reply that I usually do it.
He places his jacket on the hanger.
And lies down.
He remains silent for a few moments.

> I was out of town Monday and Tuesday. My intention was to come, but there is somewhat of a commotion going on at work. I wanted to come, but opportunities are emerging in several areas and I'm the only one that can provide assistance and follow up; for now, there is no one else. You [formal *o senhor*] ... you [informal *você*] ... know how much I value our work, because it has helped me a lot. But I foresee that at this moment it will be difficult for me to continue to come here. I even told my wife I might stop for a while and, when all this is over, I would later return. She said, "Absolutely not. No way you're leaving analysis. You go whenever you can, change your schedule when possible, but you are not leaving analysis."

He seems brisk and lively, and gives a peremptory tone to his wife's words.
I chuckle and he laughs, uneasily. I observe in passing that his wife had resorted to authority. (I did not refer to the wife per se, but to what she said, to the intonation he had given to her words.)
He interjects, "Well, yes, but she was endearing all the same ..."
He does not seem to accept a different possibility. (It seemed to me that he was addressing me directly, seeking to clarify the situation and justify his absence.)
I say something that went roughly like this: "I have the impression that you are messing with me about us working together. You even thought about interrupting our work. Yet things seem to remain outside yourself, whether it's your work or your wife setting the tone of the decisions you mentioned. It seems that you accord her great authority."

> Cecil, you know how highly I value our work. I'm getting a lot out of it, you know I enjoy it. Look, I have been going to a lot of doctors. That problem with that leg pain, they are now raising the possibility that it is a hernia. So, we're going to have to do some tests. [He emphasizes that this is something troublesome and painful.] I come here because I like it. [He seems to contrast this with his dislike of going to the doctors.] I can talk to you and let off steam, as I'm doing right now. This has been very good for me. [He seems to be trying to convince me of these facts by using an emphatic tone.] New situations are coming up at work now that are disorganizing me in what I was more or less settled in. But it's something favorable, it's not bad at all! I'm having other opportunities. But I'm the only one that can coordinate all of this; I'm needed. [He uses a very convincing tone as he tells me all this.]

As he is very near me now, I decide to try to formulate something out and see how receives it:

> Have you ever thought that it could be the other way around? It is you who are feeling agitated inside. It is you who take upon yourself what comes up in these intense and varied situations and thrust yourself upon them. Thus, the world sees a situation that complies with your needs. When this happens, you have the chance to be creative, participant, active. When this is missing, you are in trouble. So, the analysis and myself remain in the space that is left for us, the space that is possible. Perhaps the same happens with other relationships as well.

Emotional experience

From the very onset of the encounter, the client, with the questions "May I come in?" and "Should I lock the door with the key?" finds a very active way of establishing contact with the analyst. It continues with his explanations for his absence, and the analyst has the impression that the client might put an end to analysis even before actually stating it.

The client underscores the importance of his work and of his person, and emphasizes likewise the value of the analysis. The situation is very difficult to describe, because he makes it clear that our work has been beneficial to him, but the impression I have is that he *bestows* value. This pervades our work, but does not seem evident from the notes I took earlier.

The continuation of analysis is ascribed to his wife's interference in such an emphatic manner that I cannot but laugh. He is grievously surprised, bringing to light another of his singularities. He gives the impression of decidedly moving in one direction, but a mere unexpected fact or unforeseen word seems enough to take him down.

He quickly recovers and notes that his wife's response was affectionate. The impression I have is that his surprise vanished and everything is now back on track. The client seems to be singing the same tune, to which he adds the various elements that might destabilize him. So if he stumbles with a formal "you" [*o senhor*], he immediately follows it with an informal "you" [*você*] or, soon after, with a friendly "Cecil," apparently to reestablish strong intimacy.

As the session progressed, I felt it was the right time to make some comments that might touch upon a different aspect of his mental life. I said, for instance, that his wife could be responsible for his own actions. The observation did not aim to clarify domestic or personal problems, but rather to point out the pattern of a dimension unknown to himself. We thus went back to the problems of communicating one's lived experience.

I will not elaborate further, but I believe that many uncertainties and doubts that pervade my work are illustrated here. I believe that our emotional experience is accessible, but so far I have doubts whether this client is capable of learning from it.

Theorizing the concept of emotional experience

Emotional experience is something that occurs and is considered in poetry, prose, tragedy, cinema – in short, in life. The general connotation of the term "emotional experience" is obvious in human life, and thus seems to me of little use. What makes the term worthwhile is learning from experience, i.e., the use of the alpha-function. This is specific to Bion's conceptualizations[1] (1962/2014, pp. 274, 276).

Many authors do not adopt the concept of learning from emotional experience. Even though they use the expression "emotional experience," they exclude what would be rows A (beta-elements) and B (alpha-elements) of the Grid, and only take into account that which has psychic quality, that is, from row C downwards (dreams, myths, dream thoughts). I have learned to consider emotional experience as including any manifestation in a relationship, that is to say, a broader field.

In Bion's later works, we see the obscuration of the concept of learning, which, in my view, is amply developed through its assimilation, giving rise to new conceptualizations. Our attention is drawn to the complement of the title of the book *Transformations*: "Change from learning to growth."

Let us strive to examine these concepts.

The first step occurs when the knowledge link emerges, intimately connected with learning from emotional experience. This becomes clear when the knowledge link establishes partnership with the love and hate links, the basic human emotions. One may review which conditions are required for their development, among which one finds *reverie*. Therefore, knowledge, thus considered, is an emotional link.

We can use the viewpoint of learning from emotional experience to investigate our clinical example. If we consider the alpha-function, we find that the client's formulations denote great complexity, indicating they are used in familial, social, work and psychoanalytic relationships, among others.

Even assuming that the client does not learn from the ongoing emotional experience during the session, the fact remains that he is capable of developing the knowledge link. However, given the use he makes of it ("May I come in?"; "Should I lock the door with the key?"; "[My wife] said"; "at work"), we must conclude that he operates under the fantasy of expelling parts of his own self. The acquired knowledge is used to deny deep anxieties that would otherwise arise. We may consider −knowledge (i.e., less knowledge or −K) as the predominant element due to the reversal of knowledge. We are talking about column 2 in the Grid.

The more I examine my work, the more I am inclined to believe that this client tends to *not* learn from emotional experience in analysis, given that, the more he speaks, the more he tries to keep the system he uses unchanged, rather than to allow changes.

Turbulence!

Let us now attempt to examine the factors that unleash turbulence.

Bion's works introduced the possibility of psychoanalytic investigation through disorders of thinking, hence the importance of the Grid as an instrument to develop the concept of knowledge, i.e., the grid in knowledge (ideas).

With the introduction of the concept of learning from emotional experience (through the alpha-function, which transforms beta-elements into alpha-elements, and from there onward to myths, dream thoughts and dreams), we created the possibility of investigating the transition from sense impressions to the psychic quality of the mind.

Knowledge, in turn, introduces something that was already in Freud's conception: the ability to go from the unconscious to the conscious (the area of neurosis). However, through the study of psychotic situations, knowledge expands the area of investigation from the finite to the infinite.

These developments also suggest that the analyst's stance will go beyond transference–countertransference. This becomes particularly clear when the alpha-function fails and the analyst must face not only the conscious–unconscious, but above all the unknown.

2. Transition from the concept of learning from emotional experience to the concept of transformations

I will begin with the concept of invariance because, as I see it, the concept of transformations has several applications in clinical practice, whereas the concept of invariance is not considered intrinsic to transformations and often remains in obscurity.

To advance my propositions, we should restrict ourselves to the elements that were highlighted in the analytical experience described above.

Let us consider the first, longest paragraph. The patient had missed the two previous sessions and is apparently addressing this issue with the analyst. He mentions something very important, the possibility of interrupting the analysis. It is worth noting that I had indeed sensed that something of this sort was going to happen even before he made the observation. Yet he introduces a narrative of the events that had taken place with his wife, and this comes to life in the session. I even chuckle, while he laughs intensely and awkwardly.

I propose an examination using transformation and invariance as instruments. Clearly, a profound experience has undergone transformation by means of the client's manifestation.

With the first words he uttered, it is already possible to conceive a model within which he operates. What belongs to his mental, spiritual and psychic world transforms itself in such a way that he experiences it in various beings – which are, initially, the vicissitudes of work, his wife and, later, the analyst.

The narrational invariant (perceiving outside of himself and believing that therein lies the cause of what happens to him) gives rise to something more sophisticated, to wit, the theory of projective identification, which leads us to conceptualize that the ongoing transformations are those that we can group as projective transformations.

Quite possibly, the reader would not have chosen the paths I have followed here, and others would be his or her paths. So, we have here an invariant: the author of this chapter (which can be partially explored by means of the written article itself).

Possibilities for reassessing clinical material – transformations

Employing the same clinical material, we may reflect on what options we would have if we took transformations as our point of reference.

1) The first possibility is to consider the transference theory (Freud, 1920/1975, p. 12)[2] as a mode of rigid motion of transformations (Bion, 1965/2014, p. 143). So, let us take some elements – "May I come in?"; "Should I lock the door with the key?"; "You [formal *o senhor*] … you [informal *você*] … Cecil"; "Because it has helped me a lot" – that allude to an authority to which he subjugates himself, but against which he also rebels: "I might stop for a while." The experience with the analyst may be interpreted as a relationship that hints at his submissive love for, and his hatred towards, the paternal imago. Great importance is assigned to what his wife says, and we may conjecture the formation of parental imagoes in the authoritarian image of the mother, which is linked to that of the father, to which he must submit. I believe we have here a triangular situation in which parental protection both includes and excludes him. We may even find here a fragment of Oedipus complex.

It is clear, from this viewpoint, that we are witnessing "a model of movement of feelings and ideas from one sphere of applicability to another" (Bion, 1965/2014, p. 143), that is, we are verifying how unconscious conflicts manifest themselves consciously.

2) Projective transformations may be considered through the invariant template by which *one perceives outside of oneself and believes that therein is the cause of what happens to oneself.* We have discussed this before, emphasizing the use of projective identification as an invariant.

3) Let us examine transformations in hallucinosis (Bion, 1965/2014, p. 245). We can see that the client's personality is conserved and that he is capable of developing knowledge, so let us see what this unleashes in the session's emotional experience.

The analyst attempts to acquire knowledge from the events of the session through an overall impression, which may be populated by particular elements and which is impactful from the very beginning because the client *builds a place for, and the character (i.e., the personage) of, the analyst*. The focus on his own work, the possibility of not coming anymore and the wife's insistence, for example, will form an independent environment, with beings that now inhabit the room. Thus, he who was once a formal "you" and then an informal "you" becomes an intimate "Cecil." These elements, together with his mentions of "I'm getting a lot out of our work" and "You know I enjoy our work," are gradually *bestowed* on the analyst.

This builds up an emotional climate in which he somehow slithers through the analyst's observations, as a kind of fused experience between them, creating a state that the client himself produces. The emotional experience reveals an agglomeration or encompassment of the analyst – who, however, is actually left out, even as he is gradually built up as the client produces his presence. Experience shows the scale of the exclusion from the situation unfolding in the session; everything is done by the client, he is sufficient unto himself.

To this description, we would ascribe the mechanism of projective identification, in the sense of an evacuation. Given the nature of the analyst's exclusion, we might think of the invariants of rivalry or envy and of the naivety that pervade transformations in hallucinosis (Bion, 1965/2014, p. 245).

We have surmised three possible transformations, describing the knowledge that would be drawn from each of them, taking into account which vertex is used. In short, a vertex is an invariant and will differ depending on the transformations. In rigid motion transformations with regard to the transference, the invariant is that "feelings and ideas move from one sphere of applicability to another" (Bion, 1965/2014, p. 143); in projective transformations, we examine the projective identification by highlighting the beginnings of communication; and in transformations in hallucinosis, we survey projective identifications of an evacuatory nature, together with rivalry, envy and naivety.

Transformations in O

For transformations in O, let us consider the three hypotheses of transformations raised in the clinical example. Given the client's reactions, can we say that he slithers through the analyst's observations? What determines this?

Possibly, the fact that the analyst's observations contain elements that would bring truth and the possibility of getting in touch with it. We must strive to prevent "knowing" the patient from becoming "being" the patient.

In transformations in rigid motion, in the specific case of transference, we would reckon that there is resistance to the analyst's attempts at interpretation.

In the hypothesis of projective transformations, one fears becoming the one who knows the responsibility bestowed upon work, the wife and the analyst, i.e., one fears "becoming" what one does in this fashion. One fears that transformations in knowledge may evolve into transformations in O.

If we consider the transformations in hallucinosis over the course of the session's emotional experience, no learning will take place. The alpha-elements thus obtained are used as A6 elements, beta-elements, conducive to evacuation. We would have an analysand acting more vigorously, in a manner that prevents the development of the knowledge link (K) in terms of the emotional experience of the session.

With regard to the three outlined types of transformations, we may conclude that the client does not learn from the emotional experience when the transformations in knowledge (K) have the potential for transformations in O (TK → TO).

Our hypotheses assume that the three cases of transformations are capable of tending towards the truth. In clinical practice, this is not so. The invariants of each type of transformation are different, and the result is that choosing one of them precludes the others.

Therefore, there is an intimate connection between invariants and truth, as well as between transformations in O and truth. The transformations in O are linked to the development and maturity of the individual – both of the client and of the analyst.

Accomplishing (if this term can be applied) transformations in O is something that may or may not be attained during the session and in one's life. There are many who doubt anything equivalent to this exists or that it is within human reach.

Turbulence

Let us now examine which factors we might ascribe to turbulence.

With the advent of transformations, the concept of learning from emotional experience is obscured, yet it is amply developed as it is being assimilated, giving rise to new concepts. In this sense, as I have noted above, our attention is drawn to the complement of the title of the book *Transformations*: "Change from learning to growth."

An initial element of turbulence arises with the emergence of transformations in knowledge, as well as of less knowledge in relation to the aforementioned concepts of K and –K links.

Turbulence continues with the hallucinatory dimension of the transformations in hallucinosis, which introduce a basal dimension of the functioning of the psyche. As Bion (1970/2014, p. 250) points out:

> This state [of hallucination or hallucinosis] I do not regard as an exaggeration of a pathological or even natural condition: I consider it rather to be a state always present, but overlaid by other phenomena which screen it. If these other elements can be moderated or suspended, hallucinosis becomes demonstrable.

This is turbulent insofar as we introduce this dimension into the mental activity of both the analysand and the analyst, as well as into those mental activities that apprehend the unconscious dimension through the concepts of transference and countertransference.

The introduction of transformations in O generates something new: transformations in knowledge – or even the existence of knowledge (e.g., translating the unconscious into conscious) – are not enough. Because "being" (verb) or the "being" (noun) – i.e., to be in unison with O – is now imperative in the analyst–analysand relationship to attain a state of "*at-one-ment*." This concept should not to be confused with that of "insight," which, as I see it, involves a knowledgeable envisioning of mental life, the acquisition of which may be developmental or even obstructive. Insights can evolve into O or obstruct that evolution.

To summarize, we emphasized the importance of the emergence of the concept of transformations vis-à-vis that of link (as in knowledge); the hallucinatory dimension as a human apparatus for survival; and being in unison with reality rather than just knowing it.

3. Beyond transformations

In Bion's works, precious contributions follow one another, e.g., the opacity of memory and desire, culminating in his well-known recommendation, "with no memory and with no desire"; the lie and the thinker; the mystic and the group; catastrophic change; language of achievement; among many others. I believe that, even now, one may establish abstractions strongly ballasted in clinical material.

Some of Bion's developments mentioned below seem to me extremely valuable, but I find it difficult to communicate my own achievements in this regard and, above all, to correlate them with a minimally adequate clinical practice. I have selected three areas that I believe will be useful to explain these ideas: thought, embryology (vestigial tails, gill slits, etc.) and adrenal glands.

Thought

"Thought" and "thinking" are terms with multiple meanings. We will stick with those that make sense in the field of psychoanalysis.

What Bion will go on to develop "differs from any theory of thought as a product of thinking" (Bion, 1967/2014, p. 154).

The proper development of mental processes enables the development of both thought (which requires thinking to manage it) and thinking – the latter being called into existence by the imperious pressure of thoughts. This is compatible with the notion that thoughts are epistemologically prior to thinking (Mora, 1997, p. 305).[3]

Bion (1962/2014, p. 155) will restrict the term "thought" to the conjunction of a preconception with a frustration. The proposed model is that of a baby whose expectation of a breast comes in conjunction with the absence of a breast for its satisfaction. This conjunction is felt as a no-breast or a breast absent inside. "If the capacity for toleration of frustration is sufficient, the 'no-breast' inside becomes a thought, and an apparatus for 'thinking it' develops" (Bion, 1962/2014, p. 155).

The previous steps are extremely useful in clinical practice and allow the development of knowledge (the knowledge link and, later, transformations in knowledge).

The evolution of these notions leads us, firstly, to consider that the existence of a thought does not depend on a thinker; secondly, that the thinker, necessarily, when formulating a thought, will introduce elements of falsification inherent in his or her own person – falsifications that we can study in column 2 of the Grid; we are postulating the link with the lie.

Turbulence!

We are now face to face with parameters that interfere with the way we habitually exercise our clinical activity and the thoughts arising from it. Despite using colloquial language, Bion, in his later works (*The Italian Seminars, Taming Wild Thoughts* and *Four Papers*), through "imaginative conjectures" and "rational conjectures," confronts us with a new creative wave.

Let us begin with the opening passage of *Taming Wild Thoughts*: "If a thought without a thinker comes along, it may be what is a 'stray thought,' or it could be a thought with the owner's name and address upon it, or it could be a 'wild thought'" (Bion, 1997/2014, p. 175).

When examining stray thoughts by foraying into dreams, Bion suggests something ephemeral, which he will tentatively name "box." This allows us to consider both beta-elements (for things of a more physical nature) and alpha-elements (for things that are somewhat more sophisticated). Later on, he will use the horizontal and vertical axes of the Grid, including the minus (−) notation.

I was struck by the fact that Bion reintegrated the Grid so long after he had created it. And I believe that Bion presents a message of hope when he forays into Shakespeare's verses ("golden boys and girls") to refer to dandelion flowers: "It is almost an archaeological operation to excavate this knowledge [stray thoughts] in the hopes of finding a thought buried somewhere inside it, possibly even some wisdom" (Bion, 1997/2014, p. 180).

With regard to wild thoughts, I have chosen an excerpt from Bion's *The Italian Seminars*, a question asked by one of the participants precisely on this topic. I think that the question and what follows enable us to wrap up the concept.

> I thought the image with which Dr. Bion began his presentation last night was very beautiful: one quite expected to see wild thoughts floating around in the room. But afterwards I wondered whether these thoughts were an emanation of the Holy Spirit, and, if not, what is Dr. Bion saying? I then expected a solution to the mystery of the beginning of St. John's Gospel, which would tell us where the Word was and help us to understand how it had been made flesh. But none of the rest of what was said helped me with this, and, in particular, the long discussion of man's difficult acquisition of language, starting from grunts, confused me. I felt that this beginning was contradictory: in a word, does God – or whoever – grunt, or does He speak?
>
> (Bion, 1985/2014, pp. 153–154)

Another participant attempts to speak, but is thwarted mid-question by "external noise" in the room. Bion then begins to answer and mentions something about being unable to hear because of "so much noise" in the room.

To conclude the topic "thought", the expansion achieved is enormous, and I believe that the "turbulence" of the ideas was clearly demonstrated by the dramatization of the participants in the room.

Embryology: vestigial tail, gill slits, etc.

Bion's inquiries, when examining facts pertaining to embryology, resemble at times something that occurs in our experience in the analysis room, i.e., we feel that something very profound and beyond our reach is taking place there.

Bion ponders whether the mental equivalents of embryonic remains might come forth when the individual performs the highly developed function of speaking, and whether we might detect these remains: "That is what seems to me to be one of the fundamental discoveries of psychoanalysis: archaic states of mind, archaic thoughts and ideas, primitive patterns of behavior are all detectable in the most civilized, cultivated people" (Bion, 1997/2014, p. 185).

Adrenal glands

Reflecting on the most primal states of mind and their connection with states of development, Bion goes back to the beginnings of physical development, as seen in the previous item. However, he then follows on to the *embryonic vestiges* of the mind, something recessive. And his position seems again to be different when, in *The Dawn of Oblivion*, he examines the conversation that the Somites establish between themselves and the self at different ages (full-term, age 22, age 70, etc.), and also when he emphasizes the importance of the adrenal glands or of thalamic dread. He seems to adopt here a forward-looking position, as in the following quote, in which he resorts to imaginative conjectures.

> The first and most immediate of these imaginative conjectures is that the adrenal bodies do not think, but that the surrounding structures develop physically and in physical anticipation of fulfilling a function we know as thinking and feeling. The embryo (or its optic pits, auditory pits, adrenals) does not think, see, hear, fight, or run away, but the physical body develops in anticipation of having to provide the apparatus for filling the functions of thinking, seeing, hearing, running away, and so on.
> (Bion, 1987/2014, pp. 138–139)

To conclude this item, we can discern in Bion's later works a persistent inquiry into the primal mind, an attempt to perceive it in the onset of its development, that is, before a body–mind caesura is established in the observer's mind. It should be stressed how hard it is to find germane material in clinical practice.

Turbulence!

Epilogue

Closely connected with these ideas is the concept of learning from emotional experience. Learning is the basis for changes to occur.

The interest of a session lies in what goes on between analyst and analysand, and the communications of both can be considered circular arguments. Either one acquires importance when he or she establishes complementarity, that is, makes the transition from knowing about O to "being" or "becoming" O (Bion, 1965/2014, p. 264).

I believe that I have a way of working in my analytical practice whereby learning from emotional experience is the requisite condition for apprehending ongoing transformations, with their potential to transform in O as the backdrop.

Notes

1 "Alpha-function operates on the sense impressions, whatever they are, and the emotions, whatever they are, of which the patient is aware. In so far as alpha-function is successful, alpha elements are produced and these elements are suited to storage and the requirements of dream thoughts. […] To learn from experience, alpha-function must operate on the awareness of the emotional experience. […] A child having the emotional experience called learning to walk is able by virtue of alpha-function to store this experience." Bion, *Learning from Experience*, in *Complete Works IV*, pp. 274, 276.
2 "He [the client] is obliged to repeat the repressed material as a contemporary experience instead of, as the physician would prefer to see, remembering it as something belonging to the past. These reproductions, which emerge with such unwished-for exactitude, always have as their subject some portion of infantile sexual life of the Oedipus complex, that is, and its derivatives; and they are invariably acted out in the sphere of the transference, of the patient's relation to the physician." Freud, *Beyond the Pleasure Principle*, translated by James Strachey (W.W. Norton & Company: New York, 1975), p. 12.
3 These notions are in line with accepted philosophical concepts. "To distinguish rigorously between what belongs to the field of psychology and what belongs to the field of logic, it is necessary to separate thinking, on the one hand, and thought, on the other. The latter (thought) is a timeless and non-spacious entity: invariable and, therefore, not psychic, because although we apprehend it through the act of thinking, it must not be confused with it" (Mora, 1997, p. 305).

References

Bion, W. R. (1962/2014) *Learning from Experience*, in *The Complete Works of W. R. Bion*, vol. IV (London: Karnac).
Bion, W. R. (1965/2014) *Transformations*, in *Complete Works*, vol. V (London: Karnac).
Bion, W. R. (1967/2014) *Second Thoughts: Selected Papers in Psycho-Analysis*, in *Complete Works*, vol. V (London: Karnac).

Bion, W. R. (1970/2014) *Attention and Interpretation*, in *Complete Works*, vol. VI (London: Karnac).
Bion, W. R. (1985/2014) *The Italian Seminars*, in *Complete Works*, vol. IX (London: Karnac).
Bion, W. R. (1987/2014) *Four Papers*, in *Complete Works*, vol. X (London: Karnac).
Bion, W. R. (1997/2014) *Taming Wild Thoughts*, in *Complete Works*, vol. X (London: Karnac).
Braga, J. C. (2003) "*The hallucinatory in clinical practice: approaching some questions*," Scientific Meeting of the Brazilian Society of Psychoanalysis of São Paulo, May 22, 2003.
Freud, S. (1920/1975) *Beyond the Pleasure Principle*, translated by J. Strachey (New York: Norton).
Mora, J. F. (1977) *Dicionário de Filosofia* (Lisbon: Don Quixote Publications).

Chapter 2

Me and the other in the analysis room

Antonio Carlos Eva

Some ideas on the analyst I strive to be

Theoretical reflections that underpin clinical practice

To begin with, one needs a comfortable place – for myself and, perhaps, for the other. The room where I work is organized in such a way as to fulfill this requirement. Comfort begins with material elements; superficially speaking, it is synthesized by an armchair I have used for several years. Comfort also derives from a casual familiarity with the environment, and this habitual ensemble contrasts with the other – the new – that comes in each day. A contrast exists, therefore, in what I am acquainted with – the room, the furniture, myself (who I hope will almost disappear) – vis-à-vis the other who arrives.

How can the other be new to me day after day? And for what?

The next question is, How can I make myself present, not only materially, in the room, and also build a common boundary with the other, not only in the material sense, but psychically as well?

What are the required conditions to discriminate each one of us, from my perspective, in the same space and time? To be able to discriminate, I must certainly consider myself first, because without me there is no other. A puzzling and indiscriminate whole is thus formed. I take as my model the warning given on airplanes in the event of depressurization: I first ensure (mental) oxygen for myself; then, if possible, I'll check how the other presents him- or herself, how he or she is rendered in my eyes.

Undoubtedly, verbal language is widely used here, and with it, we build syntheses of the ongoing experience.

Whichever of us is able to do so, for a variety of reasons, will resort to verbal expression in this relationship.

Clearly, the relationship includes more than the verbal, which nevertheless surely influences what is said or left unsaid.

The other (the analysand) will do this by whatever means, and is entirely free, at least at first, to express him- or herself.

The analyst, in a disciplined manner, will focus on the present and, even more so, on the vertex that expresses (emotional) knowledge.

This is a huge difference. There is, I believe, asymmetry in the psychoanalytic relationship, and I actively try to attract the other to the field where I can attain hypotheses, notations, attentions, curiosities, investigations, actions, etc., etc.

In order to do this, I need to be lucid, calm and able to allot, furthermore, part of my attention to the other, that is, of what remains of my well-being in the room. I insist, first and foremost, that I must be mentally oxygenated, a condition I denote through the concept of *unsaturated*.

I am capable of being lucid, calm, unsaturated, with some attention to offer, if I see the other in the room as new. If I see the other as "old," repetitive and known, I must deduce that I am in the grip of my memory, which obliterates the lens for the new presence – an essential component for my analytical work. Perhaps memory is the fulfillment of my desire to evade the new.

A massive discussion is germane here, concerning the mental state I am outlining.

For each verbal and/or non-verbal intervention, my own and/or from the other present in the room, there is the task of examining whether the conditions that I intuit from my coeval partner, in each movement brought to pass, are confirmed or not, and with which particularities, according to my hypothesis on trial.

I must say that it does not really matter whether or not my hypothesis is confirmed. Regardless, it will always be a partial confirmation or refutation. My interest will always be the similarities and differences in this investigation based on the theoretical-psychoanalytical model that I employ. This is the model that will provide the meanings that I will espouse.

A new pair will thus be actively formed, through my own and the other's interference, starting a new cycle of the psychic movement, which I try to identify in a disciplined manner, if or while I remain with psychic oxygen. Thus, I will bring to bear a new attraction to the area that I wish to be in.

In this new cycle, there is, very often, significant loss of my contact with the other.

If I identify this loss, to the extent of my possibilities, I will remain in the room, in the dark, unsaturated. In my work, if I'm unable reach this condition, I invent – through the desire to know/understand – something with which I shed light on the darkness, so as to have at least a tenuous soothing certainty. Phenomenologically, these movements are very similar to each other, and they mingle and become equal in my mind, whether it is creating light, hastily, spurred by excessive fear or discomfort, or waiting to live out the new.

The other, depending on what lives within me or on whom he or she invents that I am, takes on varying values on this journey.

With the loss of the unknown, I need to be able to evaluate what I receive from, or perceive in, the other, bearing in mind that this is necessarily variable in terms of function. The diversity of the function depends on the components that are part of that presence. I may be confirmed or refuted depending on my significance to the other, rather than simply on the verbal content that I can offer.

Therefore, I permanently suspect the fleeting bedrock on which I find myself and on which I try to walk intuitively.

I'd like to hear from you before proceeding ...

Chapter 3

Contributions of Bion's thought to the theory and techniques of contemporary psychoanalysis

Alicia Beatriz Dorado de Lisondo

Introduction

In face of the challenges and the enormous opportunity proffered by the psychoanalytic method to follow up patients who vividly call into question the meaning, scope and limits of psychoanalysis, I have found in Bion's thought a solid theoretical and technical contribution to plunge into the depths of the souls involved in the relationship: that of the patient and mine as an analyst.

Likewise, the infant observation method of Esther Bick (1964) finds in this master a crucial revitalization, precisely because of his precious contributions on the value of *observation* in psychoanalysis (Lisondo, 2008). The analyst's presence triggers effects of meaning in the observational field.

The two vignettes that Bick provides involve adopted patients, and I will highlight the difficulties of getting in touch with the possible truth, and also of accepting the traumatic fracture between prenatal and postnatal life. There is always an unknown history that, at times, hinders affective rooting and the primary primordial link between the adoptive family and the adopted baby.

Bion in the history of psychoanalytic thought

In the history of psychoanalytic thought, common ground exists between different thinkers, e.g., acceptance of the concept of the unconscious, the importance of one's early years in the constitution of the self, and the transference mechanism. Continuity, changes and ruptures with the founding master were not always acknowledged by analysts who were themselves founders of other schools of thought, such as Klein, Winnicott, Bion and Lacan. Fidelity to the transference with their own analysts and/or dread of scientific exile are some of the epistemological obstacles. Melanie Klein preached that her thinking was a continuation of Freud's and, in this manner, sterilized her contributions. The originality of Bion's thinking is grounded on the contributions of Klein (with whom he underwent analysis) and on those of Freud, but he introduces his own epistemology in 1962 with the publication of *Learning from Experience*, after Klein's death.

DOI: 10.4324/9781003171584-3

Bléandonu (1990) divides Bion's work into different periods, and in the first two – the group and the psychotic ones – one can strongly feel Klein's inspiration. The epistemological period, in turn, heralds a shedding of waters with his analyst, namely, the place of the real external object in the constitution of the psyche and, analogously, the complexity of the analytical function.

In addition to the pain brought by the sudden interruption of F. Tustin's treatment, the psychoanalyst of thought had to physically leave England, separating and distancing himself from the birthplace of Klein's works, and going on to develop, during his Californian sojourn, in his last period, the specific originality of his work: the fantastic trilogy, the pursuit of the ultimate truth, the inquiries into the primal mind, the caesura.

The ineffable character of the psychoanalytic object does not release us from the efforts of conceptual rigor. As much as possible, one must discriminate, specify and spell out that Bion attained a new horizon when he distanced himself from the groundwork laid down by Klein's metapsychology (Sandler, 2005).

For Freud, beginning with the second topography, the id is not only indeterminate, but also infinite. For Klein, unconscious fantasy is always present as a representation of the instinctual world, a notion that limits the scope of psychoanalysis. For Bion, the mind, conceived as an open system, comprises an unconscious that is indeterminate and infinite, as it was for the founder of psychoanalysis (Lutemberg, 2007). In Freud (1962), present-day neuroses open the promising path for the non-representational and for primitive experiences. Bion, in turn, by conceptualizing the unconscious as an open system, thrusts it into infinity, thus transcending the range of unconscious fantasy. This opening up validates a different conception of clinical practice, conduces to a different place for the analyst, and makes it possible to analyze patients far beyond and beneath the neurotic/psychotic model.

What follows are Bion's original contributions to psychoanalytic clinical practice as I see them.

The analytical relationship

Psychoanalysis is a science of relationships. Bion (1989) alerts us to the importance of investigating the caesura: neither the analyst, nor the analysand, nor the unconscious, nor the conscious, nor health, nor insanity, but the caesura, the link, the synapse, the countertransference, the transitive–intransitive mood.

This epistemological stance fully commits the analyst. Thus, for example, the criteria of analyzability can only be based on, and nurtured by, the analyst's observations about him- or herself, and about the patient (Ferro, 1998); in the initial interviews and at every moment of every session, these criteria are reinstated and find their "best ally" in the patient.

In psychoanalysis, on the other hand, a *cure* is actually a *pro-cure*, i.e., also a *quest* (Rezende, 2000). In other words, conscious awareness and self-knowledge are always unfinished, relative, imperfect, and can only be achieved through successive catastrophic changes, abounding in turbulence, pain and mourning as the evolving psychic constantly grows.

In his São Paulo seminars, Bion (1979) acknowledges that he does not know if the analyst's role is merely to interpret. If the analytical function is analogous to, but different from, maternal reverie,[1] we may conjecture that the relationship can be schematized as a canal through which flows a mysterious conscious and unconscious circulation of emotions, thoughts, ideas, hopes and conceptions between the beings involved (See Figure 3.1.)

Thus, from the analyst's personality, a unique deportment and a specific manner of working emanate when sculpting the analytical object. For this reason, psychoanalysis is both a science and an art. The analyst creates a metapsychological setting (Fédida, 1988), offers unconditional attention (Meltzer, 1975) and is singularly available (Ungar, 2000).

Psychoanalytic listening is unique and special, because it strives for unconscious communication (Freud, 1955). The analyst also interprets silently, by means of interpretive acts (Ogden, 1996).

The analyst is a model of identification, as well as an inspirational model (Laplanche, 1970). Endowed with negative capability, he or she is able to tolerate doubts, uncertainties and the sense of infinity in order to attain binocular vision and avoid falling prey to theoretical, static splits.

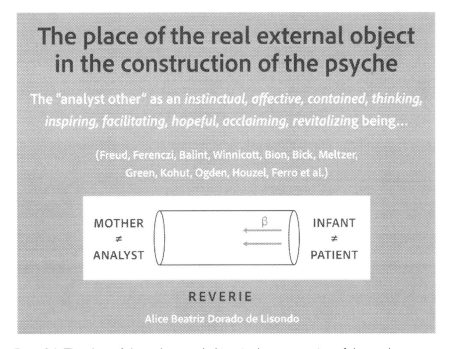

Figure 3.1 The place of the real external object in the construction of the psyche

Passion, interest, unconditional attention, respect, listening and dedication to one's work are fundamental factors of the analytical function.

For Ferro (2008), reverie is a testament to the work of the analyst's mind. Reverie can be punctiform, a flash, or be built successively as a feature film.

The use of models in psychoanalysis

Model building provides the analyst with flexible tools that are in sharp contrast with the use of theories and concepts, especially during sessions.

It should be mentioned that the *technical recommendation* for the analyst to be "*without memory, or desire, or understanding*" has not always been well understood. Bion is a model thinker, so it is not a matter of dismissing the theory and calling for *improvised guesses*; the heart of the matter is *how* theory is used during sessions. A model helps the analyst to find correspondences between clinical practice and psychoanalytic theory. It can either be discarded or become a theory. It is built with sensory elements, and makes it possible to bridge the gap between clinical observation and theories with a high degree of abstraction (Pistiner de Cotiñas, 2007). In the history of psychoanalysis, Meltzer tells us that Esther Bick sometimes clutched tightly the palms of her hands to talk about the experience of observation of certain babies. This gesture, an intuition of genius, evolved into the celebrated work "The experience of the skin in early object relations" (Bick, 1968) and inspired Meltzer (1975), in *Explorations in Autism*, to advance into the psychic dimension and the concept of two-dimensional adhesive identification.

The creation of models makes a living approach to the emotional experience possible.

Approaches to truth and to lies in Bion

We find, in the personality that has the habit of lying, a split described by Freud (1961) in "Fetishism": one part of the mind maintains contact with reality while the other belies it. The lying patient navigates this split by means of ambiguity.

This conflict implies contradictions, or vertices in disagreement. In ambiguity, there are neither vertices nor contradictions; what emerge are different shades of incongruity.

To evade reality, one must attack one's mental functions.

Lying is one of the alterations of consciousness and, when one lies, there is rivalry with "O" (Pistiner de Cortiñas, 2007). Preconceptions are replaced by predeterminations, and actions replace thoughts.

Whereas a thinker is not necessary for a thought to exist, a lie does require the presence of its creator, the liar.

Lying turns human helplessness – uncertainty, ignorance, the infinite/finite spectrum – into omnipotence and omniscience, and the notorious negative capability into positive certainty!

A lie creates a parasitic link between the container and the contained, destroying both. Falsehood, to the mind, is a dangerous toxin, for the mind cannot then manifest itself as *absolute truth*.

True experience enables contact with human helplessness.

With humility, we move closer to the possible truth. There is no single, absolute truth. Both the truth that nurtures the human soul and the lie that poisons it are conjunctions. Truth allows contact with reality and leads to mental growth; lies lead to deterioration and degeneration.

An adoptive mother in distress tells how her son suffered during a vacation at a Spanish resort, when his friend's football team won a competition. Roberto did not want to go to dinner that night just to avoid the award ceremony.

(Although I refrain myself from commenting on it for now, I perceive her pain at our separation – the vacation is for R. a metaphor of the loss of his biological mother – which she interprets as forfeiting the analyst's omnipotent control as the private life team of this "Spanish lady" [2] *enters the picture. Why isn't Alicia with me and my son the whole time? Because I am not the adoptive, biological, mature mother, you know?)*

She then tells me, sadly, that her son also won an award. I glimpse a path that might be worth investigating: Why the sadness?

When I interpret her pain in the face of losses and impotence, I ask what the award was like. With teary eyes, she talks about her son's strategy, clearly inspired by his mother, which consisted of joining the adult teams' tournament so he might beat his friends of his own age and, in this manner, achieve his goal. This wayward scheme of attempting to circumvent the law in a complex plot of "secrets and lies" was used to adopt R.

It should be noted that the adoptive father abandoned Roberto when he was 4 years old.

I reflect on his fantasy of entering the primary scene – joining the grown-ups' team – and, by means of lies, beating the boys, because he could not stand his own childish dependence and the limitations of the human condition, namely, the loss of both the biological and the adoptive father. Mother and son, in morbid complicity, circumvent experiencing the pain of frustrations, losses and acceptance of the law in order to gloss the narcissistic luster.

Because R. did not manage to win the prize in the sports competition, despite all his transgressive chicanery, a camp counselor – moved by the boy's suffering and frantic pursuits – promised my patient a stratagem that she applauded.

On the last day, the boy climbed the podium to receive a consolation trophy for his perseverance. Relieved, the mother thanked the employee for his efforts and offered him a tip.

Just between us, fortunately the false winner tossed the medal away, shouting: "This is not for real! I only won out of pity!"

In other words, a lie – the wangling – anesthetizes one's contact with the emotional life that drives growth and paralyzes catastrophic change. A lie is a predatory operation of mental activity. The penalty *disqualifies the* being.

The greatest gain here was the opportunity to be able, in analysis, to think through and become aware that mental maturity is a laborious achievement that is not for sale. The boy revealed an auspicious inner voice, a voice that alerts to and illuminates the deleterious effects of lies, transgressions and manipulations incited by the dangerous manic temptations personified in the mother and carried out by the counselor.

Humility

In supervision no. 36, Bion (Sandler, 2018) emphasizes, "*The central issue is for us to be able to learn.*"

The analyst builds imaginative or rational conjectures, and must know that he or she does not possess full and polished knowledge, the thing-in-itself.

Transference does, indeed, mean transiency.

It is not for the analyst to give opinions, to approve or disapprove. Psychoanalytic interpretation is one of the analyst's vertices of observation. It cannot be saturated or wound up as absolute truth. If it could, it would become a dogma. Roberto's mother had had a previous analytical experience in which she had felt doomed to an inability to be a mother and to resignify the lies. It was precisely when, painfully, she realized the truth about the lying games that he had set up that she became capable of being born as a mother. The analyst, who is neither a prophet nor God, is always dealing with a *dangerous, unknown and unpredictable* analytical object. Analysis, in fact, is a prelude to thought and cannot be a substitute for thinking.

As an analyst, I cannot turn Roberto into a fake winner. It is only through the elaboration of mourning and loss that he will be able to come to grips with his true mental reality and become what he is.

The analytical relationship is not perfect, nor permanent, nor always adequate, but it can offer the patient a transformative container.

In 1975, as Bion strove to tame wild thoughts, he suggested that, in addition to conscious and unconscious states of mind, there might be another, *an inaccessible state of mind*. This is a provisional name. The epistemological presence of this state inspires humility and demands that our attitude be open to contemplate uncertainty, doubt, the infinite. The uncertainty principles are summoned.

Passion

> "*Who are you?*"
> "*I am compassion. Who are you?*"
> "*I am your maid – but even then you did not see. Open my eyes.*"
> "No. I sent you prophets, but you would not listen."[3]

Passion, sense impressions and myth are the dimensions of the psychoanalytic object (Bion, 1963). Passion stems from harmony and the happy combination of the LHK links. Intensity and warmth are part of it, but not violence. The consciousness of passion is not sensory. Passion is evidence of two minds united. The dimension of passion is one of the prerequisites, a thermometer that signals the timely moment to formulate the psychoanalytic interpretation.

Passion has a respectful attitude towards ultimate reality, unknown and unknowable – the reality of "O" in Position (D).

The evolving reality of "O," in one's commitment to become oneself, is always interpretable, however painful it may be, as I try to show in the clinical examples.

The analyst's perseverance in the construction of the analytical object emanates from a personal equation, from analytical experience and from faith in the method. Tolerance towards doubt and the ability to wait for future achievements – i.e., to evolve towards new perspectives of knowledge – ensure that evidence may be sought beyond what has already been discovered. Interpretation reveals only one facet of the complicated conjugated conjunction that transference opens up in the analytical scene. This limitation is a source of pain. Finding the selected fact creates transformational possibilities.

In *Cogitations*, Bion (1992) associates compassion with truth, as human senses. Human beings must seek and find the truth to satisfy their curiosity. Who can deprive the patient from coming to know the possible truth? Truth and compassion are qualities of the relationship that nurture the soul, just as lying, indifference, contempt and rejection intoxicate it.

For Bion, the ability to love and the capacity for truth may be lacking in us, humans. This lack can be primary or innate, though some of its consequences can be changed through analysis. Put differently, transformations are always possible. The patient needs to develop compassion for him- or herself in order to feel entitled to dignity and self-respect. Clinical practice with adoptees is quite revealing in this sense.

The capacity for compassion is a source of admiration, yet it also arouses the analysand's envy, rivalry and hatred when he or she is unable to feel mature compassion (Bion, 1965).

Bion (1979) cautions that one must have the ability to distinguish between good and evil, between real truth (or real compassion) and real evil.

In *A Memoir of the Future* (Bion, 1990), Alice asks why not think of God as the source of compassion to nurture doctors, surgeons and psychoanalysts. P.A. (psychoanalyst) replies that it would not be possible to endure such painful work without compassion.

As with the sphinx, the lack of compassion and consideration leads to self-destruction. As per the riddle, the sphinx did not want to find the truth!

The onset of human life prior to chronological birth

Bion presents an open model of the mind. In his model, there are potentials to develop when the α-function is able to transform primitive experiences, anchored in the basic assumptions of the primary group. The prenatal dimension harbors thoughts without a thinker, as well as wild intuitions and undigested thoughts. In *Learning from Experience* (Bion, 1962), the brave author conceives of the human fetus as capable of perceiving the mother's emotions, albeit unaware of the stimulus or the source. In *A Memoir of the Future* (Bion, 1990), in his daring fictional work, he reveals what is beyond scientific language. The imaginary dialogues between the various characters are all part of the total personality (Bianchedi et al., 1999). Bion's self-analysis is revealed through these characters.

In 1975, the psychoanalyst of thought presented us a fetus with primal feelings and ideas to be evacuated; therefore, with the primitive capacity to develop the rudiments of projective identification: evacuation. The amniotic fluid can be contaminated with meconium; the records of heartbeats and sounds, the visions experienced above the optical cavities, the changes in pressure of the intrauterine fluid constitute the reservoir of the protomental system present in the total personality.

This contribution is an important element for us to understand, among other disorders, the therapeutics of mental orphanhood and of adoption, as can be seen in the following example.

Twelve-year-old Mario was adopted when he was 3 days old. The parents sought psychoanalytic help because the child is extremely anxious, hyperkinetic and inattentive, despite a normal neurological diagnosis.

After medicating with Ritalin, and because of the discouraging side effects, the parents gave up and sought relief along the organic route.

During the process of psychoanalytic assessment, Mario draws a swimming pool, which he shows his parents in the subsequent family interview. The pool is a triangle with a huge hole in the middle.

The psychoanalytic process begins with a hypothesis of global disorders in emotional development, given the flaws in mental continence that seem to enhance atavistic terrors. The boy's skin is the locus of his immaturity and precariousness: raw flesh, due to severe dermatitis.

The parents request an interview when M. began crying as he flipped through an album looking for a family photo to take to school. During a session, he had already chosen a photo of his adoptive mother when single, revealing both his doubts that that young girl could truly adopt him, and his expectations of finding his biological mother, a teenager.

He asks his father, "Why did she get pregnant if she couldn't have me? If she couldn't have me, she shouldn't have gotten pregnant." After the work carried out in the psychoanalytic interviews, the father replies, "But it was thanks to the fact that she was able to get pregnant that you were born, and we love having you here!"

The father tells me that he decided to research the child's history because he realized the importance of the boy's origin (which everyone seemed to want to forget). M. was the fourth child. The first two are with their grandparents. The mother had the other two in the same year. M. is the youngest one. The adoptive mother associates that, when Mario arrived, he cried so much that he lost his breath and seemed to be going into convulsions. He only calmed down when she settled him on her belly. The parents accept the hypothesis that the child's anxiety, irritability and immaturity might be related to atavistic experiences of feeling "without space," squeezed in, compressed inside an inhospitable biological womb. They also recognize their own immaturity as they struggled to raise such a difficult infant, who always disappointed them. Grievously and with much guilt, they confess to having had the idea of giving back the child. However, as an analyst, I point out how much vitality all of them display in learning to live with Mario, as well as their courage in seeking psychoanalysis, the path of possible truth.

We know nothing about what happened within that womb, of what M. imbibed from the first "impressions" of existence and of his arrival in a new home. However, we can intuitively create imaginative hypotheses and name the selected fact of constant conjunctions that lead to transformation, the caesura between the unnamed sensory life and psychic life. In this manner, atavistic terrors find a shared meaning that transcends the body level.

When the challenge is to *build the mind*, one must *build elements* to cross the caesura of the sensory world and weave the netting of the possible psychic reality. Understanding allows the transformation of sinister terrors. "O," the ultimate reality (Grotstein, 2007), is unknowable, but it is possible to be one with "O," to become who one is through the catastrophic changes in the parents that drive the transformations in the developing child.

Notes

1 To maintain requisite conceptual precision, it should be stressed that, in reality, maternal reverie has its roots in transgenerational history. Like Russian dolls, parental reverie is born from grandparental reverie, in a continuous generational sequence. The analyst does not have this historical and blood link with patients, but offers his or her α-function instead.
2 The analyst is Argentinian and speaks with a Spanish accent.
3 *A Memoir of the Future – 1975* in *The Complete Works of W. R. Bion*, volume XII, p. 42. Reference to the "First Epistle of Paul to the Corinthians," 13:12.

References

Bianchedi, E. T de et al. (1999) *Bion, Conocido, Desconocido* (Buenos Aires: Lugar Ed.).
Bick, E. (1964) "Notes on infant observation in psycho-analytic training," *International Journal of Psychoanalysis*, 45, 558–566.
Bick, E. (1968) "The experience of the skin in early object relations," *International Journal of Psychoanalysis*, 49, 484–486.
Bion, W. R. (1962) *Learning from Experience* (London: Heinemann).
Bion, W. R. (1963) *Elements of Psycho-Analysis* (London: Heinemann Medical Books).
Bion, W. R. (1965) *Transformations* (London: Heinemann Medical Books).
Bion, W. R. (1979) *Bion in New York and São Paulo* (Strath Tey: Clunie Press).
Bion, W. R. (1989) *Two Papers: The Grid and Caesura* (London: Karnac Books).

Bion, W. R. (1990) *A Memoir of the Future* (London: Karnac). Originally published in 1975.
Bion, W. R. (1992) *Cogitations* (London: Karnac).
Bion, W. R. (1997) *Taming Wild Thoughts* (London: Karnac).
Bléandonu, G. (1990) *Wilfred Bion: La Vie et l'Oeuvre, 1897–1979* (Paris: Éditions Bordas).
Fédida, P. (1988) *Clinica Psicanalítica: Estudos* (São Paulo: Escuta).
Ferro, A. (1998) "Os quadrantes do setting," in A. Ferro, *Na Sala de Análise: Emoções, Relatos, Transformações* (Rio de Janeiro: Imago).
Ferro, A. (2008) "*Videoconference: Evitar emoções, viver emoções.*" Presented at the VI Congress of the NPCR, "Na Sala de Análise", June 2008.
Freud, S. (1955) "Psycho-analysis and telepathy," in *Standard Edition*, XVIII (London: Hogarth Press). Originally published in 1921.
Freud, S. (1961) "Fetishism," in *Standard Edition*, XXI (London: Hogarth Press). Originally published in 1927.
Freud, S. (1962) "Heredity and the aetiology of the neuroses," in *Standard Edition*, III (London: Hogarth Press). Originally published in 1896.
Grotstein, J. S. (2007) *A Beam of Intense Darkness: Wilfred Bion's Legacy to Psychoanalysis* (London: Karnac).
Laplanche, J. (1970) *Vida y Muerte en Psicoanálisis* (Buenos Aires: Amorrortu).
Lisondo, A. B. D. de (2008) "*Observación de bebés: Método de observación de bebés Esther Bick: evoluciones y transformaciones con las contribuciones de W. R. Bion y Donald Meltzer al psicoanálisis contemporaneo.*" Presented at the VIII Congreso Internacional de Observación de Lactantes: Método Esther Bick: El Despertar de la Vida Mental en el Encuentro con el Mundo Externo. Observaciones y Teorías, Buenos Aires, 2008.
Lutemberg, J. (2007) *El Vacío Mental* (Buenos Aires: PP).
Meltzer, D. (1975) *Explorations in Autism* (Strath Tey: Clunie Press).
Ogden, T. (1996) "O conceito de ação interpretativo," in T. Ogden, *Os Sujeitos da Psicanálise* (São Paulo: Casa do Psicólogo).
Pistiner de Cortiñas, L. (2007) *La Dimensión Estética de la Mente: Variaciones sobre un Tema de Bion* (Buenos Aires: Del Signo).
Rezende, A. M. (2000) *O Paradoxo da Psicanálise: Uma Ciência Pós-Paradigmática* (São Paulo: Via Lettera).
Sandler, P. C. (2005) *The Language of Bion: A Dictionary of Concepts* (London: Karnac).
Sandler, P. (2018) "Comentários sobre a Supervisão A36," in G. M. Brito, H. Levine and J. A. J. Mattos (eds.), *Bion no Brasil: Supervisões e Comentários* (São Paulo: Blucher).
Ungar, V. (2000) "*Los fundamentos teóricos en el método de observación de bebés de Mrs. Bick.*" Presented at the Clínica Pais-Bebês, Porto Alegre, October 2000.

Chapter 4

α-function

Catastrophic anxiety – panic – container with reverie

Antonio Sapienza

Initially, it would be opportune to conceptualize briefly the characteristics of the α-function in its interaction with the three terms of this essay's title. This chapter seeks to show how the α-function partakes from the very moment catastrophic anxiety sets in, and how moments of panic manifest that require finesse in the functions of the container with reverie.

A myth of the Kabbalah much appreciated by Bion tells us that at the top of a mountain there was a vessel of the purest crystal inside of which a human couple lived in perfect harmony. Suddenly, there is an earthquake, the vessel breaks, fragmenting the delicate and steadfast human bonds, while despair, exile, strangeness, revolt, dissatisfaction and emotional turbulence set in.

I will use a set of questions as a means to figure out what enables the daring, injured and exhausted little bird to *recover its strength* and fly off again and again.

In the fifth New York conference, Bion (1980) proposes that the α-function is akin to providing a nest for birds that seek meaning so they may replenish and rest.[1]

In that conference, he emphasizes the embryonic character of our ability to think and introduces the term "genomene" as the precursor of "phenomenon," calling on analysts to exercise the α-function with care and comparing it to the craft of a psychological midwife.

Perhaps, when once again "fledged,"[2] the poet will fly successfully, go through emotional experiences of *catastrophic change* and, by assigning them new meanings, achieve *creative change*.

Wild thoughts stemming from unknown reality (O) bombard the "baby," who, unable to think them, is ravaged by the anguish of death. The baby then seeks out anyone who can think these thoughts, requiring the competent functioning of the container with reverie.

If we consider Bion's conception of the container ↔ contained functions, the medical model of *hemodialysis* emerges as an analog model (Grotstein, 2007). The binomial solitude/dependence is an important and constant conjunction that accompanies human existence until death. For analyst and analysand, "the psychoanalytic raft to which they cling in the consulting-room [is] a very precarious

DOI: 10.4324/9781003171584-4

raft in a tumultuous sea" (Bion, 2005). The "baby" uses its innate life impulses and, overwhelmed by the fear of a "forlorn life," will attempt to assimilate and develop inner resources to activate its self, striving to exist and struggling to find support in order to become who it is (Grotstein, 2007).

The functions of the container with reverie exist as a basic primary instrument for the "baby's" sanity. This metabolic activity will likewise require empathic receptivity, resources to perform mental detoxification and, in addition, the provision of nutritional care by the primary *container*, such as the vitalizing functions exercised by the psychoanalyst.

The thinking "psychosomatic breast" (Bion, 1963), if and when internalized, becomes the "unconscious" legislator of our inner world, bringing to mind Shelley, for whom "poets are the unacknowledged legislators of the world" (Shelley, 1821).

Meg Harris Williams (1997) convincingly reconciles the mother's capacity for reverie towards the helpless baby and the language used by analysts in the emotional experience of a session.

To maintain and support the continuous generation of symbolic productive life (so that, among other things, patients are able to think their life and anguishes), one may suggest that analysts be assiduous in their frequent reading of poetry. This mental habit will help them find a fitting metaphorical language as a valuable aid to detoxify our thalamic and sub-thalamic terrors and, thus, contribute to undo mental blocks and autistic encapsulations.

Analysts will use their ability to embrace the terror-inducing experiences generated in the analytical emotional experience and, by means of inspiration associated with α-dream-work, will be able to provide support and mental nutrition to the analysand's devitalized self. They will use a "language of consummation/achievement."

I will now stress one of the factors that activate terror-inducing nuclei in the psychotic parts of a personality (Bion, 1970). The articulation below aims to shed light on the environmental conditions that give rise to the ego-destructive superego, which, because of its trait of malignantly automatic judgment, is also called "super id" or "bad conscience."[3]

This configuration is a *result of failure* in projective and introjective interactions between mother and baby in the face of primitive anguishes in the early stages of life. This "obstructive object" is impregnated with moralistic violence and aims to "judge everything, control everything and understand nothing." It has been internalized as an agent that destroys mental life by attacking the development of feeling, thinking and verbalizing. From this configuration, "hidden" forces emanate those tyrannically poison experiences through continuous toxic inoculation, destroying the "ability to dream."

Much of the bombardment that generates mental confusion is linked to the discharge of β-elements and bizarre objects. This "obstructive object" organizes itself as a β-screen (Bion, 1962). Detecting it will lead us to the refuges and burrows where strenuous traumatic anxieties are hidden. Thus, the psychotic defenses used by the patient, basically represented by reversions of perspective and evasive movements governed by negative links in the Grid (−K, −L, −H) (Sandler, 2005), will act as subliminal clues with access to the roots of traumas, housing violently compressed radioactive nuclear material. Re-elaboration by means of a reassuring and sympathetic rereading of this threatening violence may make it possible to defuse one's intense persecutory guilt and compulsion-to-repetition, leading to a refreshing revitalization.

I find that, in clinical circumstances, Grid exercises performed after a session and focused on the analyst's notes may sharpen his or her intuitive uptake of clues from those hiding places, making for a subtle agility when addressing traps and ruses dominated by games of a murderous and suicidal nature. Therefore, in the analytical dynamic, the tenuous or glaring evidence of a moralistic setup can be used to raise suspicions that we are approaching nuclei of unthinkable traumatic suffering and residues of mental catastrophes.

I propose one should consider the evidences of this ego-destructive superego's setup by reactivating protomental and mental disasters that have already occurred, the emergence of which will require a new, re-signified reading (Sapienza, 2007). We may correlate the emanation of catastrophic anxiety with passages associated with moments of caesura, such as birth, marriage and death (Bion, 1989).

The increased contact of the analytical partnership with catastrophic change requires the analyst to have had the personal experience of bold and lucid forays into these emotional layers mobilized by impacts of primitive violence. The talents and the degrees of cooperation of the partnership are factors capable of transforming catastrophic change into creative change, of generating mental growth for the analytical duo (Pistiner de Cortiñas, 2007).

The personality, invaded and ravaged by threats of catastrophes of internal and/or external origin, is overcome by violent emotional turbulence, accompanied by premonitions of imminent disaster[4] and by intense fear of going insane, so that eventually a state of mind progressively overwhelmed by nameless terror sets in.

Our next step is to outline how the state of panic is unleashed,[5] when to the main characteristics mentioned above are added experiences of the shattering of the self, loss of emotional control and inability to think.

Let us use the model of an atomic bomb deeply embedded in the unconscious, loaded with material malignantly compressed, such as the residues of a primitive mental accident. The detonation of the bomb begins in the self and its violence can be directed towards the external world. Subjectively, what one apprehends is an increasingly destructive discharge with explosive effects of a fusional and fissional nature. We should recall here the descriptions found in the "Schreber case," with his experiences of "the end of the world" (Freud, 1958).

There is also be the possibility that, when detonated, the internalized atomic bomb will follow the intrapsychic direction, with predominantly implosive and "silent" manifestations, accompanied by varying degrees of mental death and intermittent and often inaudible "terrible screams and cries." The valuable observations of André Green on the so-called "white psychoses" are apposite here, whereby experiences of internal void, devitalization and depersonalization suddenly set in (Sapienza, 2004).

> What a pity to see a mind as great as Napoleon's devoted to trivial things such as empires, historic events, the thundering of cannons and of men; he believed in glory, in posterity, in Caesar; nations in turmoil and other trifles absorbed all his attention. How could he fail to see that what really mattered was something else entirely? Simply put, for man to go where he has never gone before.
>
> (Valéry, 1942, p. 902)

I invite the reader to a reflexive exercise on another man's delinquent episode, whose state of mind was dominated by transformations in hallucinosis. In late September 2007, a lurid piece of news on radio, television and newspapers in São Paulo appalled and horrified public opinion:

> A former psychiatric patient was captured, who upon medical evaluation had been released from the penitentiary's special ward for highly dangerous inmates. The prisoner confessed to having raped and murdered two teenage brothers in a thicket near the Cantareira neighborhood. He claims he was exasperated by the fact that the minors, after having been raped and tied to trees, denied the presence of menacing wild beasts that roared in the nearby woods and were closing in on them.

I will close this text with a brief dialogue between pope Julius II and the architect, painter and sculptor Michelangelo Buonarroti, from a 1965 film based on the 1961 novel *The Agony and the Ecstasy*, by the Californian writer Irving Stone, regarding the magnificent paintings of the Sistine Chapel:

POPE JULIUS: When will you make an end?
MICHELANGELO: When I'm finished.

Closing remarks

With a view to a new reading by a future reader of this chapter, I would like to add my eventual contribution:

> The well-disciplined, continuous cultivation of elements related to the α-function is an essential instrument for analysts to exercise their clinical practice in intimate and private partnership with the analysand at every session. Hence, the value of the setting and of the analytical contract as stable constants.
>   These factors also make it possible to preserve que requisite conditions to defuse experiences of terror related to catastrophic anxieties.

Furthermore, analysts will provide mental nutrition support to patients to enhance their ability to think realistically and encourage a generative continence capable of controlling the threats of breakdowns and actings-out related to panic syndrome.

Notes

1 Allegedly, Bion's actual words were "[Alpha function is] a kind of nest where birds of meaning might alight."
2 In poetry, the term *fledged poet* ("who can fly through air and space without fear") is used by Meg Harris Williams (Williams and Waddell, 1991, p. 115) to characterize the final stage of this journey, when the poet is able to recover his capacity for new creative "flights."
3 One should read the end of the article "Attacks on linking" (Bion, 1959, pp. 106–109) bearing in mind that the ego-destructive superego must be differentiated from the superego proposed by Freud, which develops as an heir to the Oedipus complex.
4 Etymologically, "disaster" derives from *dis/astro*, meaning the loss of the guiding star.
5 The etymology of "panic" is associated with the god Pan of Greek mythology and comprises all fears or *phobos*.

References

Bion, W. R. (1959) "Attacks on linking" in W. R. Bion, *Second Thoughts* (London: Karnac Books), pp. 93–109.
Bion, W. R. (1962) *Learning from Experience* (London: William Heinemann Medical Books).
Bion, W. R. (1963) *Elements of Psycho-Analysis* (London: William Heinemann Medical Books).
Bion, W. R. (1970) "Prelude to or substitute for achievement" in W. R. Bion, *Attention and Interpretation* (London: Tavistock), pp. 125–129.
Bion, W. R. (1980) *Bion in New York and São Paulo* (Strath Tey: Clunie Press). Originally published in 1977.
Bion, W. R. (1989) *Two Papers: Grid and Caesura* (London: Karnac).
Bion, W. R. (2005) *The Italian Seminars*, edited by Francesca Bion, translated by Philip Slotkin (London: Karnac Books). Originally published in 1977.
Freud, S. (1958) "Psycho-analytic notes on an autobiographical account of a case of paranoia: dementia paranoides" in S. Freud, *The Standard Edition of the Complete Psychological Works of Sigmund Freud* (London: Hogarth Press), vol. 12, pp. 9–82. Originally published in 1911.
Grotstein, J. S. (2007) *A Beam of Intense Darkness: Wilfred Bion's Legacy to Psychoanalysis* (London: Karnac).
Pistiner de Cortiñas, L. (2007) *Dimensión Estética de la Mente: Variaciones sobre un Tema de Bion* (Buenos Aires: Ed. del Signo).
Sandler, P. C. (2005) *The Language of Bion: A Dictionary of Concepts* (London: Karnac Books).
Sapienza, A. (2004) "Reflexões clínicas psicanalíticas sobre a memória-sonho", *Ciência e Cultura*, 56 (4), 29–32.

Sapienza, A. (2007) "Psicanálise e estética: ressignificação de conflitos psicóticos e reciprocidade criativa", *Funzione Gamma*, 20.
Shelley, Percy Bysshe (1821) *A Defence of Poetry*.
Valéry, P. (1942). *Mauvaises Pensées et Autres* (Paris: Gallimard).
Williams, M. H. (1997) "Inspiration: a psychoanalytic and aesthetic concept", *British Journal of Psychotherapy*, 14 (1), 33–43.
Williams, M. H. and Waddell, M. (1991) *The Chamber of Maiden Thought: Literary Origins of the Psychoanalytic Model of the Mind* (London and New York: Tavistock/Routledge).

Chapter 5

Learning from emotional experience and the Grid

Theory and practice[1]

Cecil José Rezze

The initial purpose of this chapter is the theoretical development broached in the title. Additionally, with the collaboration of colleagues, it is to play "the psychoanalytical game," that is, to use the Grid to examine the clinical situations presented here. Towards this end, Bion's works – *Learning from Experience* (1962) and *Elements of Psychoanalysis* (1963) – are fundamental. In the former, we have an examination of the sense impressions and primal emotions that, worked on by the α-function, allow the appearance of α-elements, essential for the development of dreams, memory, forgetfulness, etc. The inoperability of the α-function results in the appearance of β-elements.

Emotional experience is an integral part of human life and, therefore, a fundamental aspect of the multiple faces of psychoanalysis. One innovation, introduced by Bion, (1962, p. 8) is learning from emotional experience, which implies the development of the theory of functions and, particularly, of the α-function.

The α-elements allow the emergence of dreams through predominantly visual images that may, after awakening, be transformed into a conscious narrative, i.e., one with manifest content. Dreams, as Freud figured out, manifest the functions of censorship and repression, which, from a new perspective, in addition to their previous purposes, will be related to the function of preserving sleep by means of dreams that digest inner stimuli and make it possible to maintain the separation from the unconscious.

For Bion, the contact-barrier (1962, p. 17) is in an ongoing process of formation that delimits the points of contact and separation of the conscious and unconscious elements. Thus, the α-elements may aggregate, agglutinate, appear as a narrative and organize themselves logically or geometrically.

When functioning to separate the conscious from the unconscious, the contact-barrier is related to memory.

Thus, we may ask what factors are involved in the α-function, and for that we must consider whether each factor pertains to mental growth or to mental destruction.

If a baby experiences the threat of annihilation and is thus overwhelmed with unbearable anxieties, how can it possibly survive? Perhaps, if the mother is capable of "reverie" (waking dream or daydream) (Bion, 1962, p.36), she might

DOI: 10.4324/9781003171584-5

receive amply any of these elements and, through the α-function, transform them into α-elements, enabling the development of α-elements worked on by the baby. Thus, reverie may be considered a factor of the α-function.

When examining the failure of the α-function, Bion restricts himself to the envy factor (1962, p. 96).

Failure of the α-function prevents sensory stimuli and primitive emotions from becoming α-elements; consequently, β-elements arise that are not suitable for the functions described above. The β-elements lend themselves to projective identification, as an evacuation, and, thus, lend themselves to acting out.

The β-elements are storable, however not as memory, but as undigested facts. They differ from memory, which allows the operation of the α-function and enables the appearance of α-elements, which are instrumental to memory and to the possibility of thought.

When the contact-barrier (Bion, 1962, p. 17) operates, the α-elements enable the aforementioned functions of dreaming, dream-thinking, thinking, etc. The contact-barrier may undergo a reversal of α-function (Bion, 1962, p. 25) when hatred and other factors are at work. The α-elements that have already been attained will undergo fragmentation and dispersion, losing their characteristics in terms of psychic quality. They become β-elements and will now form a screen of β-elements. (Bion, 1962, p. 22) This transmutation is a living, albeit fleeting process. The screen of β-elements is directive and, thanks to the evacuatory power of the projective identifications, will attempt to reach the analyst and awaken strong countertransferential manifestations in him or her (Bion, 1962, p. 23).

β-elements are an instrument created to allow the observation of the mind and are somewhat akin to bizarre objects (Bion, 1962, p. 11). The latter, however, because they succeed the destroyed α-elements, contain traces of ego and superego.

So far, it can be said that β-elements are related to primitive relationships and are distinctly important in psychotic processes. Yet, seeing that their origin lies in sense impressions and primitive emotions, we may consider they are the matrix from which all mental developments originate. It should be noted that, in Bion's work, β-elements are considered from both these viewpoints; if this is not taken into account, the reader may misconstrue them.

The Grid

The Grid is a part of a whole or a whole into which many parts can be fitted. It is reproduced in the Appendix.

Bion (1963, p. 1) is concerned with the characteristics of psychoanalysis. When we examine psychoanalytic theories, we find that they remain distant from the clinical experiences from which they originated. On the other hand, psychoanalysts, when describing clinical facts, do so in a way that theory pervades them, diminishing the impression that they are true. Furthermore, the number of existing theories is quite large, forming a veritable Babel. How does one deal with these facts without distorting established theories, but rather creating an instrument with which to examine the facts themselves?

Bion envisaged finding the essential elements to which all theories might refer and which might become an instrument to study clinical experiences.

Thus, he created the idea of elements of psychoanalysis forming the whole – the psychoanalytic object. A comparison may be illuminating: we could compare the elements of psychoanalysis to atoms and the psychoanalytic object to a molecule (Bion 1963, p. 101).

The psychoanalytic object will contain the dimensions of the senses, of myth and of passion (Bion, 1963, p. 11).

Sensory stimuli stem from the sense organs. A psychoanalytic interpretation (psychoanalytic object) requires that something perceptible from hearing, sight and smell be accessible to the client and to the analyst.

Myth refers to one's personal myth. Thus, when the client describes his or her own person and the relationships established with others or with him- or herself, we are face to face with his or her personal myth.

The third dimension is that of passion as a manifestation of feelings that unite two minds, establishing an intense relationship of affection in which there are no traces of violence.

An investigation of what the elements of psychoanalysis are must proceed from experience and, thus, from the observation of phenomena, implying the primary and secondary qualities defined by Kant (Bion, 1963, p. 6).

I must note that Bion (1963, p. 79) will add the characteristics of the Oedipal myth to the Grid's axis of uses. Consequently, the categories of the horizontal axis will be represented by the characters of the myth. I will discuss the two presentations together, as I believe this will make it easier to apprehend their meaning.

The horizontal axis of the Grid is the axis of uses; the vertical axis is the genetic axis.

The horizontal axis (Bion, 1963, p. 17)

1   Definitory hypothesis. If, in psychoanalytic practice, the analyst comes to believe the client is depressed, this fact can be communicated. And so we have a definitory hypothesis. In myth, it is the proclamation of the oracle. What is sought is a description of the criminal, the causer of the misfortunes that befell Thebes.
2   Ψ (psi). The analyst denies the anxiety felt in the face of a situation that exposes him or her to the unknown. Thus, any interpretation will have here the quality of a denial. Tiresias represents this situation when he seeks to dissuade Oedipus from pursuing the criminal.
3   Notation. Representative formulations of present and past situations. These can be a brief summary by the analyst of facts from the current or past sessions. The myth as a whole configures the notation.

4   Attention. A function similar to what Freud ascribed to the term. Attention aims to explore the environment. And attentive will be the analyst's formulations that aim to explore mental life. It is akin to reverie, pre-conception and discrimination. One of its functions is receptivity toward the selected fact. In the myth, the sphinx stimulates curiosity, but under the threat of death if it is not satisfied.
5   Inquiry. A theory intended to investigate the unknown. The main objective is to establish communications to satisfy the patient's and the analyst's inquisitive impulses. Oedipus represents the triumph of resolute curiosity over intimidation. Symbol of scientific integrity.
6   Action. Is used as an operator. Its purpose is for communication to help patients find solutions to their developmental problems. For the analyst, the closest thing to the transformation of thought into action is the transition from thought to verbal formulations. Even so, we can also consider action, in the Grid, as the manifestation that corresponds to the evacuation of β-elements into, for example, hallucinations.

The vertical genetic axis (Bion, 1963, p. 22)

(A) β-elements. This expression represents the primordial matrix from which thoughts purportedly arise. They share the characteristics of inanimate objects and of psychic objects, and there is no way to distinguish between the two. Thoughts are things and things are thoughts.

(B) α-elements are the outcome of the activities of the α-function on sense impressions and primordial emotions. They make it possible to form and use dream-thoughts. As Bion (1963, p. 22) says:

> I do not consider that there is or can be any evidence for the existence of a realization corresponding to β-elements, α-function, or α-elements, other than observed facts that cannot be explained without the aid of such hypothetical elements. For the remaining formulations the position is different. It can be supposed that there is evidence for the existence of dream thoughts, preconceptions and the rest.[2]

(C) Dream-thoughts. Depend on α-function and α-elements. They have the same status assigned to them by classic dream theory.

(D) Pre-conception. Corresponds to a state of expectation. A primeval expectation might be that of the infant for the breast. The union of pre-conception and realization gives rise to conception.

(E) Conception. This is a variable that can be replaced by a constant. If we represent pre-conception as $\Psi(\xi)$, where (ξ) is the unsaturated element, we can say that that which replaces (ξ) with a constant comes from the realization to which the pre-conception is united. When the pre-conception of

the breast is united with the sucking of the breast, the realization of the breast occurs – and, its conception as well.
(F) This concept is conceived by the process that aims to free it from elements that might prevent it from serving as an instrument of elucidation and expression of the truth.
(G) The scientific deductive system. In this context, it indicates the combination of concepts in hypotheses and systems of hypotheses so they relate logically to each other.
(H) Calculus. The scientific deductive system is represented by algebraic calculus.

Clinical practice

Clinical development has been the outcome of the seminars I hold at the Institute of Psychoanalysis[3] – "Elements of Psychoanalysis and the Grid" – in which participants spontaneously contribute clinical vignettes pertaining to the events presented.

These multifarious participations enliven what takes place during the seminars, but some of this vitality is lost when transcribing and editing the text – not to mention that we are led to overlook that the elements of psychoanalysis refer to the psychoanalytic object (of which interpretation is one example).

PARTICIPANT 1: I have a patient who, in our conversation over the course of the session, eventually says: "I'm having the chills again, the chills." These are her bodily sensations. But while she shivers, all I feel is a profound drowsiness ... I feel so drowsy that I almost fall asleep sitting up.

The chills awaken something powerful in the analyst – a profound drowsiness. The chills cannot be expanded in the session, although they can be named – the chills – and this could be considered a *definitory hypothesis* in the Grid (column 1). Given its non-expansive character, the intensity of the emotion and the "bodily sensations," this might indicate β-elements (row A). By checking the Grid, we can compose A1 in abstract terms (β-*element* and *definitory hypothesis*).

Given the emotion triggered by the patient, we may say that the β-screen (Bion, 1962, p. 22) exerted a powerful action over the analyst – "a profound drowsiness" – and this enables us to assess the client's participation from this other viewpoint as column 6 (action). By checking the Grid once again, we can compose A6 (β-*element* and *action*). The possibility of considering different vertices of observation is what Bion (1963, p. 101) proposes as the psychoanalytic game.

Thus far we have focused on the client when examining the facts of the session. Let us now proceed with the counterpart, the analyst. She feels "a profound drowsiness," which can be seen as a reaction to the client's action and elicits the same type of response: β-*element in action* – A6.

PARTICIPANT 2: I'd like to ask you [Participant 1, the analyst] if the idea you just mentioned – of something causing "chills" in the client and a profound drowsiness in yourself – came up during the session or only now?

PARTICIPANT 1: No, no, it's something for which I don't have a name, something that makes her shiver and at the same time provokes a profound drowsiness in me. So it's not that her chills make me drowsy, or that what she says makes me drowsy. It's not that, it's something subliminal, which in her manifests in one way and in me manifests another way. But the impression I have is that it is one and the same thing that's there, let's say, at the heart of these two sensations, let's put it like this.

Someone then asks a question that seeks to clarify whether in this exercise – a psychoanalytic game (Bion, 1963, p. 101) – we are applying the Grid to the idea (Bion, 1963, p. 4) that arose during session or to the present moment in our theoretical-clinical seminar.

We surmise that both are different junctures in the space-time of Participant 1's narrative and, therefore, we will lead to different results. The paragraph above appeared during the seminar and, thus, at that present time and in that space.

So let us begin by examining this complex paragraph applying the horizontal axis of the Grid to attempt to identify the elements of psychoanalysis.

The entire paragraph can be taken as a *definitory hypothesis* – column 1 – because it presents a specific proposition. Column 2 (Ψ) does not seem appropriate, because it does not contain the *elements of falsification* that characterize this column. Column 3 – *notation* – seems insufficient to characterize the extent of what was proposed. *Attention* – column 4 – embraces the proposition contained in the paragraph in question. *Inquiry* – column 5 – adds "*subliminal*," allowing us to inquire about the workability of the theory of the unconscious (Freud, Klein, Bion), whereas the complement – "*it is one and the same thing that's there ... at the heart of these two sensations*" – leads us to cogitate on finiteness and the infinite (Bion, 1965, pp. 45–46), and on transformations in "O,"[4] as anticipated by Bion in "The Grid," in *Taming Wild Thoughts* (1997, p. 24).

Let us now proceed to the vertical axis of the Grid.

Row A – β-*element* – was extensively studied with the first quote from the text. Row B – α-*element* – is evidenced in the paragraph containing an organized expression of ideas, and from then on we may ascribe the paragraph at issue to any category from row C (*myths, dreams, dream-thoughts*) onward.

The proposal contained in the paragraph brings us a *state of expectation*, i.e., something we can appropriately call *pre-conception* (D). It should be noted that we do not need to rely on Bion's clarity when he exemplifies pre-conception with innate pre-conceptions such as that of the breast (Bion, 1962, p. 69).

The next category related to the paragraph is E (*conception*), to be evolved through realization, which bears upon our discussion of the entire paragraph at issue.

The same goes for F (*concept*) and G (*scientific deductive system*), and for the same reasons.

An important conclusion.

As we study the phenomenon – the chills – that occurred in the analyst's first description, we arrive at categories A1 (β-*element* and *definitory hypothesis*) and A6 (β-*element* and *action*) as possibilities. Continuing our study of the same phenomenon, the analyst's second description gives rise to the possibility of a *pre-conception*, where *expansion* and *inquiry* may be opportune, as well as a greater opening of the analyst's mind – thus, categories D1 (*pre-conception* and *definitory hypothesis*) to D6 (*pre-conception* and *action*).

So, we used the Grid to examine the *phenomenon* from two different viewpoints, based on the analyst's narratives during the seminar, arriving at different qualities or meanings for "the chills."

The difference is rather subtle, is it not?

It is subtle only apparently, because it allows us to discriminate very regressive states as psychotic at different levels of mental evolution. Let us examine some of the differences. The analyst "accompanies" the client in a "psychotic" experience – A1 or A6 – in the first narrative; in the second one, she portrays a state of mental expansion and the possibility of inquiry – D1 (*pre-conception* and *definitory hypothesis*) to D6 (*pre-conception* and *action of formulating*).

Moreover, identifying the *elements of psychoanalysis* becomes essential for the analyst to decide on the *psychoanalytic object*, one of which is interpretation. A psychoanalytic object is a living being and can be described as having the dimensions of the senses, of myths and of passion (1963, p. 11), which in the interpretation per se will be represented at various levels by the elements of rows B (α-*element*), C (*dream*) and G (*scientific theory*) (1963, p. 103).

At the time, I couldn't think about anything, anything ... a profound, overwhelming drowsiness ...

Let us continue to read Bion's text (1963, p. 26):

> The indications I have given in A1 show that strictly speaking A2 must be a null class, because A1 is incapable of development. Yet in some sense A1 can be used to fulfil some of the functions of A2 in that the imprisonment implicit in A1 denies any liberation of meaning.[5]

In the first narrative, a profound drowsiness was mentioned, which was placed in the A1 stratum; in the second narrative, in which "the chills" have something subliminal about them, one might conjecture an emotion that cannot be treated. If it is impossible to treat it, in this case, the perceived subliminality becomes an intuition of the analyst, an intuition that the chills have something more in them, and that this "something more" could be an emotion that, if manifested, might be unbearable. So the client goes back to A1. The second narrative holds the possibility of A2, which is subliminal.

The analyst's intuitive assertion – "*it's something subliminal, which in her manifests in one way and in me manifests another way ... it's something for which I don't have a name*" – gives us a rare opportunity to grasp the meaning of Bion's quote above, whereby A2 is a null class and "the imprisonment implicit in A1 denies any liberation of meaning" (Bion, 1963, p. 26).

PARTICIPANT 3: I treat someone who has schizophrenia and who has been reading the same page from a text by Bleuler every day for 11 years, in which he talks about autism in schizophrenia. She repeats this text, she ... every day to convince herself that there is nothing much she can do etc. She has been in analysis for about three years and, after much conversation, began to show interest in psychoanalysis and to watch videos on psychoanalysis about Bion, such and so. The impression I have is that she has an α-function capacity to develop, for instance, column C and column D from what she listens and hears. She then comes to tell me about, for instance, projection, about psychotic and non-psychotic parts. She watches, she reads, and although it seems she is having a learning experience, she then uses this learning to reinforce her theory, psychotic in my opinion, that she cannot leave the house. That would be one example. She then says to me, "Have you seen Bion's text that talks about psychotic personality? So you must understand that I can't go out, that I can't work, that I can't study."

PARTICIPANT 4: I'm wondering if we can say this learning is development. I'm thinking that a parrot learns to say certain words, it has a memory, it can even make some arrangements of words that make sense, but this does not correspond to actual development. It corresponds to a plaster-casted, memorized learning. I'm not sure it corresponds to an emotional situation of surprise, or perception, or growth.

What our colleague is saying may be one possibility, but it depends on the analyst who will say what she observes. Participant 3 tells us that this is not her impression. A diagnosis of schizophrenia was mentioned. Another quote by Bion (1967, p. 154) will be valuable here:

> The most disturbed patient can show flashes of intuition which are reminders of his mental life often lost to sight. Conversely, persons showing powerful insights are often attacked as mad.[6]

Likewise, in *Learning from Experience*, as we saw in the theoretical introduction, Bion uses the α-*function* as an instrument to study the development of *sense impressions, emotions* and even *algebraic calculus* in the vertical axis of the Grid. However, a reversal of the α-elements may occur (Bion, 1962, p. 25), and those such elements that were achieved may become *bizarre objects*, that is, β-*elements* with traces of ego and superego.

When the client reads a complex text such as Bion's, it is indeed possible that she is capable of following it and using her thought. By going in this direction, the analyst is not following the example of the parrot.

The diagnosis of schizophrenia is of no help to us, because it does not mean the client is incapable of other perceptions and elaborations. In the example, she is capable of certain conceptions, of observations occurring "after much conversation," so it is reasonable to think that the analyst's action, using her own α-*function*, enables the client to use her α-*function* as well and thus evolve.

Let us do the exercise using the clinical situation presented above.

Descriptively, the analyst tells us that after three years of work "*she then comes to tell me about, for instance, projection, about psychotic and non-psychotic parts. She watches, she reads, and* [seems to be] *having a learning experience.*" Thus, with great sophistication, the client is able to read Bion's texts and the analyst is able to follow her. We may conjecture that the client is capable of developing α-*elements* and, therefore, that she operates along rows C (*dream-thoughts*) and D (*pre-conception*) – as suggested by the analyst – but above all along rows E (*conception*) and F (*concept*) because one's impression is that she can think and talk at a very complex level. At this point, we should ask about uses. If we propose that the client is seeking authentic development and choosing rows D (*pre-conception*) and F (*concept*) of the Grid, the uses would be predominantly those of *attention* (column 4) or *inquiry* (5) – the same being true for *concept* (F). All of these movements can be seen as indicative of mental development.

However, after attaining this level, the mental disaster that affects this client's life is manifested: "*She then says to me, 'Have you seen Bion's text that talks about psychotic personality? So you must understand that I can't go out, that I can't work, that I can't study'.*"

Fear invades the scene, fear of the emotion that derives from realizing that she is capable, that she has the capacity, but that she will become accountable and will have to deal with her thoughts and with herself. The client's words continue on to *concepts* (F), which are now articulated with the function of denying the strong emotions that might overwhelm her, that is, the use becomes now that of column 2 in the Grid (F2).

We can continue the exercise with, "*It seems she is having a learning experience,* [but] *she then uses this learning to reinforce her theory, psychotic in my opinion, that she cannot leave the house.*" At this moment, the analyst sheds light on the force this client is exerting upon her, portraying this movement as a powerful projective identification, one that deserves the title of "psychotic theory" and could be considered a *definitory hypothesis* (A1) – or, alternatively, if we consider this an *action*, such as that of neutralizing the analyst's ability, we will have A6.

A clinical situation presented by the moderator (Rezze, 2003, p. 41)

The client comes in, lies down, seemingly happy, and smiles slightly. She says almost immediately, "*I'm happy*" (smiling).

And after a few minutes, "*I have nothing to say.*"

To which I say, "*Well, you already said, firstly, that you were happy; and now, that you have nothing to say. We can see that, when you're happy, you don't know what to do to live with me.*"

My words have two purposes. The first is to help her discern that she is experiencing a state of mind and that she is capable of communicating it verbally, seeing she tells me what is happening. Working with the Grid, the element would be *conception* (E) in the genetic axis, and *notation* (3) in the axis of uses – or *action* if we consider the act of speaking to inform (E3 or E6).

The second purpose is to let her know that her relationship is with me, that I am there with her, something she does not recognize. My words can be taken as *conception* (E) and, if heeded, as *exploratory function* (4) or *inquiry* (5).

There is a slight pause. She says, "*I'm now already thinking about different things. About work ... about other people ... about T. From now on we'll always use a condom* (a certain degree of concern), *but I won't feel him anymore* (sorrowful expression). *He told me that he wished to already have settled his affairs with other women and be only with me, as he truly wants* (the mood of concern is fading). *He even apologized to me* (the feeling of concern disappears and she is satisfied, relieved)."

I say, "*What was happening between us gave rise to what is no longer between us. Then, at first, you worry, but things begin to sort out in your head and, in the end, there is a successful outcome in your favor* (he apologizes) *and you are soothed.*"

The patient's words seem to respond to what I had previously uttered, that is, what I convey to her does not seem to find echo within her. Thus, she immerses herself in a state in which she creates her own visions, into which she plunges. With this immersion, she fulfills her own needs: by distancing herself from the analyst, she autonomously provides the means that satisfy her. If we consider her words as an evacuatory movement, we would classify them in row A (β-*element*), but I think it would be more appropriate to consider them in *dream-thoughts* (C) and in the uses of column 2, because they serve to avoid feeling the analyst's words or presence (C2).

My words aimed to let her know that there was a connection between us and that this connection had been broken. I also try to describe how this might be unfolding in her spirit, i.e., how the situation she creates initially brings upon her a state of concern, and how, thanks to the adjustments she keeps on making, she gradually ends up achieving tranquility. By pointing out what is "in her head," I attempt to characterize the autonomy of her action, that is, to apprise her that she does not depend on me to make this movement. What is described above, in another framework, corresponds to what I believe to be a *transformation in hallucinosis* (Bion, 1965, p. 161).

"*Do you really think it was a success? Was it good for me?*"

As I see it, the client takes what was said and realizes what it is about, which would correspond to *pre-conception* (D), or, taking into account the speculative level, possibly to *attention* (4). However, her perspective changes, like that well-known figure that if you look at in one way you see a chalice and if you look at in another way you see two faces. We can say here that she reverses the perspective (Bion, 1962, p. 41), that is, what was said to her to illustrate a certain view of reality is used to set her at ease and allay for her the reality that had been pointed out. It can be seen that the patient's reaction is possibly related to the pain she would probably feel if she came into direct contact with the analyst's words.

I then add, "*How could I say that? Actually, I don't know anyone, I don't know what's going on and I only have what you tell me. I was talking about what you do, how you have to mend everything in your head.*"

My words serve two purposes: the first is to help her discern what is happening from the analyst's viewpoint; the second is to allow the client, by assessing the situation, to create a distance, a space, a *crevice* through which she may observe the ongoing facts.

We can see this observation corresponds to a *psychoanalytic object*, that is, in the evolution of the text I used the dimensions of *sense, myth and passion* (Bion, 1963, p. 11), whereas abstractly my words reveal aspects of α-*elements* (row B), *dream-thoughts* (C) and *scientific theory* (G) (Bion, 1963, p. 103), although I believe that my observation is more fitting in *concept* (F). As for uses, given the fact I am communicating with the client, we have column 6 – *action*.

The clinical fragments we are studying here are leading us to consider both the *elements of psychoanalysis* (according to their places in the Grid) and the *psychoanalytic object*, of which interpretation is an example.

"*So, I take one thing that you say and use it for something completely different?*" (She seems to become aware of the fact and shows interest in it.)

This is a rare moment in the relationship with this client. (Actually, it may be uncommon in the relationship with any client.) She seems to establish a relationship with me, a connection, a realization, through her experience, of what I am trying to bring closer to her. And, last but not least, she seems to conceive a thought.

I say, "*Yes, you take what I say (which may even be consistent with an actual need of yours) and transform it into something else that immediately satisfies and soothes you.*"

I remain within the situation, striving to maintain the connection that was established between me and her, between the part of her that lives and the part that acknowledges herself living and even capable of conceiving a thought. She goes on and remains within the situation as well, which is a rare event in the relationship that has been maintained between us.

She says, "*So, it's not the truth.*"

She continues in the situation and, through our experience, acquires a knowledge, something that had never possible until then. She maintains that knowledge until this moment. And judging by the emotions that accompany her words, I believe she is able to realize the situation in which she finds herself, becoming aware of it. We can consider her idea as a *psychoanalytic object*.

I say something else about what was discussed above, particularly her acknowledgment that she takes facts and uses them in different ways, as well as her recognition that this is not the truth. I emphasize both realizations. She then says, "*Did I say that? I don't recall.*"

This is a very important moment. A rupture has occurred. There has been a split. She really finds the events odd, and they do not seem to concern her.

On the genetic axis, we find that the client evolved from the lower levels of the Grid to those of greater development (A→G), but due to the strong emotions aroused by the analytical work she also makes the reverse movement (G→A).

Final considerations

This chapter was written bearing in mind that senior analysts express their difficulty in understanding the workings of the Grid and its use in their clinical and theoretical experience. We have tried to develop a dynamic that fosters the perception of the *psychoanalytic game*, a dynamic that performed after a session will allow a clinical situation to be rethought. This same instrument may be opportune not only to show when different theoretical systems are applied to the same clinical situation, but also in clinical meetings that can be clarified by the participants, regarding discrimination, if they can make use of psychoanalytic "elements" and "objects."

We have tried to adhere to a theoretical system by following as closely as possible the original text while bearing in mind that, in 1963, Bion (1997, p. 12) presented "The Grid" at the British Psychoanalytical Society – "*In our work, 'O' must always be an emotional experience*" – anticipating the changes it will undergo as it evolves into transformations in "O."

With the successive developments of Bion's theories, we will have the opportunity to examine the clinical situation from other viewpoints, such as transformations in rigid motion, in hallucinosis, in knowledge, in "O" – thus, the concepts of "at-one-ment" and common "O," among others, that have greatly expanded our horizons.

Notes

1 Paper presented at "The Journey of Psychoanalysis: Bion, Transformations and Developments," Brazilian Society of Psychoanalysis of São Paulo, March 14 and 15, 2008.
2 Bion, *Elements of Psychoanalysis* (London: Karnac, Maresfield Library, 1984), p. 23. Also in *Complete Works V*, p. 23.
3 The Durval Marcondes Institute of Psychoanalysis of the Brazilian Society of Psychoanalysis of São Paulo.
4 "In our work, O must always be an emotional experience." Bion, "The Grid" in *Taming Wild Thoughts*, in *Complete Works V*, p. 106.
5 Bion, *Elements of Psychoanalysis* (London: Karnac, Maresfield Library, 1984), p. 26. Also in *Complete Works V*, p. 26.
6 Bion, *Second Thoughts – Commentary*, in *Complete Works VI*, p. 194.

References

Bion, W. R. (1962) *Learning from Experience* (London: William Heinemann Medical Books).
Bion, W. R. (1963) *Elements of Psycho-Analysis* (London: William Heinemann Medical Books).
Bion, W. R. (1965) *Transformations* (London: William Heinemann Medical Books).
Bion, W. R. (1967) *Second Thoughts* (London: Heinemann).
Bion, W. R. (1997) *Taming Wild Thoughts*, edited by F. Bion (London: Karnac Books).
Rezze, C. J. (2003) "A fresta," in P. C. Sandler and T. R. L. Haudenschild (eds.) *Panorama* (São Paulo: SBPSP Departamento de Publicações), pp. 41–56.

Chapter 6

Emotion, non-emotion and analyst language

Celia Fix Korbivcher

I.

Writing about emotion is a challenge. This may seem paradoxical as we need to put into words experiences which we have no way of translating. We don't have access to the emotion itself only its approximations. Emotions are experiences of the individual, far from the rational field of knowledge.

The word emotion means e-motion, in motion, the act of moving. According to Bion, a movement, a storm, is created when two minds meet. Emotion will connect these two minds. Bion tells us that: when the storm comes, "one does not immediately know what the emotional storm is, but the problem is how to make the best of it, how to turn the adverse circumstance into a good cause" (Bion, 1976). In our clinical work, we are often exposed to specific situations in which states of intense emotional turmoil predominate. Some patients who are immersed in this atmosphere are unable to contain the emotions in their minds, transform them, and think about them. Instead, they violently discharge them into the analyst's mind.

Other patients invite us to share experiences in which manifestations of the primordial mind – unintegrated and autistic states – prevail. The latter are dominated by sensations which have not acquired representation. Such patients avoid psychic contact with emotions and mainly express themselves through the body. For them, the body is the stage on which they find a state of some cohesion and a sense of existence.

My question is, what tools does the analyst have to operate in such apparently adverse situations to enable patients to live their emotions, become aware of them, contain them in their minds, and transform them into thoughts and language that can be communicated?

In one of his lectures, Bion (1978) asks:

> Who is the patient we are meeting when starting the session? Is he a small, primitive creature or a grown person, and what language will we use to make contact?

Paraphrasing Bion, I ask what language the psychoanalyst should use with his patients when facing highly emotional states of mind. What language should he

DOI: 10.4324/9781003171584-6

speak with the primordial states of mind of his educated and developed patients? What language will the psychoanalyst use to communicate with the body of his patients, their unintegrated states, and autistic barriers? How may the analyst use his capacity for reverie and α-function when facing such situations?

In this paper, I aim to examine the type of language used by the analyst faced with strong emotional states and primordial states of mind, states in which emotional avoidance is predominant and the body is the patient's main channel of expression. To this end, I make use of Bion's theory of *Transformations* (Bion, 1965), particularly, transformations in "O". I propose that the analysts' language for accessing such states of mind should be the "language of emotions", specific to transformations in "O", with the analyst being at one with his patient, "being" the emotion of the moment. I suggest that this could be an experience of aesthetic fruition. I also report clinical material from Lia and Arthur to illustrate these issues and stimulate discussion.

II. Emotion

According to Meltzer (1998), Bion in his work builds the foundations of a theory of emotions, in an unprecedented way. Bion locates emotion at the centre of mental growth through learning from experience. Emotion results from the relationship between container–contained; that is, through the contact between two minds. The α-function, a function of the mind, converts sensory impressions and emotions into α-elements; these elements are conducive to dream-thoughts. When the α-function fails to act on sensory impressions and emotions, they remain unchanged, becoming β-elements, which do not lend themselves to thinking, but only to evacuation.

The emotion that results from the container–contained relationship is the first step towards thinking. Awareness of emotion results in an emotional experience. For Bion (1962), this is the analyst and patient field of work during the session – "learning from the emotional experience".

When an emotional experience does not achieve a symbolic representation to be used in dreams and thoughts, it may somehow be discharged from the mind. The analyst's task, therefore, using his trained intuition, is to contain this emotional experience, and with his capacity for reverie and α-function, to name it. The patient, then, would be able to keep that experience in his mind, think about it, which would allow him to become "the experience".

Emotions, just as atmospheric changes influence a reflection on the water's surface, become constant elements in a transformation that will affect the resulting representation, whether or not this representation is distorted or preserved in its invariants (Braga, 2016, personal communication).

For Bion (1962), emotions have a potential for linking function. It is only after emotions are connected with representations or ideation, that they can link. The links between objects constitute emotional experiences. Bion highlights three types of emotional links that will apply α-function: love, hate, and knowledge (L, H, K) and their negatives (−L, −H, −K).

Bion considers the K link, learning from experience, to be the evolution of basic emotions. This notion is associated with a "model of the mind as a thinking apparatus with the capacity to learn from and understand the emotional experiences that impact it" (Meltzer, 1998).

In turn, negative links are expressions of hatred directed towards links that connect objects, instead of the objects themselves. It is not the objects which are attacked but, rather, the links between them. Patients operating in −K despise "any new development in the personality as if the new development were a rival to be destroyed" (Bion, 1962, p. 128). This hinders the activity of knowing.

III. Transformations

For Bion, the analyst´s field of work is to learn from emotional experience, and the theory of *Transformations* (Bion, 1965) is an observational theory of the mental phenomena in this field.

Bion suggests different types of transformations: transformations in rigid motion, projective transformations, transformations in hallucinosis, in K, in −K, and transformations in O.

I understand Bion's concern in discriminating different groups of transformations as an attempt to guide clinical analysts facing the various communication levels proposed by patients.

For Bion (1991), the fundamental discovery of psychoanalysis would be the contact with equivalents of embryonic traces and archaic mental states found in civilized and educated individuals with a developed speech function, despite presenting primordial behavioural patterns. Such archaic mental states, in my view, would be what Bion (1997) terms "inaccessible states of mind", embryonic mental states that are accompanied by sub-thalamic manifestations of fear. I propose that this area of phenomena is related to the unintegrated area.

Unintegrated phenomena (Bick, 1986) are characterized by an absence of the notion of limits capable of keeping emotional contents joined, resulting in the lack of discrimination between internal and bodily substances. From the introjection of an external object interacting continuously with the surface of the infant´s body, a psychic skin will be formed, giving birth to fantasies of internal and external space. If for any reason there are disturbances in the functioning of the primary skin, a second skin will be developed to protect the infant from intolerable unintegrated experiences. The threat of falling into an endless space, of dissolving, and spilling are expressions of these states. Autistic maneuvers are often developed as a protection against such experiences. Relationships between "me" and "not me" in the autistic realm occur through adhesive equation (Tustin, 2012); the individual will adhere to continuous surfaces, avoiding any space and thus maintaining experiences of continuity with the object.

In 2005 and 2009 I proposed including in Bion's theory of transformations the autistic transformations and unintegrated transformations (Korbivcher, 2005, 2009, 2013, 2016). Autistic transformations are characterized by being formed within an autistic medium, which implies the absence of the concept of internal and external object. Some of their invariants would be the presence of auto-sensual activities, the "absence of emotional life", and the experience of "emotional emptiness". Relationships between "me" and "not me" occur through sensation objects – autistic objects and autistic shapes. Unintegrated transformations occur in an unintegrated medium, characterized by intense unmetallized bodily manifestations without mental representation. Some of its invariants would be the presence of corporeal manifestations, a constant state of extreme vulnerability, the threat of dissolving, of spilling and of falling into a black hole. This means a constant state of terror of losing the sense of one's own existence.

IV. Transformations in "O"

Writing about "O" and about transformations in "O" may seem paradoxical because, as defined by Bion, "O" is unknowable. We may only make some conjectures about it.

In regard to "O", Bion (1965, p. 26) writes:

> I shall use the sign O to denote that which is the ultimate reality represented by terms such as ... absolute truth, the godhead, infinite, the thing-in-itself. O does not fall in the domain of knowledge or learning save incidentally, it can be "become", but it cannot be "known". It is darkness or formlessness, but enters the domain K when it has evolved to a point where it can be known.

Bion defines "O", the thing-in-itself, as a phenomenon that can only be experienced and not known. My question is how this concept is considered in clinical practice. Bion suggests that the interpretations should do more than increase knowledge. They should enable the patient's "being" emotion which could eventually evolve to knowledge, K.

Bion (1965, p. 148) states that the gap between knowing phenomena and being reality resembles the gap between knowing about psychoanalysis and being psychoanalysed. I suggest that there may be a gap between the analyst "knowing about psychoanalysis" and "being psychoanalysis". Analysts "being psychoanalysis" involves the analyst using his mind, his personality, his psychoanalytically trained intuition, and incarnated theories, interacting and existing with the patient at each movement in the session.

Regarding "O", Grotstein (2007, p. 114) writes:

> Bion crossed the Rubicon of psychoanalytic respectability in London ... and launched a metapsychological revolution whose echoes are still reverberating across the psychoanalytic landscape worldwide. ... [He] introduced inner and outer cosmic uncertainty, infinity, relativism, and numinousness as its successor.

Grotstein states that Bion promotes a key paradigm shift in psychoanalysis by conceptualizing "O". Bion abandons positivism and expands the field of psychoanalysis to an infinite and unlimited field, "dark" and "formless", in which the unknown, uncertainty, mystery, and doubt prevail.

V. Language

As we know, the word is the main medium of work for the analyst. The word transforms emotional experience into α-elements to enable thoughts. However, it may reveal or conceal, depending on the type of ongoing emotion. Therefore, it may become an actual obstacle to communication. The analyst's intuition and imagination are key elements in the process of choosing the language that he will use with his patients.

This issue is further complicated when unrepresented mental states prevail, states in which individuals predominantly express themselves through sensations and corporeal manifestations. In this context, it is difficult for the analyst to find a suitable language to access the patients' experiences and to reach them. We must be able to listen to the non-verbal language which translates more accurately than words the emotion of the moment.

We may establish a link between the type of language in circumstance as described above and the language used by mothers with their pre-verbal infants, motherese. In this language:

> Infants read their mothers' lips and facial expressions and understand their emotional meaning when there is a concordance between lexical (verbal) and non-lexical (sounds, intonations, gestures) aspects of the spoken language.
> (Norman, 2004, quoted in Reiner, 2012)

The content, the meaning of the words used by the mother with the infant, is not relevant, but its prosody is. Infants are more attracted to the music of the mother's communication than to its lyrics. It is through this musicality that the infant captures the emotion of the mother. The "mother being emotion", just as the "analyst being psychoanalysis" uses a "language of emotions" which is conveyed through the tone of her voice, of her facial expression, her muscle tone when carrying the infant, etc.

This mode of expression, in my view, is close to the notion of transformations in O. Transformation in "O" is an experience that emerges at a specific moment in the analytical session when patient and analyst are at one with each other, sharing a common emotional experience. This would be considered an experience of aesthetic fruition that cannot be known or translated into words, but only lived. The language that promotes such experiences would be the "language of emotions", the analyst "being emotion", far from the language of knowledge, K.

According to Bion, (1970) this would be the "language of achievement".[1] The language of achievement not only expresses something but also that enables a new experience. It is not a random language but instead is based in the analyst's trained psychoanalytic intuition. The analyst spontaneously and genuinely communicates at that moment with his discipline of absence of memory and desire (Bion, 1981) and his negative capability, something that provokes a rupture during the session. From that moment on, analyst and patient are no longer the same. Both begin to operate in the dimension of "O", "being emotion", which would eventually evolve towards K.

VI. Clinical material

Arthur

When seeing me in the waiting room for one of his sessions, Arthur, 8 years of age, plunges his flaccid body to the floor and proceeds to drag himself towards our room. He throws himself onto the couch, where he remains sprawled out for some time. Then he gets up, grabs two large plastic swords from his toy box and very carefully sticks one down each pant leg. He carefully checks whether his right leg is firmly supported and then repeats the same procedure on the other leg. He changes the position of the sword, now tucking it under his shirt against his back, covering his spine. He starts walking proudly around the room, showing off his upright, firm body.

In another session, when calling Arthur, I find him completely in the waiting room sprawled out across the body of his driver, totally absorbed in his iPhone. He fails to react to my presence. Finally, he walks to our room, with his flaccid body half-stumbling, and throws himself onto the couch, where he remains for a while. Then, he asks me to make him a paper airplane and unsuccessfully attempts to make it fly, but it soon falls. Arthur becomes very angry, throws away the plane, and suddenly throws himself onto my lap. I am impacted to see that big, strange body on top of me, a flaccid mass, lifeless, giving the impression that it would dissolve and spread out. I feel very uncomfortable because he awakens no tenderness and care, unlike other children who use to sit in my lap.

I tell him that he got angry because the plane did not fly and fell, perhaps similarly to his body's inability to stand up straight. I add that he feels like he has nothing firm inside of him, that his body is soft and shapeless. Then I move him towards the sofa. I then search for a puppet in his box and show him the puppet's body, a flaccid, shapeless body. I tell him that perhaps he may feel like this puppet, with a flaccid body, without nothing firmer inside it. I slip my hand inside the puppet and show him how firm it is now. I tell him that he feels his body becoming firmer when his body clings to mine, and that makes him feels safer. Arthur listens to me carefully. Then, he slides to the ground. He grabs the family of dolls and retreats saying: "Heal me, heal me!" I tell him, "You are asking me for help so you do not feel so afraid of spreading out and disappearing for ever. You feel less terrorized if I hold your body and everything you have inside, if you cling to my lap." He continues playing with the dolls and says, "Hold me, Celia!

I will ooze out and melt. Hold me, please! Please, hold me! Someone is falling from a building; if you hold him, you will save him." He grabs a doll and talks about a parachute. He says: "I have a parachute! Parachutes save people when they are falling, but some people die when the parachute doesn't open. If you fall slowly with the parachute open, it saves you. Save me! Save me!"

I say, "You are afraid of falling and having nothing to hold you up. You hold on to me like a parachute that will not let you fall and disappear for ever. Now, you are able to talk about what makes you so much afraid, and you are able to communicate all this and ask for help."

Lia

I find myself apprehensive when meeting Lia (40 years of age) for her session. She had some absences, and there have been tense situations between us in prior sessions. I did not know what to expect. On this day, Lia arrives calm. She walks in, lies down, and says in a somewhat cheerful tone, "I had a different weekend. I went out three nights, I went to three parties, I drank way too much, and I was very, very happy. It has been a long time since I have felt this happy." She speaks enthusiastically about the parties and the different people she met over the weekend. Next, more discouraged she says that she never felt as lonely as when she arrived home after her parties.

I think about the polarity between excitement and depression. I feel like I am walking on eggshells with her, fearing her unexpectedly explosive reactions that often occur whenever I speak.

I tell her that we are meeting after several days of separation and that perhaps she had felt abandoned and the parties may have made her feel momentarily supported.

She says in an angry and hostile tone that the connections she made were particularly good at the parties, but she continues to feel very discouraged.

To minimize her suffering, I invite her to question whether both her joy at the parties and her loneliness need to be so intense. I add that perhaps she could recall moments when she felt good, such as at the parties, and consider that both loneliness and joy come from inside of her.

She reacts angrily, "I knew you would talk about that! You always talk about the same thing; you always say that I should do things differently from the way I do them! It is always like this! I even already know what you will say! It is always like this!"

I am taken aback by her overreaction. I understand that she heard something completely different from what I said. Spontaneously I ask her, "What did you hear me say, could you repeat it back to me?" She became very grumpy and refused to respond. I insist and she unwillingly repeats my words.

I tell her that she seems to listen to something inside her; she always hears the same thing: criticism and mistreatment. I tell her that it is difficult for her to accept that I am a separate person who tells her things that come to mind that are different from the things she hears.

Lia listens to me carefully and I realize that her tone is changing as she talks, seeming less irritated and angry. Her emotion changes, and the hostile environment disappears. In a more depressed tone, she says, "I understand what you are saying." After a while, in silence and shrouded in considerable pain, she says, "I remember a verse I wrote many years ago where I talked about it."

It is a palindrome; she goes on to explain what a palindrome is. They are words that can be written the same way from left to right and from right to left. She tells me about the verse she wrote.

In Portuguese, the phrase is "S.O.S. SÓ SÓS SOMAMOS!" She explains the meaning of the verse. She says that in order to become two, a pair, one must be on one's own, be separate. She says she wrote it a long time ago and that only now does it make sense.

I was impacted by her association, an aesthetic creation erupting at that very moment, impacted by the way she transformed what we had experienced moments earlier.

I say that something seems to have changed throughout the session. Now she was able to form a pair with me. I say that through the palindrome she poetically expresses her perception that she is on her own, that we are separate, and that it is very painful to accept this condition. It makes her feel very helpless and vulnerable, as she said at the beginning. The session ends.

VII. Discussion

How does one consider the important psychic changes that occurred with Lia and Arthur as related to the language used by the analyst? Is the therapeutic action rooted in the semantic meanings (K) of the language alone?

We could ask what makes us think that the analyst operating with transformations in O, using a language of emotions, "being" the emotion, makes important emotional changes possible for the patient. Why when operating only with transformations in K, that is, with a language that increases knowledge, would the analyst not be able to provide such experiences?

Both materials reported illustrate these issues.

Facing the impact of projective transformations, and transformations in hallucinosis manifested by Lia, the analyst realizes that Lia had not heard the analyst's words but she had heard herself. The analyst, immersed in this experience (transformations K → O) using a simple and informal but straightforward language, spontaneously asks Lia to repeat what she had just heard. While listening to herself, Lia immediately changes her state of mind. The course of the session is ruptured. Lia gets depressed and creatively and poetically communicates the palindrome. The palindrome is a verse with the same meaning when read forwards and backwards. Using the palindrome, Lia reveals that inside of her there exists the opposite of what she had experienced until that moment in the session.

A new dimension arises, poetically and painfully indicating the awareness of "being on one's own". At that moment, the analyst, and the patient with each other "being" the emotion (transformations in O). This would be considered an experience of aesthetic fruition, a unique moment of strong emotion that cannot be translated into words, but only experienced.

We could surmise that if, instead of asking Lia to repeat what she had heard, the analyst had offered a classic interpretation with persecutory content, she would have possibly invited the patient to also operate at levels of rational knowledge, distant from emotion, which would make important emotional changes more difficult.

When meeting with the analyst, a separate person, Arthur feels the threat of losing his body support (unintegrated transformation). With the swords – a concrete, hard, and firm object (autistic object) – he seeks to obtain a cohesive state within his body to allow him to remain standing. His frenetic search reveals a constant threat of dissolving, spilling, and falling into an endless space (unintegrated transformations). Arthur has failed to develop an endoskeleton that is capable of keeping his body upright and cohesive or a psychic skin capable of gathering and containing his internal contents and establishing a boundary between inside and outside. Arthur proposes further exploring his body support with the paper airplane game. In the absence of support from the plane, Arthur abruptly throws his flaccid body onto the analyst's lap (non-integrated transformations). Faced with that sprawled "volume" on her lap, a lifeless body, the analyst experiences a strong emotion that intuitively leads her to resort to the puppet figure, a doll with an empty and flaccid body. The analyst explains to Arthur how she believes that he feels about his body (transformations in O → K). The analyst's language triggers a rupture in Arthur's pattern of communication. He becomes aware of his vulnerable state and can ask for help (transformations O → K). Arthur says, "Heal me! Hold me ... Celia, I will melt." Using the parachute, he also enacts his request for the analyst to operate as a parachute, to hold, support, and protect him from falling and disappearing for ever.

I think with patients such as Arthur, in whom unintegrated states predominate and who resort to autistic maneuvers, it becomes crucial for analysts to plunge into that idiosyncratic patient world, so they emerge later when they are able to assign some meaning to it. In other words, they operate in transformations O → K.

In end, I quote Meltzer (1998, p. 77), who proposes the following question:

> Has Bion succeeded in constructing a theory of the mind that will lend itself to a substantial concept of emotions that will distinguish modern psychoanalysis from other psychologies, including Freud's, where the emotions are either primitive insertions, noises in the machine, or bodily manifestations of mental states perceived as emotions?

Note

1 Language of achievement is based on Keats' concept of "negative capability, that is, when a man is capable of being in uncertainties, mysteries, doubts, without any irritable reaching after fact and reason".

References

Bick, E. (1986) "Further considerations on the function of the skin in early object relations: findings from infant observation integrated into child and adult analysis", *British Journal of Psychotherapy*, 2: 292–299.
Bion, W. R. (1962) *Learning from Experience* (London: Karnac, 1984).
Bion, W. R. (1965) *Transformations* (London: Karnac, 1984).
Bion, W. R. (1970) *Attention and Interpretation* (London: Karnac, 1984).
Bion W. R. (1976) "Making the best of a bad job", in *The Complete Works of W. R. Bion*, vol. X (London: Karnac).
Bion, W. R. (1978) *Conversando com Bion: Quatro Dicussões com Bion. Bion em Nova York e em São Paulo* (Rio de Janeiro: Imago, 1992).
Bion, W. R. (1981) "Notes on memory and desire", in R. Langs (ed.) *Classics in Psychoanalytic Technique* (New York: Jason Aronson, 1981), pp. 259–260. First edition 1967.
Bion W. R. (1991) *A Memoir of the Future* (London: Karnac).
Bion W. R. (1997) *Taming Wild Thoughts* (London: Karnac).
Grotstein, J. S. (2007) *A Beam of Intense Darkness: Wilfred Bion's Legacy to Psychoanalysis* (London: Karnac).
Korbivcher, C. F. (2005) "The theory of transformations and autistic states: autistic transformations: a proposal", *International Journal of Psychoanalysis*, 86: 1595–1610.
Korbivcher, C. F. (2009) "A teoria das transformações os fenômenos não integrados: diluição e queda" [Bion's theory and unintegrated phenomena: falling and dissolving], *Revista Brasileira de Psicanálise*, 47: 111–125.
Korbivcher, C. F. (2013) *Autistic Transformations: Bion's Theory and Autistic Phenomena* (London: Karnac).
Korbivcher, C. F. (2016) "Bion's theory and unintegrated phenomena: falling and dissolving", in H. Levine and D. Power (eds.) *Engaging Primitive Anxieties of the Emerging Self: Papers from the 7th International Conference of the Work of Frances Tustin* (London: Karnac).
Meltzer, D. (1998) "O significado clínico da obra de Bion", in *Desenvolvimento Kleiniano*, vol. III (São Paulo: Editora Escuta).
Norman, J. (2004) "Transformations of early infantile experience: a six-month-old baby in psychoanalysis", *International Journal of Psychoanalysis*, 85: 1103–1122.
Reiner, A (2012) *Bion and Being: Passion and the Creative Mind* (London: Karnac).
Tustin, F. (2012) *Autistic Barriers in Neurotic Patients* (London: Karnac). Originally published in 1986.

Chapter 7

Clinical use of myths in psychoanalysis

Myth, psychoanalysis and psychic reality

Celso Antonio Vieira de Camargo

Preamble

Firstly, thanks to the Yanomamis, it is possible to substantiate the universality of certain overarching themes in the imagination of peoples. Besides the beauty and poetry of mythical accounts in a "raw" state, such as those that emerge from descriptions of Yanomami cosmogony, we can see the impact that nature overall and the psychic reality of each human being has on all of us. We have, thus, descriptions of the genesis of the world, of the first couple that will give rise to all other Yanomamis, and of animals, alongside accounts of the suffering of living beings in the face of the beauty and power of nature. Rain that does not cease (the flood), scarcity of food (the great hunger), fire, intimacy with animals, anxieties of annihilation (everything ends …) – each of these events triggers the mythical imagination and emerges from these accounts, some of which we transcribe in this chapter. Next, we establish some correlations between the myths of Oedipus and the Garden of Eden and the labors of knowledge, as perceived by Bion. To conclude, we discuss a correlation between the myth of Dionysus (as described in Euripides' *The Bacchae*) and a specific clinical situation, and attempt to show that myths can be used as stimuli for the facts of a session and provide models for us to think about psychic events.

We endeavor to discuss these myths from a psychoanalytical conception, and from this perspective our main concern is to acknowledge that myths, among other approaches, can be seen as dramatizations of mental contents.

Introduction

The Yanomamis, with the help of Cláudia Andujar and some missionaries, bequeathed us their history and their version of the creation of the world, fortunately recorded by the excellent photographer and her friends.

This compilation of myths, titled *Mitopoemas Yãnomam* [Yanomami mythpoems], was published in book form by Olivetti do Brasil (Andujar and Bardi, 1978). The process of producing this book is quite interesting and deserves to be described.

DOI: 10.4324/9781003171584-7

In 1974, photographer Cláudia Andujar completed a documentary record of the Yãnomam Indians in Roraima. Due to the difficulties in communication, she asked them to draw and describe the characters and situations from their mythical space. Taken together, these descriptions reconstructed elements from a Yanomami cosmogony. They were later translated by missionaries directly from the original, in "raw" form, so to speak, and then received a literary treatment.

This approach associated images and language, and a process of "translation" into a modern Western language – a process that, one way or another, we all face in our daily lives whenever we have to convert that which arises from the unknown in each one of us into a better articulated language. It is more or less the same process we observe in dreams, when we also have to "translate" images into a verbal narrative. And we can say it is also very similar to the workings of the α-function, a term Bion coined for our cognitive perception of the inner and outer worlds.

Interestingly, the Yanomamis have several versions of the creation of the world. The "transcreation" of these versions into a literary language, as suggested by the book editors, is as follows.

The beginning of the world, 1

An immense part of the sky split itself. Everything ended. The feet of heaven are far away. The sky above is propped upon them. The sky is suspended overhead. Its wooden legs have been thrust into the ground. Another rift appeared in the sky attached to a fork. The heavens rip open once and again. The weather is cloudy. Everything is over. There are no more woodlands. The toppled forests made a hole in the earth and plunged in very deeply. Small-leaved and short-trunked trees are uprooted and are split in half as they fall. High above in the sky there is still water; rainwater.

The second version was also transcreated:

The beginning of the world, 2

The small hut way up there, in the sky. Everything has ended. Far, far away the Yanomamis cry. Everything ends. A small hut way up there, far away. Another hut built nearby. Up here, my ancestors' hut. At the beginning of time everything ended, everything fell from above. The Yanomamis all cry in the *tapiri* [thatched shack]. Anguished, they pummel the *hiima* [pets]. They pummeled a lot; they also pummeled the pots and pans. All the boys cry. Shamans brace up the sky. The shamans held up the sky. Slowly they raise heaven up; not too high they suspend it. Another piece of the sky, filled with trees, rifts apart. A part of the sky remains in place (the one we still see today). The great shaman props up the sky, props it up a lot.

The cosmogony proceeds with the appearance of the primal Yanomamis, Omam and Yoasi, then the women, animals (tapir, armadillo, possum), followed by stories of floods, fires – the appearance of fire through the alligator – and the destruction of the world. In short, the cosmos populated by characters and facts that are significant for Yanomami culture. Parallel worlds existed as well, and every Yanomami had an alter ego called řixi. Each Yanomami had his or her řixi, that is, they were born, grew, hunted and died together, but never met. When a Yanomami died suddenly, it was because someone had killed his or her řixi.

At a certain point, we see an ancestral Yanomami copulating with his own leg, which becomes pregnant! This reminded me of one of the vicissitudes of Dionysus, who, to be born, had to be sewn on Zeus' thigh after Semele's death. Men giving birth: might we see here a reference to what Freud would later call the constitutional bisexuality of each one of us?

It is interesting to note the construction eventually arrived at. For the representation of a myth to be accessible to a 20th century Western mind, it was necessary to transcribe the indigenous story through visual images, each associated with a written depiction, which in turn had to be "retranslated" into a more "understandable" literary form. As I mentioned above, this is the process of the α-function.

This procedure allows us to access a form of mental functioning that might be called *more primordial*. I found this term in André Green's paper presented in Turin (Green, 1979) on the celebration of the centenary of Bion's birth. In fact, I believe we are here on the very edge of the unknown, on the threshold of the source of creativity itself – that formless unknown within each one of us.

In the Yanomami myth-poem, the onset of the creation of life is described as taking place after a destruction, an end. As I see it, this expresses a very germane element of life when observed from the viewpoint of the vertex of psychic reality. To be sure, everything in life succeeds something else. This made me think of the symbology often expressed through the image of a snake curled around its own tail, an image representative of the cycle of life itself, where everything begins and ends, in an endless circular movement, at least for the duration of life. At the same time, we can also identify this description with the notion of unconscious as the psychic locus where opposites coexist and where there are no contradictions.

This characteristic, as described in myths where the creation and destruction of the world are associated, may serve as an introduction to an idea of Bion, the notion of "catastrophic change," that every significant psychic change is accompanied by intense feelings of calamity. We will delve further into this when we discuss the myth of Oedipus.

Another noteworthy aspect in these indigenous myths is the emergence of the Yanomami race from a first couple, the narrative of the flood, the catastrophic fire in the forest, and the appearance of other Yanomami.

It is legitimate to imagine that, mythically and intuitively, the Yanomamis depict not only the origin of each one of us from a primal couple (our parents), but also the tragic impact experienced in the face of the forces of Nature (flood and fire) and the feeling that we are all faced with annihilation, the end, death. We are confronted with psychic truths here, which acquire a clearer meaning through psychoanalysis.

Freud proposed an interesting idea that established a very significant relationship between myth and psychic reality. In *Psychopathology of Everyday Life*, he writes:

> In point of fact I believe that a large part of the mythological view of the world, which extends a long way into the most modern religions, *is nothing but psychology projected into the external world*. The obscure recognition (the endopsychic perception, as it were) of psychical factors and relations in the unconscious is mirrored [...] in the construction of a supernatural reality, which is destined to be changed back once more by science into the psychology of the unconscious. One could venture to explain in this way the myths of paradise and the fall of man, of God, of good and evil, of immortality, and so on, and to transform *metaphysics* into *metapsychology*.
> (Freud, 1960, p. 256)

Definitions of myth are many, but here I only wish to say that *myths, for psychoanalysts, ultimately, concern the organization of fantasies and how we establish contact with our psychic reality*. The more universal and accepted by a culture a myth is, the more it presents itself as a paradigm of that culture's values. By the same token, it will also propagate collective fantasies.

In our clinical work, it is essential to consider what takes place inside the room from the perspective of the emotional experiences[1] lived by the analyst and the analysand. Even though we can see that the apprehension of emotional experiences is observational and, above all, intuitive, those experiences are a central aspect of psychic life and one of the cornerstones of the concept of the mental universe as put forward by Bion.

We may say that emotional experiences develop invariably within a relationship, whether it is a person's relationship with him- or herself, with another person or even with an inanimate object. A complicating factor immediately arises, because clinical practice shows that all of us often treat emotions and human contact as if they belonged to the inanimate world, and then behave accordingly. Another important fact, as I see it, is that we are always undergoing emotional experiences, which are characterized by a continuum from birth to death.

For my part, a template for emotional experiences and for psychoanalytic sessions can be found in myths and dreams. In the latter, something of external reality can be perceived in what we have learned to call "day's residues," i.e., the elements of reality that stimulate inner, often totally unexpected experiences. However, dreams contain the intrapsychic factor to a degree greater than myths do – we can say they expand within the individual. Myths, even personal myths, open us up to the social, therefore to the group, and to the group's emotional implications for the individual. For this reason, I believe dreams and myths, as signs of psychic reality, complement each other. Much like dreams, myths have a "make-believe" dimension. For the psychoanalyst, it matters that myths can be a way of organizing fantasies, and this is all the more significant because they are accepted by the social group. This allows us to treat myths as a model for emotional experiences and for sessions of analysis. This concept, of course, does not preclude other approaches, such as those developed by Walter Burkert in his excellent *Structure and History in Greek Mythology and Ritual*.[2] I believe that for us psychoanalysts, however, myths make sense particularly because they refer to the fate of the individual within his or her social group or cultural context. And, as such, they juxtapose in a single articulate narrative both emotional "complexes" and intense fantasies, as well as one's early experiences, from which one may extract very dense experiences of internal relationships (with our own mental world) and of external relationships (with other people or things) that are foundational to one's psychic life.

It was a frustrating experience to realize that, when formulating a myth-based model of emotional experiences, it made more sense to me than to the analysand. Often, the analysand took this model more as a cultural perception of life than as something that could deepen and develop their own life experiences.

Little by little, however, I became aware that, for me, contact with myths opened up the possibility of expanding our intuitive knowledge of psychic reality. And that it also led to a type of fundamental mental exercise for psychoanalysts, namely, to improve our instruments to establish contact with this type of knowledge. Or, perhaps, it might be more accurate to say we have here a tool to "sharpen" our precarious perception, always subject to crashing and burning in the face of the "pathos" incited by contact with certain types of intense emotional experience.

There is yet another important element to consider, for myths are meant to be used to study, not replace, the individual.[3] *In other words, in the type of approach I am proposing, myths are a template with which to approach the emotional experiences lived in the here and now of a session*. We can also use them to reflect upon the events of a session after the session has ended, as a kind of intuitive exercise.

As I've said, in this chapter I propose to examine relationships that might be established between myths, certain concepts of Bion and psychic reality. I will attempt to delve deeper into them, using mainly the myths of Oedipus, Paradise (described in the Bible) and Dionysus, and will try to relate them to the idea of catastrophic change, α-function and certain remarks by Bion.

The Oedipus myth acquired fame in psychoanalysis after Freud used it to elucidate aspects of our mental world. In his first theory of instincts, Freud opposes the instincts of ego conservation to the sexual ones, establishing a conflict that will give rise to the first theories of neuroses. The Oedipus myth, or better yet, the tragedy involving Oedipus – as recounted by Sophocles in his superb masterpiece, *Oedipus Rex*, and later in *Oedipus at Colonus* – tells us how this hero, after consulting the oracle of Delphi, learned he was doomed to kill his father and marry his own mother. Trying to escape this prediction, Oedipus turns away from his parents (whom he did not know were adoptive), monarchs of Corinth, and goes to Thebes, where his real parents live and where the prophecy is eventually fulfilled: Oedipus kills Laius, his true father, and marries Jocasta, his mother.

Before that, however, Oedipus had to face the Sphinx, which killed anyone that did not decipher its riddle: "Which creature has but one voice and yet is four-footed in the morning, two-footed at noon and three-footed in the evening, and is strongest when it has the least and weakest when it has the most?" When Oedipus answers "man," the Sphinx kills itself.

Freud brings this myth to bear upon a situation that every one of us faces in our development, namely, that we "fall in love" with our parents but also have to "kill them" internally to constitute our personality.

Bion proposes to view this myth as containing a "model" of the vicissitudes we face in our quest for knowledge, and even more so in the process of "knowing ourselves." This does not disagree with the Freudian proposal regarding sexuality, since Freud himself said that "the ego is first and foremost bodily ego." The sensations that the infant experiences in its own body are actually its first attempt at knowledge, and among them those that bring pleasure are fundamental. And if we consider the later evolution of the theory of instincts as comprising both a death drive and a life drive, this becomes even more evident, as I see it. The infant needs a "training wing" for its loving and hostile impulses, which is provided by its relationship with itself and its parents. Whether this training terrain is adequate or not will depend on the intensity of the impulses and on the infant's and the parents' (reverie) ability to "contain" and elaborate them.

For this purpose, in *Cogitations*, Bion specifically addresses the myths of Oedipus and the Garden of Eden, but places greater emphasis on the K and −K aspects (knowledge and minus-knowledge) than on instinctual conflict.

> The story of the Garden of Eden and the story of Oedipus each contain a character whose attitude to knowledge is hostile – or perhaps I should say, "two-faced," since the Sphinx demands the answer to a question and may therefore be supposed to be favouring a search for it, and God of Genesis plants the tree of knowledge of good and evil in the garden. Psychoanalysts have concentrated attention on the sexual pair and have left discussion of the attitude to knowledge on one side. Yet in man's search to know, few disciplines have penetrated so far in illuminating that source of his difficulties that lies within himself. This adds significance to the neglect of the material that might be compacted in the roles attributed to Sphinx, God and Devil (also Tower of Babel – verbal thought attacked).
>
> (Bion, 1992, p. 233)

Bion proposes a psychoanalytic investigation not only of Oedipus, but also of other characters that appear in myths. These characters, by way of their function of storing personality characteristics, can serve as a tool to survey the emotional obstacles that can prevent developments in "K" and also the possibility of transformations in "O" (to be "what one thinks" or to be in a state of "at-one-ment").

Melanie Klein shows us that several emotions interfere with the possibility of knowledge, but envy is one of the most fundamental, because it interferes with the relationship that the infant establishes with the mother's breast, the primary source of affection, gratification and knowledge. The way the infant and the breast relate to each other gives us an indication of the infant's later ability to establish stimulating and vitalized communication with life itself. If the linking is attacked,

> these attacks and their effect are clearly manifested in the destruction, namely projective identification, ideogrammatic expression, sound (as the matrix of that specialized form which in its maturity we recognize as music), and indeed the ideational counterpart of all the senses.
> (Bion, 1992, p. 199)

If envy, hatred and anguish are excessive, whether in the mother or the infant, the container–contained relationship can be shaken up – the contained might explode the container, or the latter might not be able to "contain" the emotions.

What Bion is considering here is the formation of the α-function, essential for the development of one's "mental space," where emotional experiences can be elaborated and knowledge can begin to emerge.

The myth of Oedipus lends itself to many ideas that Bion elaborated in psychoanalysis. Offhand, we can think of the α-function, the α- and β-elements, and, if we include *Oedipus at Colonus*, we can also see Oedipus' opportunity to learn from experience. It would even be possible to include the transformations in hallucinosis by considering Oedipus' blindness and Jocasta's suicide, enabling us to imagine that what happened was what Bion calls catastrophic change.

In 1966, Bion writes an article on the concept of catastrophic change (Bion, 1966). He begins the essay saying he will describe a recurring configuration in psychoanalysis. At a certain point, he addresses the relationships between the genius (which he alternatively calls "mystic") and the group, both of which would contain the "messianic idea," i.e., the new idea that, if true, always has a disruptive character. A distinction is made between nihilistic mystics and creative ones, but I would rather emphasize the concept of an idea that confronts all well-established things (i.e., the creative idea that produces changes that are turbulent in greater or lesser degree) and of an "establishment" or "status quo" that resists these changes. Fables, says Bion, may be considered a pictorialization of our inner world. And, indeed, for those familiar with Kleinian theories, his descriptions may be seen as dramatized, personified, socialized and pictorial representations of the human personality.

These ideas, which Bion draws from great revolutions in the history of humanity, can be brought to bear upon the path that everyone who undergoes the analytical experience must follow, a path that implies a psychic shift that moves us from a sensory appreciation of life to a psychic one. (I will use these terms for the lack of better ones.)

As I see it, change can be catastrophic when it entails a profound reformulation of how we view our psychic reality and the external world. On the other hand, change can also lead to great personal enrichment when it finds a personality capable of containing it and elaborating it. From another angle, or vertex, we could also say that a catastrophe, whether silent or exuberant, occurs when we cannot follow the inevitable processes of change in life.

This is the process that Oedipus lived through. Unable to use his α-function to reflect upon the prophecy uttered by the Delphic oracle, he flees (full of good intentions and wishing to protect his parents). However, by doing so – and, therefore, by evading contact with his psychic reality – he plummets even deeper into the fate predicted by prophecy. We may perhaps distinguish pre-catastrophic stage (up until the moment when it is revealed that he is his father's murderer and his mother's lover) from post-catastrophic stage, when he literally blinds himself in order "not to see." Evasion (which constitutes an inability to see) turns concretely into blindness. The proud monarch gives way to the banished wretch. Only later, in *Oedipus at Colonus*, will he excogitate, in his famous reply to Creon: "If someone were to march in here right now and attempt to kill you, you righteous man, would your first response be to ask the killer, 'Are you my father?' or to fight him back?"[4]

Yet earlier, at the outset of the myth, I believe we already have a harbinger of the catastrophe. When Jocasta becomes pregnant, the myth tells us that Laius is frightened by an oracle proclaiming that the boy who would spring from that union would kill his father and marry his mother. He therefore commands that Oedipus be killed as soon as he is born.

But it immediately becomes clear that another reading is possible, namely, that what we have here is a "psychic truth," the truth that whenever a child appears the familial relationships change. Laius and Jocasta cannot contain the anguish brought about by the appearance of a new being, Oedipus, and the catastrophe is set in motion.

On the other hand, I also think, less dramatically, that these events are part of our daily life and help us think about it. For instance, an analysand of mine observed how his wife's pregnancy had stirred up the curiosity of their other young children. Among many questions, one of them wanted to know if the baby would eat all the mother's food, clearly revealing the anguish sparked by a new child, who represents the unknown and shakes up an existing situation. We may even infer that children project on a baby their own greediness, which, if not contained, might pose a risk to the survival of the family group.

To conclude this chapter, I would like to examine a myth I particularly appreciate, as it addresses two fundamental issues in life, creativity and the hallucinatory facet of the human mind. The myth tells the story of the Greek god known as Dionysus, while exposing the catastrophe experienced by the royal family of Thebes – Cadmus, Harmonia and their descendants. I will describe it briefly so we can ponder over it.

Every myth has several versions, which add new dimensions to the story or reveal new angles of existing versions. The myth of Dionysus was described by

Euripides in his well-known play *The Bacchae*, so a brief consideration of this work might be useful. The play was written while the Greek tragedian was living in Macedonia, towards the end of his life. Dionysian rites were still held there, and, according to Marie Delcourt-Curvers, (1962, p. 1207), they were quite wild. Hence, the poet writes a play that, while containing some elements of a living ritual, is an artistic creation in addition to a description of facts. Euripides portrays, among other things, situations that resemble demonic possession as depicted in the Middle Ages and extant to this day. Dodds has made a profound study of these states of mind and mentions "this strange rite, described in the *Bacchae* and practiced by women's societies" (Dodds, 1951, p. 270–272). He tells us that "their character may have varied a good deal from place to place, but we can hardly doubt that they normally included women's ὄργια [orgies] of the ecstatic or quasi-ecstatic type described by Diodorus, and that often, if not always, they involved nocturnal ορειβσία or mountain dances." He continues: "There must have been a time when the maenads or thyiads or βάκχαι really became for a few hours or days what their names implies – wild women whose human personality has been temporarily replaced by another." By collating these descriptions with "spontaneous attacks of mass hysteria," Dodds seems to believe there are invariant elements both in Euripides' description and in our mind today.

Marie Delcourt-Curvers (1962) observes that "the Greek legends represent Dionysus as a god that, coming from abroad, was initially unwelcome on Hellenic soil and with great cruelty breaks down resistance to him." Dionysus, in mythological narratives, son of Zeus and the Theban princess Semele, is born a first time when his mother is fulminated by lightning for having contemplated the magnificence of Zeus. She is consumed by fire and the still-fetal child would have suffered the same fate were it not for the intervention of Zeus himself, who sews it to his thigh, where it continues to develop safely. In Euripides' play, Dionysus appears in Thebes, already an adult, bent on introducing his rites to the city, birthplace of his mother. Facing defiance from Pentheus (who, incidentally, was his cousin, being the grandson of Cadmus, the mythological founder of Thebes, and son of Agave, sister of Semele), Dionysus teaches the women of the city (including Agave) to go into a trance and run around exultantly through the woods. He then convinces Pentheus to go and watch them in their practices, on the sly, after having him "bewitched," as it were. Once there, Pentheus is discovered by the bacchantes, who tear him apart by dismemberment, mistaking him for a wild animal. The play ends with the expulsion of Cadmus and Agave from Thebes, after the episode in which Agave, still in a Dionysian trance, shows Cadmus the bloody head of Pentheus, believing it is that of a lion.[5]

In reality, over the course of analysis (as of life), we go through many different types and qualities of states of mind and emotional experiences. I consider it important to have contact with pain, anxiety, transformations in hallucinosis, ecstasy and aesthetic emotions, among others. It is also important to experience disappointment, hatred of analysis itself, boredom, and disenchantment with psychic life and analytical work in order to avoid establishing an idealized relationship whereby psychoanalysis itself is felt to be an access route to paradise (incidentally, also one of the most frequent mythical configurations within life itself). The myth of Dionysus, in its manifold presentations, reveals to us several of these emotions in an extremely rich and enlightening manner, crystallizing our observations on mental life.

First, the unknown. Dionysus appears as a god[6] who has to impose himself because he bears an unknown element and appears as a foreigner. Historically, we know this was not so. Among the Greeks, Dionysus is very ancient.[7] Second, the god has to impose himself even though he was already known. We could say that this is also a characteristic of the experience of making contact with psychic realities, especially the most significant ones that imply inner change – we have called this "insight," and one could associate it with catastrophic change as a phenomenological element, all the more catastrophic the less developed the mental life that must contain it. Using the portrayal of Dionysus and of the bacchantes as a model for emotional experiences leads us, thus, to the unknown, to its destructive irruption into consciousness, to possession, to momentary loss of personal identity, to the confrontation between female and male and between order and disorder, to hallucinosis and to the reorganization of creative elements. (This experience, if tolerated, can be very enriching and enable the PS↔D transformation.)

An episode from my clinical practice might shed light on the possible interrelationship between myth and emotional experiences. The patient is a successful professional, approximately 30 years old and recently separated from his wife, has two small children and came to analysis because of depression and frequent use of alcohol and cocaine.

The first session I will mention takes place on a Monday. We are nearing the end of the year. The patient says,

> I'm fine today, but I was feeling very bad on Tuesday and Wednesday. I don't know what happened, but I was really craving cocaine. I felt that "itch" to snort. I became depressed. I was with my girlfriend and ended up drinking a lot. I just couldn't take it. It was really bad. But not today, today I'm fine.

I tell him he was describing a kind of "crisis" experienced over the weekend. It would be useful, I add, if he could provide additional associations to what he had gone through and also to what he was calling depression.

> It all started when I spoke to my ex-wife. There are certain things I simply can't stand, like her telling me she is going to travel and spend Christmas with my kids and her current boyfriend. This really got to me and made me very sad. I drank a lot, although I didn't snort, but simply because my girlfriend stayed with me. Then, when she left, it was horrible. I went to my parents' house, a sad, joyless Christmas.

I observe that one of the major difficulties he had been facing was to be able to stand his own company, and also to tolerate the painful feeling of absence from his family – from his children, his ex-wife and especially the family they had formed. The separation had had an unbearable dimension.

> It was horrible, I was shook up and sad. [And, after a pause:] Funny, I thought you would be working only with me today ... that you would see me and then you would go away.

The patient didn't say it, but he might as well have added, "leaving me alone with all these painful and uncomfortable feelings."

I believe that, at that moment, the patient was referring to a strong conflict in himself between having to live the absence and separation (tolerating the ensuing pain and suffering – depression) and a strong tendency to evade everything through drinking, snorting cocaine, etc. The whole situation was aggravated at that time of the year (Christmas, New Year), when family reunions and group celebrations are common – as social (and also mythical) symbols of things ending and being lost side by side with the new year arriving. We could also think that, unable to bear "being himself," the patient might seek a Dionysian experience where he can let himself be carried away by drugs to the point of losing his identity. To elude this pain and the feeling of having destroyed something that might have had potential value for him (wife, children), he might depersonalize himself. I say "potential value" because he was actually incapable of truly living out his familial relationships and resorted to cocaine and alcohol in these circumstances as well. Indeed, this was one of the factors that precipitated the separation.

On the date of his next scheduled morning session, Tuesday, December 31, he does not come. Around lunchtime, I receive a phone call from his sister, in distress, informing me that he has gone missing. (This had been a frequent occurrence before he started analysis.) She agrees to let me know when he is found.

I now see that, by disappearing, he was forcing me to undergo the experience of being abandoned. For some time at least, I "became" a part of his self.

When I return to work on January 2, I receive a message from his family that he would come for his evening session.

As he comes in, he sits down as usual, but seems worried, self-conscious. And he immediately starts talking.

> It was irresistible – I left here on Monday, walked around a bit, then took a taxi and went downtown. I drank, talked to a transvestite and went to a small hotel. The transvestite had cocaine, I snorted, thought about having some sexual activity with him, but I wasn't turned on and continued to snort ... At times, another transvestite came to bring me the drug. The difference from the other times I took drugs is that I was unable to have any type of sexual activity, I didn't even take pleasure in using the drug. It was as if there was a

voice within me saying, "Get out of here, get out of here." Previously, when I snorted cocaine, it gave me great pleasure, I was momentarily happy and able to release myself sexually. I had active and passive sex with transvestites, sometimes I even paid to see a couple having sex – until I got tired. When I didn't feel like doing that anymore, I would phone someone to pick me up. I felt terrible guilt, a very intense depression, I would cry with my family, ask for forgiveness, a painful and very humiliating scene.

Psychoanalytically, we have here a serious and complex emotional situation. We may surmise that, when faced with an extreme experience of loss (and, consequently, of pain), this patient acts out with great intensity, through cocaine and alcohol, his impulses to evade reality and to loathe frustration. I believe the frustration of being separated from his family, and from the analyst (in our last session he alluded to his fantasy of me seeing him – and only him – and then leaving), causes a pain so intense that he needs to act out a series of fantasies of his most primitive mental world – fantasies that are not elaborated and are mobilized by these emotional experiences. It is as if the child that exists in him (and in all of us) took control of his mental life. And because he is subjected to these fantasies and begins acting them out, we *perceive them as being concretely experienced*. Some are fantasies of sexual liberation, involving an attempt to achieve unlimited pleasure and delight, and we could say that he experiences a momentary sense of triumph over a frustrating breast (to use a Kleinian framework). As in the Dionysian rites, the contours of one's personal identity are temporarily obliterated and the patient hallucinatorily acts out various fantasies of the primary scene. He is an observer of a couple in coitus (possibly, as a child, he was excited by his parents' sexual relationship – as Pentheus was "bewitched" by Dionysus and excited by the opportunity to "see" the bacchantes, one of which was his own mother). At the same time, when he penetrates the transvestite, or a woman who happened to be present in that milieu, it is the penis that penetrates (i.e., he fantastically becomes the father); and when he passes over to passive sexual intercourse, he is the woman who is penetrated. It is also pertinent that the patient goes out looking for transvestites, individuals who, caricaturally, can be seen as representatives of man and woman at the same time, that is, of a couple. They "incarnate" in their own body the visual elements of a couple – the penis and the breast in the same person. By bringing the myth of Dionysus to bear, what I am able to observe is enormously enriched.

The Oedipus myth seems very useful for observing neurotic situations. I propose *The Bacchae* and the myth of Dionysus as complements to reflect on certain psychotic aspects of our mind (which, by the way, can also be very creative). For instance, Dionysus is a male god, but is often described as effeminate. Ambiguity (that is, dissociation[8]) is the central element of the play. His retinue is composed of various types: satyrs, sileni (woodland deities usually associated with wild, unconstrained sexuality) and especially women, with plentiful wine as a backdrop. At the end of the play, we clearly see the experience of hallucinosis in

Agave. From the viewpoint of creativity, we are justified in presuming that the play poses us the challenge of accomplishing within ourselves the "marriage" of the male and female aspects of our personality.

Collating the myth of Dionysus with psychotic experience allows us to approximate (before, during and after the session) the myth and the emotional experiences recounted by the client. Here are some possibilities: a) I may undergo an important life experience in terms of its potential for knowledge and development, but due to our natural resistance to the suffering that everything new brings, I may ignore it. If the challenges posed by this experience are not summoned by life itself, I may even keep myself happy, but at the cost of great personal impoverishment; b) I perceive the experience, but am unable to elaborate it. This may result in a psychiatric clinical condition (involving much pain and suffering) or in analysis, which also involves pain and suffering, but where these can be used as means to make contact with the unknown in each of us; c) I perceive the experience, I have the requisite inner conditions to elaborate it, and I personally enrich myself.

Essentially, the Oedipus myth refers to the transformations that occur when three people relate, forming a couple and an excluded third (possibly the invariant element in the myth). The Dionysus myth basically refers to the hatred of the unknown (a fundamental component of life), the split between male and female, and the realization of fantasies involving the primary scene at a different level from that of the Oedipus myth. When these elements can be elaborated, we can experience a burst of creativity, or, as Bion says, the possibility of transformations in "O" opens up. We should do well to bear in mind that tragedy and the entirety of Greek theater emerged from the Dionysian rites.

Our work must include the interpenetration of clinical material, the different possibilities that our chosen myth allows us, and the relevant psychoanalytic theories. In so doing, I think we can use the myths in ways similar to those proffered to us by the Grid: as exercises to stimulate our psychoanalytic intuition.

Notes

1 I use the term "experience" according to the basic dictionary definition: "Experience: the act or effect of experiencing." Because the term can refer to numerous types of experiences, "emotional" is a necessary complement to delimit our field of work.
2 A myth is a traditional narrative, usually revolving around gods and heroes, about the origin of a culture and a world, but it is also a "metaphor at tale level" or a "structure of sense" (Burkert, 1982, pp. 28, 15).
3 What I am here ascribing to myths can naturally be expanded to short stories, anecdotes and literature in general, all of which may or may not enable a greater or lesser degree of expansion of one's mental universe, which is the essential factor in the analytical situation or even outside it. Myths, however, generally have a broader cultural scope, as Bion emphasized in the chapter "Tower of Babel" of *Cogitations* (Bion, 1992, p. 226).
4 Translation by Ian Johnston, Vancouver Island University.
5 The chorus ends the play with the following lines: "The gods appear in many forms, carrying with them unwelcome things. What people thought would happen never did.

What they did not expect, the gods made happen. That's what this story has revealed" (Euripides, 2015).

6 Creativity is, perhaps, the closest manifestation of divine manifestation in ordinary life – when we wake up each day, we create (or kill) a world from the one that already exists. Of course, the results may be enriching or impoverishing, depending on one's momentary internal conditions. In the Bible, we find a mythical description of this process when God literally decides to "create everything that exists." Likewise, the Brazilian poet Orestes Barbosa, when he says "The moon, piercing through the zinc roof of our shanty, sprinkled our floor with stars," and adding that his lover "treaded upon the stars, distracted," gives us a description of a very peculiar and sui generis shack full of holes that configured his private world.

7 The archaeological research of Chadwick and Ventris (the decipherers of Linear B writing, which, together with Linear A, were the forms of writing of the Minoan-Mycenaean civilization), reveals the presence of his name as "Diwonusos" in two tablets from Pylos, at the time of the Minoan-Mycenaean civilization (which flourished in the 20th to 12th centuries BCE). One of the tablets also contained another strange word that might be a compound of the word for "wine." Dionysus' "divinity" cannot be safely established from these tablets, but his name does appear – and next to wine (Chadwick, 1976, pp. 99–100).

8 It is quite intriguing to notice that, in the play, when Pentheus "accepts" Dionysus' invitation to go and watch the bacchantes, he dresses in a feminine way and says, "Fancy that! I seem to see two suns, two images of seven-gated Thebes. And you look like a bull leading me out here, with those horns growing from your head." And, immediately after, "How do I look? Am I holding myself just like Ino or my mother, Agave?" (See Episode 4, translation by Ian Johnston.)

References

Andujar, C. and Bardi, P. M. (1978) *Mitopoemas Yãnomam* (São Paulo: Olivetti do Brasil).

Bion, W. R. (1966) "Catastrophic change," *Bulletin of the British Psycho-Analytic Society*, 1966 (5): 13–26.

Bion, W. R. (1992) *Cogitations* (London: Karnac Books).

Burkert, W. (1982). *Structure and History in Greek Mythology and Ritual* (Berkeley: University of California Press).

Chadwick, J. (1976) *The Mycenaean World* (Cambridge: Cambridge University Press).

Delcourt-Curvers, M. (1962) *Les Bacchantes*, in *Euripide: Tragédies Complètes II* (Paris: Éditions Gallimard).

Dodds, E. R. (1951) *The Greeks and the Irrational* (Berkeley: University of California Press).

Euripides (2015) *Bacchae: A Dual Language Edition*, translation by I. Johnston (Oxford, Ohio: Faenum Publishing).

Freud, S. (1960) *The Psychopathology of Everyday Life*, in *Complete Works*, vol. VI (London: Hogarth Press). Originally published in 1901.

Green, A. (1979) "The primordial mind and the work of the negative," *International Journal of Psychoanalysis*, 79 (1): 649–665. PMID: 9777446.

Chapter 8

Issues related to "cure," "improvement," "normality" and "abnormality"

Psychoanalysis and psychotherapies[1]

Claudio Castelo Filho

1.

A patient tells me about an episode with a friend of his, who suffered over a short period two serious health setbacks and had to be submitted to at least two surgical interventions one after the other. He says his friend had always been someone who appeared to deal courageously with his hardships. This time, however, he was summoned by the friend's relatives to provide "moral" support, because the friend had suffered some kind of breakdown and was having grievous crying fits. My patient went over and, together with the family, tried to comfort him, but realized there was little he could do, as the friend remained dejected (even as he strove to show himself off as "getting better" for my patient). My patient resented that his friend was more aloof and reserved than usual towards him.

I reasoned with my patient that, facing such unfortunate circumstances, it seemed natural that his friend felt depressed and disheartened, that this was actually a normal reaction. On the other hand, there is the idea that feeling sad or discouraged is the equivalent of being ill, making my patient and his friend's relatives do their utmost to heal him, to change his state of mind.

I pondered and said to my patient that, possibly, his friend was more reserved and aloof towards him because it might be very painful for him, in view of his own pain and consternation, to have to produce, for those around him, a state of apparent improvement, because he saw all their anguish and felt their pressure on him to show himself getting better or cured.

This conversation arose when we were talking about my patient's expectations that I might "cure" him of feelings he considered very painful but which I considered quite natural given the circumstances of his life (dire family problems) at that time. I implied that any attempt of mine to heal him of his distress would be akin to an attempt at mutilation – because what he was feeling, however painful, was natural, was part of his own nature given he was living through rather painful situations. His suffering and pain, therefore, were natural and normal.

DOI: 10.4324/9781003171584-8

II.

Another example is that of an analysand who was suddenly stricken by a very serious disease, leading to her death in a very short time. When she found out about it, she was desolate and felt she was being persecuted. But she told me that her entire family was adamant she show herself off as high-spirited and combative in face of the disease. They reproached her for being prostrate and bitter. Considering the seriousness of the menace and the gravity of the context, I thought it would be surprising if she behaved any other way, because her shock had truly been overwhelming. (Although it was not I who was sick, I was sorely aggrieved when I was informed of her illness and, later, was very deeply touched by her death.) It was not up to me to be one more person trying to boost her morale; quite the opposite, I should be someone who might help her embrace her own pain and depression, and accept them.

III.

In a further episode, I remember a young mother who tortured herself for not giving her baby all the attention she thought she should be capable of. She expected that she should never feel bored, never get in a bad mood in the face of the chores the baby required from her.

I was apprehensive that the patient might expect from me some kind of reprimand for her inability to be totally, consistently available and tolerant towards the child, as she presumed she should be. I, the analyst, would most certainly possess the skills she thought she lacked, and it would be my natural right to despise her for her limitations. Inversely, she also hoped that her contact with me might endow her with the means to become omnipotent and omniscient, just as I, in her idealization, probably was.

I reasoned with her that, of course, it is beneficial and profitable for a mother to have the emotional fortitude to not make her baby's life more distressing than it naturally is. Having said that, this parameter should never become a moral obligation, seeing that each mother can only offer her child what she herself has.

I told the patient it would be useful for her baby to be able find out that she was just an ordinary woman, and that she should likewise accept in herself feelings of hatred, irritability, exhaustion, limitation. Perhaps, living out these feelings without wanting to excise them would be a healthier attitude than "pushing the envelope" to show herself available when she actually was not. If she insisted on holding herself up to the moral obligation of being an inexhaustible breast, the model of mental functioning that the baby might "assimilate" would be one of superhuman requisitioning, i.e., a demanding superego with no regard for experience.

IV.

The patient, a young man, is markedly irritated when I propound the need to be sad, to be depressed, because these emotional experiences, with which he refuses to make contact, would be essential for him to give meaning to countless experiences of his own, especially those taking place in the analysis room with me or before my eyes.

The assertion above may seem surprising, shocking or absurd, especially if the vertex of the analytical work is psychiatric or medically oriented, so I will attempt to clarify how I came about it.

To begin with, I should stress that the patient's manners and how he treated me in my office were recurrently high-handed and habitually lacking in basic courtesy and politeness. Often he was downright coarse. Mustering all my patience, I strove to show him the brusqueness of his ways, but he refused to acknowledge there was any truculence in his behavior. As he saw it, his hostile deportment was perfectly natural. I tried to convey to him that what he believed to be perfectly natural might not be perceived as such by others, starting with myself. Numerous times I explained that I was trying to help him realize something important by pointing out that how he treated me caused me considerable discomfort and unease. I indicated that, outside my office, surely no one would put up with what I had to endure with him, or tell him, communicate to him, what was actually going on so he might assess whether anything in how he willfully acted might be responsible for his difficulties and hardships. In his relationships, if he behaved in the same way as he did towards me (and he certainly could not be one with me and another with others), people probably reacted with irritation or even aggressiveness to how my experience told me he acted towards them.

If he grasped what I was trying to show him, he would feel dejected and depressed, but a different depression than the one he was used to, and more like that of a boy who bemoans seeing all his toys broken but suddenly realizes that he had broken them himself and was continuing to do so. It would be depressing to acknowledge this, but it might be the only way to stop him from carrying on as he did. Only the pain of the sadness of acknowledging his responsibility for the damages he caused might lead him to reconsider his ways and, eventually, if he so discerned, to reorient his conduct.[2]

I observed that the only way for him to see a meaning in what I was proposing would be to endure the experience of sadness and depression arising from what he might become aware of; otherwise, he would never see what I was trying to show him.[3]

From the medical point of view and from the perspective of other possible psychotherapeutic approaches, the depression he was suffering from should be attacked, i.e., he should somehow be freed from it. From my standpoint, however, this depression was the counterpoise of a realistic perception of his lack of prospects and hope. This depression, if acknowledged and respected, might lead my patient to think about what was happening to him. On the other hand, if one's goal is to get rid of this "disease," one is deprived of the vertex by which depression corresponds to a real situation that must be taken into account and worked on. This, in my view, is what enabled Freud to realize what none of his contemporaries did; instead of trying to rid patients of what tormented them,

Freud was willing to assess, before any other initiative, what might be the meaning of their distress.

There are two types of depression and I consider both realistic, as they correspond to apprehensions faced by the analysand. The second type, the one the patient already experiences, implies a situation in which the person becomes depressed because he or she is being persecuted, i.e., trapped in a mental state that effectively annihilates any and all eventual hope. This state leads the patient to mental inanition (which can lead to the death of the psyche). The suffering experienced is natural, so to speak. Any attempt to purely and simply eliminate the state of suffering would prevent the individual from accessing whatever might alert him or her that something is not going well, or rather that something quite serious is actually occurring. It would be equivalent to sedating or anesthetizing the patient and thinking this made the malaise go away, without considering that pain is a signal that something is getting complicated and that it is a natural and necessary way to make him or her aware of their condition, and, if able to reflect upon it, to effectively deal with their problem. With regard to the patient, the issue would be one of intolerance to contact with pain, hindering the ability to acknowledge and take care of whatever needs to be taken care of. The more one tries to get rid of the symptom, believing it to be the problem, the more difficult it becomes to recognize and deal with the suffering itself, in a kind of infernal vicious circle.

It is up to the analyst to maintain the psychoanalytic vertex, seeing that psychoanalysis might be the only opportunity to verify the "reasons" of the phenomenon. The psychoanalyst's job is not to relieve patients of their difficulties, but to help them develop their own ability to think about them, thereby making the psychoanalyst ultimately unnecessary.

The psychoanalytic vertex I am considering here, and with which I work, is the one that focuses on the unknown (Philips, 1997), a notion that is equivalent to and expands Freud's idea of unconscious – in essence, that which is not known.

V. Expectation of improvement and cure, and certain consequences

> That the analyst works on his patient's emotions as a painter might work on his canvas would be repugnant to psychoanalytic theory and practice. The painter who works on his public's emotions with an end in view is a propagandist. [...] He does not intend his public to be free in its choice. [...] The analyst's position is akin to that of the painter who by his art adds to his public's experience. Since psychoanalysts do not aim to run the patient's life but to enable him to run it according to his lights and therefore to know what his lights are.
>
> (Bion, 1977b, p. 37)

One of the problems of patients expecting improvement and cure is that they may be led to produce the improvement and cure desired by the analyst, intending to please and be accepted by – or, inversely, to outwit – him or her. Even if unaware of them, patients intuitively perceive the analyst's expectations of healing and betterment, and contentment when they are presented. Patients may become experts in producing cure and betterment that delights and flatters the analyst. In general, these improvements appear in their accounts of how their life has improved outside the analytical context. For instance, patients may state they got married, started treating their children better, found a better job, ceased being inconsiderate to others, stopped being selfish, no longer wished to betray their husband or wife, alongside a series of other changes, often intimately associated with conventional moral values. Patients, however psychotic they may be – or, possibly, particularly if they are psychotic (Bion, 1977a, p. 32) – intuit and capture values and desires from the depths of the analyst's mind. And, once wise to the analyst's expectations, they may begin to enact on a large scale what the analyst expects even without realizing it. To undergo analysis themselves is crucial if analysts are to get an intimate grasp of their own values and biases, and acknowledge their expectations and desires, so as to be able to drive them out when they perceive them or to drive away their own desire to have their expectations and values accepted by the patient, however alien they may be to him or her.

The analyst who naively believes (Bion, 1977c, p. 102) their analysands' accounts of what is going on in their lives outside analysis and does not keep a keen eye either on what they actually do in the analysis room or on the relationship they establish with him or her, will become ensnared by their productions and may assume things are going quite well and that they are very committed and collaborative patients. Patients (albeit unaware or unperceiving), for their part, tend to commit themselves to producing what the analyst wants from them. This is quite different from developing one's own mental abilities and, thus, from assuming postures and values that might diverge from those of the analyst but are, rather, genuinely theirs.

In my clinic, I once had a patient who, as soon as I said anything, would immediately mobilize to show me his agreement with what I had proposed. In my observations, however, it was clear that he had not, not by a long shot, had time to "digest" or verify my propositions. Furthermore, in his endorsements, he did not bother to check if they had anything to do with what I had actually proposed that he reflect on. Apparently, they were the same thing, but in reality they were not. Often his movements aimed to show me he was free from certain prejudices of the groups to which he belonged, believing that was what I expected of him. However, by trying to show me he was emancipated from the supposedly "old-fashioned" values of those groups, he became submissive and adherent to the values he attributed to me, and with which he confused me, believing I expected him to adhere to them. It was clear that when he tried to portray himself as emancipated, he remained submissive as always and merely changed the external form of the authority figure. If I had not realized this situation and actually assumed the role assigned to me, I could very well have become an authoritarian non-authority figure. In a somewhat simplified manner (and not an exact depiction of this case), this is what happens when analysands seek to show they have renounced the "backwardness and moral obscurantism" of whatever religion they profess and take on a more "modern" religious non-religiosity that they believe would be that of the analyst, never developing a true discernment of their own. A "cool and hip" analyst may believe that the analysand has evolved from a medieval situation to a more contemporary and freethinking position without noticing that the analysand's status quo has not changed at all.

With this particular patient, I had the impression (which I conveyed to him) that he believed all the resources on which he depended to survive lay outside himself, within a certain group or outer authority. Much like a newborn baby, he was desperate to be adopted, for me to adopt him, and despite being a middle-aged man and, from what he implied, professionally well-established, he believed, in his heart, that if he was not assimilated, adopted, accepted by me or by some other group that was the real possessor of all resources necessary for survival, he might starve to death in utter destitution. Thus, there with me, he struggled – even without really understanding what I was saying – to show he also believed in what he believed to be my ideas and my values. Had the values been different, he would have partaken in them as well, because discernment of the actual ideas was unimportant. The imperative was to render as his own the ideas of the authority of another person or group, because upon this depended not only him being accepted and assimilated by the authority or group(s), but also his immediate survival. Again like a newborn baby, he was desperate to be and to see himself as "important" to me, to his group or to his parents, for a baby indeed needs to be important to its parents or to those on whom it depends (Bion, 1992, p. 122). Only after many conversations and by depicting this situation from various angles did it seem to make some sense to him and to actually lead him to reflect on his state of mind and its consequences.

VI. Panic

Panic syndromes are now in vogue and seemingly the order of the day. As I see it, however, this clinical condition is an old acquaintance of psychoanalysts, for panic syndromes are what Freud called anxiety hysteria or phobias with a new guise or nomenclature to give the impression they are something new. With regard to the psychoanalytic practice that addresses this condition, I believe that if we maintain a work posture devoted to the medical model, we face the danger of losing the psychoanalytic vertex and the distinguishing features this vertex can bring.

Under the curative medical bias, panic situations are addressed as diseases that must be extirpated. Panic is seen as abnormal, for which there is no place at all. However, I believe there is confusion here between the symptom and the problem itself. The symptom is likewise perceived as something wrong, as something that should not exist. This is a serious issue because, as I see it, symptoms, even from a medical viewpoint, are both proper and appropriate – they indicate that a problem is occurring – and their manifestation is possibly the best thing that can happen while the problem persists.

I am not advocating that psychoanalysis is a panacea and can handle any situation. I do not think that people in the midst of an intense panic attack, who are barely able to leave their home or their bed, can do without medication or some kind of help to allow them a modicum of mobility. I do believe, however, that such approaches are palliative.

In my clinical practice, I have met numerous individuals who manifested these famed "panic syndromes" and often declared, after being medicated, that they felt as if something put their life in a state of suspension, but that the thing itself, although apparently shut off or suspended, might be reactivated at any moment. The fear persisted. To a certain extent, the only reactions that had been suspended were those that this fear would have led them to. These persons also complained that the medications left them listless and apathetic, incapacitated for the other activities they had to undertake in life. Not to mention the issue that, after some time, according to statements from these patients in my practice, medication starts to lose its effect and must be switched, or the dosage has to be continuously increased, bringing other secondary consequences.[4]

What I have borne out *in my clinical practice* is that, overall, people who complain about experiencing panic attacks adopt ways of dealing with what anguishes them that result in them experiencing panic – panic with real motivation.

In my observations, in their contact with me, what I often see in patients is an attitude of "setting upon with ignorance"[5] toward any attempt that could put them in touch with what distresses them or contradicts their expectations of how things should be. Someone who, in order to avoid having an insight into what is displeasing or distressing, punctures their own eyes, pierces their eardrums and shuns any stimulus that might shed light on what they so adamantly strive not to know, is indeed in a very complicated situation. Imagine yourself blind, deaf, with no sense of touch or smell, and lacking any kind of perception that would indicate what is happening around you – or, even if you retain your perception of stimuli, imagine that any and all emotional feeling these stimuli might arouse is compromised, so you can "see" the stimuli but can no longer give meaning to them. In face of such a situation, I think panicking is the most natural reaction possible. Panic, in this context, is a healthy reaction! It is one's common sense (or what remained of it) manifesting itself. To attack it – or to want to deprive the person of this reaction – is to attack what is still healthy and pertinent. From other, more mundane points of view, panic is something wrong and sickly that must be purged. From the psychoanalytic viewpoint *I am proposing here*, it is a perfectly adequate manifestation indicating that the patient must revise how he or she deals with what is harrowing or distressing.

Running amok, dismissing a hateful reality or denying the meanings of what one perceives is probably one's first resort in the absence of other alternatives. To deny reality when one can still count, however precariously, on adults (parents or guardians) to help face the facts of life is one thing; to deny facts when one is in a situation where one must face them alone is quite another. What may have been reasonably useful in one stage of life to face one's fears or discomforts (felt as insurmountable, or at least undesirable) can, in another stage, become detrimental.

The analyst's job should not be to point to the panic as the problem to be solved; quite the contrary, it should be to indicate that panic is probably the proper reaction to the "solutions" patients have given to their anxieties. If this is verified by the patient, the analyst, who supposedly is better equipped to maintain contact with anguishes and discomforts, should help the analysand develop the ability to accept, assimilate and get along with situations of even greater anguish, discomfort and frustration that might lie ahead. The most emotionally developed person is not the one who has got rid of anguishes and frustrations, but the one who tolerates increasing levels of anguish and frustration. Only this can enable someone to deal with life's difficulties. The more someone feels unable or refuses to deal with sentiments mobilized by adversity or frustrations (i.e., by facts that differ from one's own desires), the more he or she will be incapable of dealing with real life situations. The more someone finds him- or herself in this situation (without realizing it), the greater the tendency to panic when faced with facts of life that are impossible to avoid – much like a newborn baby may react who has no life experience or resources to deal with what happens to it. It is not for the analyst to spare or save the patient;[6] being spared or saved from what one considers frustrating and unpleasant is precisely what the patient suffers from. On the other hand, being able to recognize adversities and frustrations does not guarantee immunity from depression, sadness or helplessness. Real development implies the possibility of accepting and assimilating these experiences in the face of adversity without those feelings necessarily preventing the individual from continuing to think, to function and, eventually, to perceive auspicious opportunities.

However, not sparing the patient does not entail being violent towards analysands or wanting to push "truths" down their throat; on the contrary, it means helping them confront not only the facts they have always refused to deal with, but also anything else they may find unacceptable because it does not conform to their expectations and desires. In order to do this, the analyst must tolerate anguish and adversity – in one's own clinical practice, to begin with. Analysts need not present themselves as heroes or superheroes, but merely as individuals who, when faced with painful and adverse situations, can accept themselves in all their suffering and remain respectful to themselves even in the face of their ignorance and insufficiency – waiting, in a state of faith as defined by Bion in *Attention and Interpretation* (1977c, pp. 31–32), for the appearance of some kind of evolution.

VII. The issue of truth and honesty

Freud, from the very beginning, used to say that psychoanalysis is inseparable from truth and love of truth. Bion (1977b, p. 38) rounded off by writing that truth is inseparable from, and indispensable to, mental health. I believe this is the limiting factor in clinical practice, as well as the benefit one can derive from psychoanalysis. The analysand must be at least minimally interested in the truth for the analytical work to bear fruit. As for the analyst, to be capable of practicing psychoanalysis and not another type of supportive psychotherapy, his or her vertex must be that of truth and honesty with patients, since it was a lack of psychic truth that led them to a state of penury in the first place and made them seek help.

I often hear comments that one should not say this or that to patients because they cannot take it. First, I would argue that it is highly presumptuous to say it is up to *me* to ascertain and decide what a person is or is not able bear or perceive. This concern becomes clearer when we think of adoptions in which the parents decide they cannot tell their children they are adopted. Everyone who has ever worked in our area is tired of knowing how this attitude eventually leads to considerable complications in the mind of the adoptees. Somehow they know that something is being hidden from them, that something is not being said, that there are lies in the air – lies that, as Bion pointed out, are poison to the mind (1977b, ch. 11). Furthermore, a fact of life (adoption, in this case) that cannot be stated becomes, in the minds of both those who do not say it and those who are left without access to the truth, something truly terrible and hideous that must indeed remain hidden. A simple fact becomes a stigma. Something with no actual exceptionality becomes a stain tarnishing the child's personality. (To be sure, the stain is not *on* the personality, but in the concealment, whereby adoption is experienced as a stain *of* the child's personality – both by the parents and by the child itself.)

I am reminded of Oedipus' tragedy, as his drama unfolded from a truth that was hidden from him and from which he was "spared" by his adoptive parents.

Likewise, everything that a psychoanalyst perceives yet hides from his or her patients as something they cannot bear to perceive eventually creates a situation similar to that of adoption I just mentioned. Patients somehow sense when the analyst knows something and will not tell them. Whatever the analyst does, in principle at least, to spare patients ends up stressing them even more, increasing their sense of persecution, as they intuit something is being hidden from them, that the conversation is not entirely frank. Conversely, when the analyst is forthright, this may seem brutal at first sight but, over time, as the patients find that the analyst is being honest with them and hiding nothing from them, in my experience they start feeling more at ease, reassured, certain that there are no "skeletons in the closet." When they realize that the conversation is really sincere, they sense they are being truly respected in their integrity – and not perceived as foolish or incompetent. To assume, *a priori*, that analysands are incapable of getting in touch with facts is a cavalier attitude. Conversely, by being sincere, the analyst is also stressing his or her belief that patients can deal with problems differently than how they have done so far (for every neurosis or psychosis is, ultimately, a distortion or denial of a reality deemed intolerable or unacceptable). If the analyst really thinks a patient-to-be is utterly resourceless, why accept him or her as a patient in the first place? I do not think psychoanalysis creates resources in those who lack them; it can only develop existing but unevolved resources.

A similar situation occurs in how doctors relate to patients who suffer from serious illnesses. I find it disastrous and disrespectful when doctors and family members decide they can hide from the patient whatever they think the patient might not bear to make contact with. It is an affront to the patient's right and autonomy. Wryly, however, in such circumstances, reality ends up imposing itself. And when this happens, the person who was deceived regarding a lethal disease, for instance, may feel aggrieved for not having had the opportunity to decide what he or she would like to have done in the last months, days or hours of existence. When the concealed reality finally imposes itself, there may be no time left to do anything.

Freud and Klein did not spare their patients from what they considered to be the truth. The repercussions they suffered for not reneging on their sincerity were considerable. I think it is often forgotten, when someone says, "How can you say that to a patient? It is overwhelming!", what Freud (1978) and Klein (1975), for instance, dared say to their patients and their contemporaries of scientific practice. In the midst of the Victorian age, Freud spoke to puritanical maidens and ladies, and to men of the strictest moral reserve, about their desires to kill their father (or mother) and sleep with the parent of the opposite sex – or even of the same sex. Nowadays we lose sight of how impactful such utterances probably were in Freud's day, of how they must have shocked and horrified their listeners – patients and colleagues. Yet, despite these reactions, he continued to say what he thought, because, as I pointed out, Freud did not distinguish between psychoanalysis and the pursuit of truth (know thyself!).

Do we not recall the initial impact of our readings of Klein? Do we not recall she wrote down what she said to her patients?

I am not advocating being rude – there are manners and manners of talking to someone. We must never forget that the person in front of us is suffering, often from a "raw flesh" sort of suffering. But this is no reason not to perform the required procedures on someone whose flesh is raw.[7] Nor should we neglect their condition. In addition, we must find a way of speaking so the listener may understand what we say. One should not talk metaphorically or abstractly to a very material person (on the other hand, if the person is truly unintelligent or overly concrete-minded, perhaps the option for analysis is not feasible). One must seek the *language of achievement* (Bion, 1977c, p. 125).

I think we should wait to say things to patients if we have not yet found a clear and evident way to express what we aim to communicate, or while we assess if our own judgment was not compromised by undigested emotional turbulence or contaminated by some bias of ours. Nor should what we say be an accusation of a moral or religious order. I think it is up to us to present facts for patients to think about them, not accusations of improper conduct (after all, who but self-styled moral authorities can pronounce what this might be?). Freud, when he spoke to patients about their Oedipal condition, was certainly not accusing them of it, but merely proffering elements they had never previously perceived or thought about, so that by making themselves aware they might reflect on and elaborate them. Elaboration does not imply enjoining some type of purportedly more proper conduct, behavior or functioning supposedly more consistent with established normality. The end result of the elaboration should be unknown to the analyst (and to the analysand as well) and there should be no *a priori*s about it. Otherwise, if the result is indeed known in advance, what we do would no longer be psychoanalysis, but rather some other type psychotherapeutic, medical or pedagogical activity, or moral and religious preaching.

I do not deem it a problem for a person to receive catechesis or pedagogical guidance, or even undergo psychotherapy with pedagogical characteristics, if that is what one is seeking or really wants to achieve. These approaches allow many people to organize and function in their lives, and can actually be quite useful for those who seek them out. The analyst, however, must inform their patients, as soon as possible, the differences between these approaches and what psychoanalysis aims at, namely, the patients' autonomy through the development of their ability to think, which is only possible if the focus is the unknowns of their psychic reality. This must be carried out in the analyst's own praxis so as to make his or her vertex and premises perfectly clear. It is up to analysands to decide whether or not they are interested in what the analyst proposes – and this applies even to children, as Bion pointed out (Bion, 1978). The analyst must offer prospective patients that which is peculiar to psychoanalysis and cannot be found elsewhere. If the analyst provides something other than psychoanalysis, he or she may deprive prospective patients of what was actually proposed (i.e., psychoanalysis), implying, in effect, that psychoanalysis if actually of no real use.

The relief that patients may derive from psychoanalysis, but which should not be its aim, must come from the development of their ability to think, which enables them to see from different perspectives the issues they struggle with in life in the present and in the days to come, and endows them with discernment, autonomy and the ability to choose. The development of the ability to think evolves from the proposed counterpoint between the analysands' beliefs of how things are and what the analyst perceives them to be from his or her viewpoint, i.e., between what the analyst can see from his or her perspective and what analysands cannot from theirs. The analyst must contrast the analysands' perception angle with his or her own – conveying whatever perceptions of a situation he or she may share but which the analysands do not perceive. If the analysands are able to withstand this contrast, they will ascertain there is more than one point in the universe from which to view the issues that afflict them – and, eventually, they will perceive alternatives for what they now experience as an impasse by considering the existence of different perspectives that can completely reframe what they initially saw. This is, to be sure, a didactic proposal in the Socratic sense. By contrast, in the pedagogical vertex the idea of authority is maintained, i.e., of a single viewpoint to be considered, whereas in the didactic vertex (which would be that of psychoanalysis, as I conceive it) it becomes possible to develop the notion of the analysands' authority and responsibility.

To avoid being authoritarian or brutal, while remaining frank, the analyst must be capable of compassion. One way to achieve this is through his or her own analysis. If it is fruitful and profound, the analyst will hardly be able to cast the first stone, having been made aware of that which is human in the other.

In any case, the fact that the analyst is capable of compassion and seeks an accessible and respectful language towards the patient, without ever withholding the truth, does not in itself guarantee successful communication with the analysand. Interest in, and consideration for, the truth cannot be a prerogative of the analyst, and must also be present in the patient. For the analyst to be heard, he or she must somehow find in the client an interlocutor who is willing to listen and who recognizes the importance of honesty (Bion, 1978).

It is also worth noting that Bion drew attention to the dogmatization of psychoanalytic theories, as well as to the intention of making psychoanalysis and psychoanalysts respectable – authorities in conformity with an establishment. He, on the other hand, continued his investigative work beyond what was considered acceptable and settled, and ended up being labeled crazy[8] by many of his own colleagues.

Psychoanalysis does not exist to produce respectable citizens. If analysis is to help someone find him- or herself, it must not have *a prioris* of what this should be, let alone prescribe that that person should eventually think and function according to some pre-established value. Respect for the patients' autonomy must take into account the outcomes and directions they might want to for their own life, regardless of what they may be.[9]

I believe the only way for someone to have access to a certain degree of happiness in life is that in which one feels sufficiently autonomous and free from any type of authority (including that of the analyst) to live in accordance with one's own aptitudes, values and desires. Over the course of the analytical experience, the analysis must allow a person to verify what these truly are. But this should never be known beforehand – otherwise, as I have said, we would be performing some form of indoctrination (and, consequently, doing violence to the patient's autonomy), not psychoanalysis.

The respect one needs is, above all, one's respect for oneself. As I see it, it was this self-respect that allowed Freud, Klein and Bion, for instance, to remain true to themselves despite being perceived as outsiders by the groups to which they once belonged.

Freud was regarded as an aberration for drawing attention to Oedipus and child sexuality – as if these notions could only spring from a degenerate mind (see Jones, 1961, pp. 272–279). If his main concern had been to become a respectable citizen, he would have done like Breuer[10] and succumbed to the establishment, which would have been the "normal" thing to do. Still, the only real way for a person to develop true consideration for others, a proper and genuine ethics, as advocated by Socrates, according to Cornford (2014), in contrast to the moral values imposed from the outside in, it to have real consideration for oneself, for one's autonomy and options, whatever they may be. Freud and psychoanalysis only became effectively respected – albeit only to very limited extent – because he had real consideration for himself and his thoughts, despite them being perceived – not only then, but even today – as deviant, abnormal, disturbed and disturbing.

Finally, I must mention the matter of psychoanalysis' wish to become pleasant, respectable, normative and norm-driven. Associated with these first three factors are the interests to make it commercially profitable, a mass consumer good. This concurrence, if it prevails, will place psychoanalysis on a path that will lead to its annihilation, much like all other types of mass-marketed goods. As Hannah Arendt (1961) pointed out, every product for mass consumption is discarded as soon as it is consumed, having exhausted its consistency and usefulness, except as a fleeting entertainment.[11]

Notes

1 Paper presented at the conference "Psychoanalysis – Bion: Transformations and Developments" on March 15, 2008, on the premises of the SBPSP. Originally published in the journal *Psicanálise em Revista*, v. 5, no. 2/2007 and v. 6, no. 1/2008, pp. 29–50.
2 He also found it enormously difficult to acknowledge and recognize other behaviors that were quite harmful to his own interests.
3 I am aware that this is a paradoxical situation. The patient would have to tolerate what he cannot stand in order to be able to verify something relevant. On the other hand, the presence of the analyst could help him consider revising his beliefs regarding what is or is not intolerable. Something that might not be bearable in early childhood may be so in adulthood, and something that might be excruciating to address with his family, with his mother or father, would not be so with me. In any case, there is a point that depends only on the patient, namely, his decision to venture into unfamiliar territory. This is a task that only the analysand can decide and take upon himself, no matter how much his analyst might deem it beneficial. If the analysand is not willing to take such a step, there is nothing the analyst can do. In this specific case, failure to acknowledge a strong feeling of envy might also be a major factor in producing this type of condition.
4 This does not correspond to the experience of most psychiatrists regarding the use of these drugs, but to the testimony of those patients who came to me. I want to make it clear that I hold no position against psychiatry or the use of medication. I do not advocate that a patient in the midst of a psychotic break will benefit more from psychoanalytic treatment. Indeed, the use of medication can be of great value in stabilizing an acute condition. Psychoanalysis should not be mistaken for a panacea and psychoanalysts must bear in mind the limits of their work and assess the patients' condition when accepting them for analysis. I do not deem sensible to attempt to analyze someone whom I perceive is about jump out of a window. However, if the person is not acutely breaking down, the psychoanalytic vertex can be useful to investigate and clarify what led the individual to such a state of despair.
5 A Portuguese idiom (*partir para a ignorância*) which roughly means "I'm so fed up I might well fly off the handle." It is used here with double entendre, so the expression should be taken in the sense both of patients not wanting to know or to have any kind of contact with what they dislike, and of actually going berserk, that is, having uncouth and violent reactions. (Translator's note.)

6 José Longman, a training analyst at the SBPSP who passed away in the early 1990s, used to say that analysis is for those who want to save [in the monetary sense as well], not for those who want to be saved or spared. For him, development is not possible for those who want ease and to be spared. For growth to occur one must use the resources at one's disposal; if they are not used there is no development.
7 Except when patients explicitly say they do not want our intervention, help or the type of care we propose – a decision for which they must also take responsibility.
8 From what can be inferred from his last sentences of *A Memoir of the Future*, this also ceased to be relevant to him. In two different conferences on different occasions at the Brazilian Society of Psychoanalysis of São Paulo which I attended, two prominent British psychoanalysts who were his contemporaries did not hesitate to call his later production the works of someone who had become insane, senile or gaga.
9 I must make clear, however, that in my practice, as a promoter of life, I will always aim to collaborate with the patient's life. If the patient wants something else, it will have to be without my help.
10 I want to make it clear that Breuer's decision and choice for the establishment and for respectability are legitimate and in no way a demerit, as I see it. Each of us must know where our shoe pinches, as one says in Portuguese. However, it should be emphasized that psychoanalytic research and practice are incompatible with pursuing the establishment's recognition and assimilation.
11 To produce mass entertainment products, as Arendt highlights, this industry needs to use real original works of art, but stripping them of their essence and making them "pleasant" for rapid digestion. In this process, however, the original work of art ends up being destroyed.

References

Arendt, H. (1961) "The crisis in culture: its social and political influence," in *Between Past and Future* (New York: Viking Press).
Bion, W. R. (1977a) *Learning from Experience*, in *Seven Servants: Four Works by Wilfred R. Bion* (New York: Jason Aronson). Originally published in 1962.
Bion, W. R. (1977b) *Transformations*, in *Seven Servants: Four Works by Wilfred R. Bion* (New York: Jason Aronson). Originally published in 1965.
Bion, W. R. (1977c) *Attention and Interpretation*, in *Seven Servants: Four Works by Wilfred R. Bion* (New York: Jason Aronson). Originally published in 1970.
Bion, W. R. (1978) *Supervisão 19** no Brasil*. Transcribed by J. A. Junqueira de Mattos, senior member at the Brazilian Society of Psychoanalysis of São Paulo and training analyst at the Brazilian Society of Psychoanalysis of Ribeirão Preto., Unpublished.
Bion, W. R. (1992) *Cogitations* (London: Karnac Books).
Cornford, F. M. (2014) *Before and after Socrates* (Cambridge: Cambridge University Press). Originally published in 1932.
Freud, S. (1978) *Complete Works*. Standard Edition (London: Hogarth Press).
Jones, E. (1961) *The Life and Work of Sigmund Freud* (New York: Basic Books).
Klein, M. (1975) *The Writings of Melanie Klein*, vols. I–IV (London: Hogarth Press).
Philips, F. J. (1997) *Psicanálise do Desconhecido* (São Paulo: Editora 34).

Chapter 9

α-function ↔ psychoanalysis

An investigation process (on the *quality of presence* in analytical session models)

Cícero José Campos Brasiliano

> In art, there is neither past nor future.
> The art that is not in the present will never be.
> Pablo Picasso (Picasso Museum, Barcelona, Spain)

I. Following Marco Polo's example

I was outside Brazil for forty days in December 2007 and January 2008, visiting Portugal, Spain and Germany (Berlin). To paraphrase a great traveler,[1] "I hate traveling and I hate explorers," but in the face of the inevitable, I strove to make the best out of a bad business.

From a very early age, the travels of the Venetian Marco Polo made a strong impression on me. At the end of the 13th century, having arrived in China, Polo remained there for sixteen years, where he joined the Court and even performed administrative functions for emperor Kublai Khan (Polo, 1908). The Venetian was not a "tourist," but someone interested in, and attentive to, the physical and human characteristics of Asia, which he portrayed in his book, clearly stating that "some things, however, he did not see, but heard them from other men, sincere and true" (Polo, 1908).

Before starting on my journey, I had received an invitation to participate in a seminar on Bion's work. A peculiar thing happens to me, and perhaps to the reader as well, whenever I have to present a paper at some scientific meeting: my attention becomes selective and, in my mind, various ideas begin to gestate, often springing from lived experienced or visual elements. Perhaps the reader remembers the model used by Freud to introduce the concept of free association of ideas: "Act as though, for instance, you were a traveler sitting next to the window of a railway carriage and describing to someone inside the carriage the changing views which you see outside" (Freud, 1958, p. 134).

Freud's model seems valuable as a metaphor for the psychic flow, which occurs, for instance, in a session of analysis or when writing *about* psychoanalytic situations. In this paper, I intend to highlight certain *factors* related to the *quality of the presence* of the analyst and/or analysand in a session, using for this purpose *three models* that I deem useful to signify the topic.

DOI: 10.4324/9781003171584-9

II. Discovery during a walk

In the investigation of psychic phenomena, the *qualitative*, that is to say, non-sensorial aspect seems of fundamental importance. The same can be said of psychoanalysis, which is essentially a *qualitative* investigation of psychic facts.

It so happens, however, that we often have to deal with *quantitative* situations in the clinical environment. I am referring, for instance, to patients who are very adept at manipulating words, hiding behind them and, therefore, precluding access to their self. Words are frequently not used to communicate feelings or ideas. Quite the opposite, their objective is to provoke an *action*, more often than not upon the analyst, thus encumbering the analyst's thinking process, distracting him or her from the heart of the issues and attempting to turn the session into something anodyne.

I remember an intelligent, captivating 30-year-old analysand with excellent command of verbal language who had been under analysis for two years. He arrived punctually at every session and, after lying on the couch, began an outpour of words describing situations in his life with intense emotional colorfulness, always in the guise of someone powerful and strong. Gradually, over the course of therapy, I realized he was simply *not present at the sessions*. He was more like a *non-presence*, as it were, because in rare moments it was possible to glimpse, amid all the verbal torrent, something of that which might have led him to analysis in the first place: his extreme *frailty* and *helplessness*. These moments were elusive, for his thundering voice toned down and became almost a whisper, difficult even to hear. It seemed to me that he himself did not want to hear. This analysand, however, had a favorable trait: it struck me that he actually listened to some things I said. I had shown him how his ways resembled those of a seesaw, oscillating from arrogance and a superior attitude to helplessness and frailty.

After I made these observations, his reaction toward me began to change very slowly. I found that, from then on, his *presence* in the sessions underwent a change in quality and he was able to perceive the need for *intimacy* and to value it.

This clinical situation resembles what Bion, in chapter IX of *Learning from Experience*, describes as β-screen (Bion, 1977, p. 20). One could object and say that this patient's garrulous communication might be the only way possible for him to be present at the session. But I emphasize the need for analysts to assess the quality of presence and show this to our analysands. If they listen to us (as was the case here), favorable changes may occur in terms of bettering their contact with themselves and with me.

Returning to the title of this topic, I will provide an image to represent pictorially what I exposed above: just before my trip of 2007/8, I had gone with my youngest daughter, who was studying to take the Architecture admission exam, to the huge campus of the University of São Paulo to visit the School of Architecture and Urbanism (FAU).

The purpose of our tour was for her to take a break from her studies and perhaps even to feel more motivated, because visiting the beautiful building designed by Vilanova Artigas is always exciting. Upon arriving there, a photographic exhibition was being held in the main lobby. As I said earlier, before writing a paper my mind goes into a kind of gestational state and my *attention* is stimulated towards the subject I am studying. Thus, I noticed a photograph (see Figure 9.1) that seems the very image of what I have exposed above. As the photographer explained to me, the photo was taken at a meeting of FAU students and shows one of them speaking into a megaphone, with a reddish background behind her. The interesting thing is, of course, that the megaphone completely hides the person's features. We see a few letters in the back, perhaps some sort of slogan, but the speaker's individuality has disappeared. Neither does the speaker appear nor was it possible for even the audience to see her. The megaphone, a device that amplifies words, is the central element. The photo also renders a feeble hope that the individual who is speaking might emerge, as we can notice the gestures of her hands conveying some emotion.[2] The title of the photo is very suggestive: *Auto-Falante*.[3] That is, the speaker speaks to herself. But can she hear herself?

Figure 9.1 Auto-Falante (2007)
Source: Camila Picolo, photographer and architect from FAU-USP

III. A visit to the Picasso Museum in Barcelona

On my last trip to Barcelona, I visited the Picasso Museum. In it, a room particularly caught my attention: a comfortable environment had been created where the viewer could contemplate, as a background, a reproduction of the famous painting by Velázquez, *Las Meninas* (or *The Family of Philip IV*).[4]

Upon *Las Meninas* were projected the 58 studies that Picasso made of Velázquez' painting between August and December 1957 (Rafart i Planas, 2008, p. 29).

Much has been written about this painting by Velázquez (Lacan, 2002). As I am not an art critic, but a psychoanalyst, I will use this canvas together with Picasso's *Las Meninas* to illustrate certain clinical situations involving *quality of presence in sessions*.

Velázquez' *Las Meninas* provokes certain peculiar sensations in me. The main one can surely be called strangeness (*unheimlich*). The same word can designate a psychoanalytic session when we manage to enter into that which appertains to it, namely, the dream world.

The painting causes another particular sensation, that of the spectator and the model permanently reversing their roles. As Michel Foucault says in his essay about this canvas: "Because we can see only that reverse side, we do not know who we are, or what we are doing. Seen or seeing?" (Foucault, 1989, p. 5). Another point of interest is the question of the visible and the invisible: much like a session of analysis, the picture sends us toward something non-sensorial, mysterious. In other words, it presents us with an unsaturated scene that allows multiple interpretations. Going back to Foucault, "the painter's gaze, addressed to the void confronting him outside the picture, accepts as many models as there are spectators; in this precise but neutral place, the observer and the observed take part in a ceaseless exchange" (Foucault, 1989, p. 5). Velázquez, therefore, suggests with his canvas not the classic situation of the painting as an *object* of observation by the *subject*, but rather, it seems to me, as a *relationship* much like the one that occurs in a psychoanalytic session.

The milieu at the Picasso Museum in Barcelona, where Picasso's 58 studies were projected on Velázquez' canvas, constitutes an interesting model for the clinical situation in the analyst's office. Let us admit for a moment that Velázquez' canvas is, indeed, a depiction of what is taking place in an analysis room (including its strangeness). Picasso's *Las Meninas*, in turn, would be the analyst's observations of the clinical material, *portraying the facts from another angle* and, therefore, presenting something new, surprising, unexpected and original that happened at that moment of the session. *Las Meninas* are now Picasso's, and no longer Velázquez', although they are based on the latter's. Let us listen to what the artist from Malaga had to say about this, premonitorily, in 1950 (his *Las Meninas* was painted in 1957):

> If one were to copy *Las Meninas*, in perfectly good faith, let's say, upon reaching a certain point and if I were the one who was copying, I would say

to myself: "What would it be like if I placed this a tiny bit more to the right or to the left?" I would attempt to do it my way, forgetting Velázquez. The proof would surely lead me to have to change or alter the lighting, because I had displaced a figure. Thus, little by little, I would paint a *Meninas* that might seem detestable to a professional copyist. This *Meninas* would not be the one he thought he had seen on Velázquez' canvas; they would be my *Meninas*.

(Rafart i Planas, 2008, p. 28)

It is interesting to think that, to paint his *Meninas*, Pablo Picasso proposed *forgetting* Velázquez. This is somewhat similar to an analyst who works with the emotional experiences that take place in a session but is not primarily concerned with understanding them. The analyst can change the angle of observation, and something new and surprising may emerge, something that most of the time would never have been considered by the analysand (or by the analyst).

The aesthetic model I employed here is just another way of talking about *quality of presence* in a session. If the analyst can tolerate the strangeness of the analytical situation and can maintain discipline irrespective of concerns about using memory and/or understanding, he or she will be able to make observations on new vertices and completely change the situation at that specific analytical moment.

I remember one analysand who, after retiring from the company where he had always worked, began to display plaintive attitudes in the sessions and, somewhat theatrically, to unravel his misfortunes and complaints about life, his own imminent demise, his great suffering, etc. I noticed that there was a certain pleasure in his grievances, with which he hoped to draw attention to himself and obtain secondary benefits (love and caring from his wife, children and even me). In one session, histrionically as ever, he said he was "suffering so much that it would be better to just get sick and die." I told him that, at that moment, death would solve nothing, because it would put an end to all the "suffering" from which he actually derived pleasure by drawing everyone's attention. The patient seemed to have actually heard what I said and, after remaining silent for a few minutes, replied: "I think you're right, but I'd never thought about it this way."

Sometimes, observations from experience, but also from different angles, can be useful for analysands to achieve a new perception of themselves. This new knowledge might enable the *evolution* of quality of their presence with themselves.

We can consider *evolution* a form of transformation. Or, perhaps, that

> the goal of *evolution* is to give meaning to the relationship at that moment, regardless of any isolated signification it may have in the analytical situation, centered on the premonitory aspect of satisfaction-seeking impulses and linked to the analysand's de-involvement, for which I must be available to observe. Towards this end, one must deprive oneself of any desire, of any need – even of the need to understand the analysand.

(Longman, 1997)

I reemphasize that Picasso, to paint his *Meninas*, had to *forget* Velázquez, even if, as he says, he was not a copyist but a creative artist. Regardless, he clearly used Velázquez' painting as inspiration to create 58 other autonomous, free and absolutely innovative works.

To establish an analogy with the moment of the session, the analyst must, within the "canvas" that emerges from the emotional experience (which includes words, but transcends them), use his or her α-function to paint a new picture or to alter its emotional "colors," or to change the viewing angles of the characters of the original painting (as Picasso did).

It is always useful to insist that the analysts' *quality of presence* and use of their α-function involve many factors, among which, especially, is the personal analysis and re-analysis they should undergo.

IV. Psychic flow and time

When we make contact with our psychic world we become aware of its constant flow in time. We are forever dealing with moments in unceasing transition. As Freud (1957, p. 305) wrote, "Transience value is scarcity value in time."

Much has been written on psychoanalysis; so much, in fact, it is difficult to keep up. But is there really so much research going on to justify the huge number of publications? Let the reader decide.

For my part, I am concerned with reading and elaborating on the classics. So, striving to be consistent, I will not expand upon this text.

Before finishing, however, I would like to highlight, on this last trip of mine, an interesting fact that I observed at the Nationalgalerie in Berlin involving an exhibition of the works of Anselm Kiefer. Those pictures of Kiefer are exquisitely beautiful, having transience as their overriding theme, and are premised on a biblical quote supposedly from Isaiah: "Grass will grow over your cities." Their point is the passage of time and the changes humans undergo towards the unknown. This artist is so radical in his approach to transience that his own paintings are gradually falling apart (and, according to the museum's guide, create a problem for janitors, who have to clean up parts of the paintings that disintegrate every day).

Perhaps the meaning I intend to convey has to do with the epigraph by Picasso that opens this chapter: what exists is the *present* and, contingent on this perception, we can either deal with the analytical session (and with life) in a *real* way, or not.

With this text, I have invited you, my reader, to travel with me (I hope I was good company), in an effort to make myself *qualitatively present*.

This brisk promenade through the experiences and ideas jotted down here may have provided some information about how I work, and, hopefully, some pleasure as well.

Regarding pleasure in writing or reading, I recall a phrase by Paul Klee: "a line is a dot that went for a walk" (*Eine Linie ist ein Punkt, der spazieren geht*).

Notes

1 Claude Lévi-Strauss (1981) in *Tristes Tropiques*.
2 I remember a supervisory group that I organized with Frank Philips many years ago, in which someone outlined the clinical experience with a very psychically disturbed woman. There was, however, a particularity: this woman liked ballet. So Philips suggested, "We can start from there."
3 A clever wordplay. In Portuguese, *alto-falante* is a loudspeaker. Thus, *auto-falante* (which sounds almost identical) would be a selfspeaker or an autospeaker. [Translator's note.]
4 The original, painted in 1656, is on display at the Prado Museum.

References

Bion, W. R. (1977) *Seven Servants* (New York: Jason Aronson).
Foucault, M. (1989) *The Order of Things: An Archaeology of the Human Sciences*, translated by A. Sheridan (London: Routledge Classics – also New York: Vintage Books, 1994).
Freud, S. (1957) "On transience" in *Complete Works*, vol. XIV (London: Hogarth Press). Originally published in 1916.
Freud, S. (1958) "On beginning the treatment (Further recommendations on the technique of psycho-analysis I) ," in *Complete Works*, vol. XII (London: Hogarth Press). Originally published in 1913.
Lacan, J. (2002) *The Seminar of Jacques Lacan*, vol. XIII: *The Object of Psychoanalysis* (London, Karnac).
Lévi-Strauss, C. (1981) *Tristes Tropiques*, translated by J. Russell (New York: Criterion Books). The quote in this chapter was freely translated from the French edition.
Longman, J. (1997) "O objeto psicanalítico," in Sandler, P. (ed.) *Ensaios Clínicos em Psicanálise* (Rio de Janeiro: Imago).
Polo, M. (1908). *The Travels of Marco Polo* (London: J.M. Dent & Sons).
Rafart i Planas, C. (2008) *Las Meninas de Picasso* (Barcelona: Editorial Meteora).

Chapter 10

Transference–transformations

Evelise de Souza Marra

The Freud–Klein–Bion axis has raised and led us to issues that can be thought of as contents in search of a container. Transference–transformations is one of them, which will be expanded through the following pairs:

1 trans-ference–trans-formations;
2 transferential relationship – analytical relationship;
3 interpretation of the unconscious – description of emotional experience;
4 theoretical conjunction–disjunction;
5 expansion–rupture.

These issues seem to have originated more from the exercise of the analyst's clinical practice than from theoretical conflicts apprehended in the writings of the aforementioned authors.

1.

The idea of transference, conceived by Freud, was ensconced in psychoanalysis as falsehood, with mobile cathexis, resistance, the separation between idea and affection, and the theory of repression as its theoretical substratum. The "patient" *repeats* in lieu of *remembering*, and it is up to the analyst to decode the "false links," interpret the unconscious, and revoke the resistance. The "presentification of the past" proved to be useful and central as a means of access to repressed content. The concept of transference expands into a theory of Transference and separates what is analyzable from what is not. Even with the notion of constructions (i.e., less dependence on memory to reconstruct the past) and the development of Freud's second theory of the instincts postulating an irrepresentable death drive, the idea of falsehood remains in the analytical relationship, as opposed to something true or ongoing.

With Melanie Klein, based on the notions of object relations from one's early life and of an inner world intimately connected to the outer world through the intricate interplay of projections and introjections, transference acquires the connotation of *totality*. The transferential relationship is now the stage set where the representation of this world takes place, whereas projective identification (a brilliant conception) enables the analyst to apprehend relationships – internal–external, real–fantasized, partial–total. Thus, the theory is expanded: transference interferes in perception through objects that are internalized early on, and is enacted in projections of fantasies and events from the inner world onto the outer world, i.e., onto the object. The inner world is externalized in the immediacy of the relationship and the analyst represents both total objects (people) and partial objects. The inner and outer worlds become essential, rather than the past and present. Transference is a structure in which there is always movement and activity.

Bion discusses transference in his early works and, with *Learning from Experience, A Theory of Thinking* and *Elements of Psychoanalysis*, he will gradually propose that analysis is not a decoder of the unconscious, but a means to alphabetize the β-elements. He emphasizes *learning from emotional experience* through container–contained relations, with the development of thinking as its "goal." In other words, the emphasis is on the "newness" in experience as a possibility for growth and for the transformation of something not yet "alphabetized" or thought or lived.

2.

With the theory of observation presented in *Transformations*, transference is no longer synonymous with *analytical* relationship, that is, it does not comprise the whole of the analytical experience. When considering the various groups of transformations – projective, in rigid motion, in hallucinosis, in knowledge (K) and in O (field of being) – Bion approximates transformations in rigid motion to transference, but with a specific use. He reconciles them by identifying origin and destination, that is, both in the rigid motion transformations and in transference there is an idea of where they begin (past, primary objects) and where they are going to (the receptor, i.e., the analyst). However, the use of the starting point is descriptive and unidentified with the theory of transference as a whole, which stresses the elements of projection and repetition, and alludes to the Oedipus complex. The descriptive aspect of the analytical relationship gains status alongside "interpretations," whereas the other groups of transformations (projective, in hallucinosis, in knowledge and in O) are part of the analytical field.

This brings the projective transformations closer to what, for Klein, is contained in projective identification.

This is a complex discussion, because transference is not only a concept, but also a theory, and has acquired different connotations in each of the three authors.

3.

However, to conceive of the analytical relationship as a field of *living and learning from emotional experience* that, through this, develops thinking and being, is something that draws one's attention to the "mystical" dimension of psychoanalytic activity. This conception of the analytical relationship also enables interventions of a different nature from those that aim to *interpret the unconscious*. Descriptions, or rather, the "*transformations*" of the analyst concerning the ongoing emotional experience in the session, and the communication of these transformations to the analysand gain amplitude in motley expressions. Interferences by the analyst that stimulate attention and inquiry, the proposition of models and his or her own associations (dreams) acquire a function without necessarily aiming to explicate unconscious contents, anxieties and defenses, or the vicissitudes of the inner world in its relationship with the outer world. The analyst's focus of attention either shifts or expands.

4.–5.

To consider both the analytical relationship as the stage set for the *new* – and not, by definition, as the place of the repeated and fantasized (i.e., transferred) – and the influence of the analyst's "*real*" (far from neutral) person in the relationship leads to significant changes in clinical practice. The "real" person is inevitably present in an analyst who operates with "transformations," i.e., who does not have access to the experience "itself" and seeks to operate with transformations in knowledge (K), knowing, however, that he or she is dealing with the unknown and the unattainable. Compared to Freud and Klein, the space assigned to the analyst's "real" presence in the session has grown immensely, as has the search for descriptions or interpretations for what is lived and experienced by the analyst/analysand duo in the analysis room.

The relationships between learning *with* or *from* emotional experience, transformations and theory of transference (the pillar of clinical practice in Freud and Klein) are open to reflection. In *The Italian Seminars*, Bion will say that:

> The idea of the transference and the countertransference has been extremely productive, provocative and growth-stimulating. But, like every really good idea, like anything which provokes or stimulates growth, it makes itself out of date at once. [...] Your feeling that I am your father or mother can be compared with other ideas you have: you can bring together both the idea that I am your mother or father and the idea that I am a stranger whom you do not know. Then you can decide for yourself who or what you really think I am – that is your affair. In that way a new idea is born. The idea that you had before – namely, that I am a blood relation, a father or mother – is transient; it is a temporary idea on the journey of your life. From that point of view the technical term "transference" can be seen to have a resemblance to ordinary usage. It is an idea that you have "on the way" – you transfer it to me as a temporary measure on your way to what you really think or feel. At the same moment the new idea that you have is a temporary one and will be discarded sooner or later. [...] You might be able to trace a sort of map

showing the stations of your journey from point A to point Z. Where you are now, when you have just seen this point, is already out of date.

(Bion, 2005)

The theory of transformations and the emphasis on newness in the analytical experience point to a space-time in psychoanalysis that tends to infinity. The theory of transference is compatible with the conscious–unconscious field, but does not cover the finite–infinite field now being proposed.

How these and many others matters stressed by other outlooks – e.g., theoretical conjunctions–disjunctions, or even expansion–rupture – are used will depend on the psychoanalytic group subject to specific scientific, political and emotional interferences. Here, the intended use is that such matters reflect shared or shareable concerns and find a container conducive to mental growth by identifying and developing theoretical and clinical issues.

Two proposed inquiries

- If the theory of observation proposed in *Transformations* does indeed expand the field of observation to comprise both what antecedes and what goes beyond transference, how will this affect the practice of psychoanalysts?
- Do the theory of transformations and its derivations imply a new paradigm for psychoanalysts?

I outline below two clinical situations as an approach to these issues. They involve the following.

I.

A session with content involving remembrances of the analysand's history (or story) and establishing direct links between past and present, symptom and trauma, current and reported anguish – all of it bringing us closer to the theory of transference in Freud and Klein. The anguish, the complaints, the physical symptoms associated with pain, the resentment towards the mother, the traumatic loss of the father and the mournings come together into a coherent and very plausible "understanding" for me and for the analysand. The content of the session is pervaded by "My mother used to say … When my father died … During adolescence … Now …" amidst strong emotions, crying, pain and desolation.

All this brings to bear upon Bion's "transformations in rigid motion," that is, I am led to consider historical propositions (such as the origin of the current transformations), that is part of the theory of transference. What happened then and there influences and explains the here and now. However, I prefer to use the idea of "lived" experiences rather than that of "re-lived" ones in the current analytic relationship to buttress the ongoing emotional experience, an experience of intimacy, trust and (seemingly, to me) great relief and elaboration. The newness in this situation is an intimate and trustworthy relationship to deal with life and its accidents. We undergo, and respond to, intense compassion and pain.

I realize that I feel comfortable in the situation, with both my feet on the ground, "understanding" what is going on, and clear-minded with regard to my role.

2.

In this other situation, the experience is centered on the active and immediate interaction between analysand and analyst. It resembles a game that unfolds without clear outlines. Stories or histories establish no direct connections with the present; the links have to be deduced, interpreted, built. The current experience is central and demanding. The "then and there" is far away. It now occurs to me a relationship between this state of events and the analysand (child and adolescent) recalling his hyper-activity at home and at school, where he was the center of attention. His accounts of family or work situations succeed in making me a participant in his world, agreeing with and admiring his opinions and referrals. The atmosphere is playful, joyful, fun although serious, pervaded by my slight discomfort at not knowing what to say that might have some kind of "psychoanalytic relevance." From time to time, I press one foot on the floor as I formulate something that enables me to proceed. This analysis has been going on for several years and the analysand has shown himself interested, satisfied and grateful ...

The topical "symptom" is the vital disposition, creativity, responsibility, cooperation. Pain, when it emerges, presents itself with the same intimacy and trust.

Right now, my role in the relationship seems unclear to me and the experience often resembles a relationship in the ordinary sense, although the asymmetry is quite clear (I am the "doctor").

The two situations above involve lively and intense approximation. One in joy, the other in pain. I realize I am more comfortable with my own role and more down to earth in the situation of pain, and more at a loss in the situation of joy and its lack of complaints requiring a solution. It seems to me that when the experience is closer to the medical model, the situation is better known and more comfortable than when we are in a more symmetrical situation, with less well-defined contours.

With the awareness that these formulations are also transient and are evolving into continuously ongoing psychoanalytic thinking, doing and being, I expect new resonances and developments.

Reference

Bion, W. R. (2005) *The Italian Seminars*, edited by F. Bion, translated by P. Slotkin (London: Karnac Books).

Chapter 11

Complementarity and clinical practice

Isaias Kirschbaum

Quite possibly, the selected fact that hastened and organized my ideas was Frank Philips' admonition about the importance of addressing psychoanalysis scientifically. One's aim must be to avoid the interference of habits and beliefs (Philips, 1997). This made me curious as to what constitutes the foundations of any scientific activity, or what they consist in. What follows is the outcomes thus far of my research.

Freud, from the very beginning, with his first works, expressed evident concern for developing psychoanalysis on scientifically acceptable bases. The models derived from archeology, physics and medicine give us an idea of his steadfastness in this matter. His manifest interest in methods and techniques explicates his goal of establishing a scientific basis for psychoanalysis. In "The unconscious" (Freud, 1957), he follows up on Kant in his pursuit of a respectable scientific basis, resorting to the concepts of "noumenon" and "phenomenon." The former, the "thing-in-itself," evades apprehension but is amenable to intuition, while the latter can be apprehended by the senses. However, he also seems to imply that the psychoanalytic object lacks the sensory characteristics that make for a classic scientific approach. In turn, among other things, this scientific approach would make for predictability, an essential quality for a classically established science.

What we call Western science emerged with Thales of Miletus. He suggested one fundamental principle in nature, water, from which a theory was required to explain the phenomena of nature. This has been so for approximately 2000 years and was accepted by all renowned researchers, including Galileo, Copernicus, Newton and Einstein – a truly long tradition brought off by truly notable scientists. However, when moving from the investigation of macroscopic phenomena to the sphere of microscopic ones, it was found that the existence of only one theory (or model) was insufficient to apprehend, describe and communicate the observed phenomena.

It is interesting to note that during that period when physics had plunged into crisis, Freud developed the concept of "complemental series" (in 1917), published in the twenty-second of his *Introductory Lectures on Psychoanalysis* (Freud, 1963). He formulated the concept after studying the etiology of neuroses, in which he observed a complemental relationship in the variable proportions of

DOI: 10.4324/9781003171584-11

these two factors, the constitutional and the traumatic. He observed the existence of a duality and assumed the possibility of a joint concerted view that would complement itself in the resulting effect. This was, to be sure, a profound intuition of Freud, seeing that Nobel Prize-winner in physics Niels Bohr would only present his complementarity principle ten years later, in Como, Italy. This specific contribution by Freud – observation of a phenomenon derived from incompatible but coexisting factors that complement each other – has not yet been properly appreciated by the scientific community. For Bohr, this is the basic essence of any observable expression in nature, including psychic ones. Freud, anticipating Bohr by ten years, presented his theory of complementarity in the field of psychoanalysis and named it "complemental series." I very much wish to pay my respects to this psychoanalyst, thinker and scientist.

The search for the touchstones that determine the criteria of what is called contemporary science leads to Niels Bohr (1927) and Werner Heisenberg. The latter, essentially, contributed with the uncertainty principle, derived from indeterminacy, i.e., from the impossibility of determining with certainty the location of an electron when measuring its velocity – and vice versa, the impossibility of determining with certainty its velocity when ascertaining its location. Bohr's contribution is vast, but what interests us here is his description of an incompatibility one gleans from the nature of light, for light both behaves as a particle and manifests itself as a wave. Bohr suggests that any and every aspect of nature exhibits this dual constitution.

Possibly, nature is apprehended as dual because of a human limitation, our inability to apprehend it integrally, and this shifts the matter to the conditions required to observe and apprehend nature.

Heisenberg's contribution provides tremendous relief to everyone whose object of interest and inquiry is the phenomena of nature, for it released them from the need to be certain. In a seminar organized in Buenos Aires in 1968, Bion stated that "another important point remains, which sooner or later psychoanalysts will have to face; it brings to mind an unresolved problem concerning light as corpuscles and as waves – though apparently incompatible, both views have thus far proven to be correct." And, as far as we know, they remain so to this day.

Thus, indeterminacy, derived from the principle of uncertainty, is one of the two paradigmatic outlooks of contemporary sciences, the other being the pursuit of the unified field, which consumed many years of investigation and research on the part of Einstein. Had his labors succeeded, he might have resolved the question of uncertainty. Regardless, complementarity is a result of both *uncertainty* (indeterminacy) and of the *incompatibility* of the manifestations apprehended from the object under observation, which nevertheless coexist.

Bohr, going against every traditionally established scientific and philosophical current, tells us that to describe a phenomenon of nature what is required is not a model, or a theory, but rather at least two models or two theories. He also suggests that what we have is a situation where it is possible to construe the same event through two different modes of interpretation. The two modes are mutually incompatible, but they also complement each other, and it is only through their juxtaposition that the perceptual content of a phenomenon can be fully apprehended. I hope this will contribute to a broader appreciation of Bion's contribution to the theory of reversible perspectives, which I will explain below. Complementarity does not establish *conflict* – neither of the patient with him- or herself, nor of the patient with the analyst – but rather *coexistence*.

Bohr, with his theory, not only explicitly rejects Thales' postulate, but also suggests that the models we use to describe observed phenomena pertain not to the investigated objects themselves, but to what we can say about the nature of their interaction. Certainly, models are not the investigated objects; we build models because of our incapacity to describe the object.

I believe Bion's description of the state of mind he called "reversible perspective" is an exceptional illustration of how he used concepts from another sphere in a kind of interdisciplinary fertilization. In *Cogitations* (Bion, 1992) he spells out how he selects and uses the contributions of quantum physicists, especially those of what came to be known as the Copenhagen School.

Taking Bohr's complementarity principle as a model, we can see how Bion used it in his theory of reversible perspective.

Reversible perspective, an expression of the psychotic area of the personality managed by its non-psychotic area, is described as two apprehensions of modes of functioning that take place in parallel, as if one is traveling along two tracks that never communicate. Patients are extremely skilled in ensuring that the two modes of functioning (which are observed and apprehended by the psychoanalyst) never intercept each other. Much like what happens to train tracks, they may meet in infinity, in "O."

This state of mind is characterized, on the one hand, by an apparent agreement between analyst and analysand on the facts of the session. The agreement, however, occurs in the area of sense impressions, as in the drawing where one sees a vase and the other sees two faces. Yet, there is also a silent, tacit disagreement regarding the principles (premises) that guide the activity carried out by the analytical duo. Assumptions are denied and replaced by others, as the analysand aims to turn a dynamic situation into a static one so as to avoid mental suffering. Lastly, the divergence between analyst and analysand, which might entail conflict, is not discussed and is kept confined to an area in which it is not deemed a divergence at all between them.

The situation that results from diverging opinions about the known facts that take place in the session is explicit; from the reversed perspective, however, discordance, in general, only becomes evident when an apparently unwary analysand is caught off guard.

It is very difficult to distinguish the pause that occurs in this circumstance with this patient and the one that occurs with a neurotic patient. The latter uses the pause to process and to elaborate an interpretation, whereas the former uses it to make an "adjustment," that is, to adapt the interpretation to his or her premises so that nothing happens.

In the reversed perspective, patients caught off guard feel they need to rearrange their thoughts and align them with their changed assumptions of analytical work. For instance, the assumption that the psychoanalyst is the psychoanalyst is preserved insofar as the patient will readily agree with the analyst's interpretations. Silently, however, everything that clashes with the patient's vision simply has its perspective reversed so as to conform with it. This is usually accompanied by a pause, a brief moment required for the adjustment. In this fashion, the patient preserves the incompatibility (by means of devices such as reversing the perspective) in order to evade the conflict that would be established with him- or herself – and, eventually, with the psychoanalyst.

If I was somewhat loquacious describing the reversal of perspective it is because I wish to make clear how Bion uses concepts from other fields and builds bridges to overcome the gaps that exist on the threshold between known and unknown territories in psychoanalysis.

The clinical example of "reversible perspective" described by Bion (1989) in *Elements of Psychoanalysis* reveals a paradox: Bion suggests that the episodes reported by the patient during the analysis sessions were probably incomprehensible to him (the patient). The patient agrees. It is something that cannot be explained by an alleged lack of intelligence or sensitivity on the part of the patient, for the examples he gave might even be used to illustrate psychoanalytic theories. A baffled Bion asks himself:

> If the patient has no psycho-analytic acumen how is the evidence of careful selection in accordance with psycho-analytic principles to be accounted for? If the evidence of selection is admitted how is one to explain the failure of comprehension?
> (Bion, 1989, p. 57)

It is as if, on one track, the patient apprehends an admirable selection of episodes, all of them quite adequate and consistent with sensitivity to psychoanalytic principles, and, on another, parallel track, there is a complete failure to understand the meaning of such episodes. These differing apprehensions are apparently incompatible, yet they coexist. Furthermore, they complement each other in the function of paralyzing the psychoanalytic process.

One may compare this apparent paradox with the situation in which the α-function, producing α-elements, creates a contact-barrier that both separates and preserves the separation between what is conscious and what is unconscious. We have two incompatible yet coexisting states of mind, naturally preserved by the α-function and complemented by other functions mainly to establish propitious conditions for psychic development.

Perhaps a concerted view of the two tracks, when possible, would permit construing the patient's mental functioning. The contradictions and paradoxes of dreams are likely different from the contradictions and paradoxes of the α-function. The dream experience, as described by Freud, is a failure because it attempts to reconcile and satisfy incompatible activities. It fails in its efforts to evade frustration and it fails in its attempt to modify frustration. On the other hand, a successful reversal of perspective in terms of paralyzing the analytical process implies failure in developing the patient's personality. Let us consider, for instance, the psychic phenomenon of emotional turbulence. This mental state is noticeable when the analysand, as a result of the self-knowledge achieved in his or her development, feels compelled to decide between evading and modifying psychic reality. The driving force behind the decision is mental pain. Thus, we can observe efforts to paralyze the process by reversing the perspective, or, on the contrary, efforts towards being-to-oneself with all the turbulence and suffering this entails.

A supervisee reports an experience with his patient. The experience is described with overblown hues, adding dramatic coloring to the story. What seems relevant to me in this episode is that his supervisor said that, because he knew the patient, he believed that the entire dramatics might be related to the fact that the supervisee had canceled the previous two sessions with her. The supervisee conveys this to the patient, who then seems to calm down. The patient's reaction seems to confirm what the supervisor knew about her.

From this, we can see how a psychoanalyst's knowledge of a patient can be used to clarify what happens at a given moment, in a given session. The analytical duo seems to feel it can evade situations where turbulence, uncertainty and the unknown prevail, and will be allowed to navigate calmer waters and move through known and safe areas. In other words, if a psychoanalyst has a theory about a patient and "applies" it to explain what happens at a given moment with that patient, the analyst will be replacing the analytical duo's unknown and uncharted emotional experience in the session with his or her foreknowledge of it. In this manner, both the patient and the experience with the patient are reduced to the theory that the psychoanalyst holds about the patient, nullifying the otherness that is implicit in complementarity.

Knowing of a patient prevents the emotional experience from evolving and, thus, the psychoanalyst from coming-to-know the patient and, inversely, the patient from coming-to-be-known by him- or herself.

Freud conjectures that early on the ego is corporeal. Gradually, an ego of a psychic nature develops. Obviously, the two aspects coexist, although, in terms of their intrinsic nature, they are incompatible. This allows us to speculate that what we call "psycho-somatic disorders" or "soma-psychotic disorders" are, perhaps, expressions of an atypical form of coexistence. Resorting to a kind of "mental embryology," Bion suggests that the onset of the non-sensory aspects occurs much earlier than proposed by Freud. Indeed, he locates the beginning of psychic development in the fetal period, coexisting with bodily development.

Another area where Bion seems to have been inspired by Freud and used Bohr's complementarity principle of the dual constitution of nature can be gleaned from his novel proposal to address jointly the instinctual and relational models (paradigms?).

Bion describes the coexistence of both approaches in a spectral dimension using the theoretical concepts of narcissism and socialism, as well as their interaction. In clinical experience, this is expressed by the analysand alternating between placing the analyst now in one segment of the spectrum and then in another, and reversing this at any moment.

In short, narcissism and socialism are the two poles of every drive, and concern the individual's relationship with him- or herself and with the (social) group. The bipolarity of all drives affects the individual's search for satisfaction as an individuality, and, on the other hand, also impacts aspects of his or her life as a social animal. Whatever the prevailing drive, we can observe, in clinical practice, a permanent conflict between narcissism and socialism at some point of the spectrum.

When writing, Bion separates the suffix -*ism* to highlight the direction of the drive. Clinical observation suggests that when the love drive follows the direction of the ego (ego-ism), the hate drives are simultaneously directed towards the group, towards the social (social-ism) – and vice versa: when the analysand's hate turns against him- or herself (one's self, the narcissistic tendency), the group will likewise become the object of love. The two apprehensions complement each other in a spectral gradation.

The instinctual or relational dimensions or models are intrinsically incompatible. However, the prospect of considering narcissism and socialism as the polar extremes of every drive creates a bridge between the two models, making a concerted vision possible by which they can coexist. This makes complementarity possible and expands our apparatus to the observation and apprehension of what occurs in the psychoanalytic field.

Clinical experience may reinforce the impression that complementarity, much like splitting, as described by Melanie Klein, can be used to promote or paralyze the development process of one's personality.

I believe that the state of mind I am provisionally calling "complementarity," borrowing from Freud's concept (complemental series) and from quantum physics, constitutes a paradox whose function will depend on one's degree of tolerance to frustration. It can be used to avoid mental pain, as in Bion's example of reversible perspectives, paralyzing the process of psychoanalysis and, by extension, the patient's mental development; or, inversely, if the insight is tolerated, it can foster the development of the personality – for instance, the complementarity established between what is known and what is unknown of the individual's personality. Using the known to replace the unknown, in the case of intolerance to frustration, leads to the annihilation what is left unheeded or ignored, paralyzing the development of the personality. One has only to consider the Church's historic intransigence toward scientific research and discovery, and the regrettable episode in 2008 involving pope Benedict XVI and Sapienza University of Rome. On the other hand, observations of children suggest that attraction to the unknown may be a natural process.

Bion is of the opinion that apprehending and describing the psychoanalytic object requires three conceptual models, namely: a model that extends into the area of the senses; another one into the area of myths; and, lastly, one into the area of passion. An interpretation can only be considered satisfactory when it illuminates the psychoanalytic object, and this can only be achieved when, at the moment of interpretation, it is possible to visualize it in all these dimensions.

Possibly, the dimensions that extend into the areas of the senses and of myths express the dual nature of the psychic phenomenon, whereas the dimension of passion, resulting from the encounter, establishes the context in which the other two dimensions express themselves. Passion is revealed in the emotional encounter of two personalities. This dimension encompasses everything that is derivative and lies in the spectrum that comprises love, hate and knowledge – i.e., the links, as described by Bion.

The presence of the psychoanalyst and the patient, as I see it, in one and the same place and time, is the minimal condition for the process of psychoanalysis to occur. Considering they form an irreducible duo, with respect for, and preservation of, their otherness, and the uncertainties that pervade the relationship as well, we will likely have an essential complementarity, one with the potential to expand our mental universe.

References

Bion, W. R. (1989) *Elements of Psycho-Analysis* (London: Karnac, Maresfield Library).
Bion, W. R. (1992) *Cogitations* (London: Karnac Books).
Bohr, N. (1927) *"Complementarity principle,"* Volta Conference in Como, Italy.
Freud, S. (1957) "The unconscious," in *Standard Edition*, XIV (London: Hogarth Press). Originally published in 1915.
Freud, S. (1963) "Lecture XXII: Some thoughts on development and regression," in *Standard Edition*, XVI (London: Hogarth Press). Originally published in 1916–1917.
Philips, F. (1997) *A Psicanálise do Desconhecido* (São Paulo: Editora 34).

Chapter 12

Empowered by failure – vicissitudes of *Transformations*

João Carlos Braga

> I asked him once in Los Angeles what he now thought of a former statement of his which had impressed me some years before: "Psychoanalysis aims to produce that change in the mental apparatus which enables it to learn by experience." He smiled and said, "You know, rather like catching a tiger and saying: 'nice pussy cat'."
>
> Hanna Segal (1981)

The theory of transformations (Bion, 1991) is the psychoanalytic theory that has interested me most over the past 20 years. This recognition has raised some questions: What have I identified in *Transformations* that has drawn my attention for so long? Which ideas in the book have influenced my psychoanalytical thinking and my clinical practice? Why do I privilege these ideas instead of others? Where do Freud's and Klein's theories stand among the theories in *Transformations*? Have I overestimated the theory of transformations while idealizing Bion's ideas?

The core of the present chapter addresses the questions above, but some prior clarifications are necessary. In a broader sense, *Transformations* has improved my perspective on the human mind. In more specific terms, the theory has changed the way I perceive myself as an analyst and how I incorporate fundamental ideas from the book by leaving aside what I already know (including the classic theories) when I face an experience and become receptive to elements evolving at the moment. With *Transformations*, I started paying attention to emotional experiences in the analytical session, thinking of them as *stem cells* evolving to different dimensions: knowing, not-knowing, hallucinatory, and being-at-one with reality. Another realization, possibly a more significant one, is an intense emotional mobilization from my involvement with the theory of transformations: interest, challenge, frustration, enchantment, and moments of serene thinking.

The opposite side of these improvements includes strong feelings of failure, incompetence, and helplessness. I often feel unable to organize these different mental states into a logical system. I can only understand my experience at each moment in a partial and precariously integrated manner. Most psychoanalysts are unfamiliar with the way that the ideas are communicated in the book and the areas of knowledge serving as models for most theoretical formulations. Trust

DOI: 10.4324/9781003171584-12

from feeling aligned with the ideas proposed by Bion is hardly achieved, and when this happens, the theory itself imposes with the concern that the trust achieved may be a transformation in hallucinosis.

This sense of failure also emerges when we recognize that among Bion's works, *Transformations* is the least appreciated one. A strong rejection of the book is easily recognizable in criticisms of hermeticism and insinuations that the theory is a half-delirious construction (Meltzer, 1978).

This paradoxical combination of empowerment by failure reminded me of Freud's concept of being *wrecked by success* (Freud, 1957) and offered me an approach to *Transformations* by the theory of transformations.

Transformations unfolded

The observations below are based on my understanding that Bion was successful in his choice of communication when he wrote *Transformations*. In the book, Bion creates an environment that favors personality growth rather than knowledge accumulation, seeking to stimulate the experience and resources of the readers' own thinking instead of merely communicating his ideas. This successful form of communication is opposed by a sense of failure, in which the book becomes painfully demanding for those interested in studying it. Bion's ideas are difficult to apprehend and require the analyst to be persevering and confident in the psychoanalytic possibility of being open to intuition, which is a sharp contrast to the demands of understanding a scientific study.

Bion seems to have been struck by how Kleinian theories were wrecked by success: valuable insights treated as revelations. Also, we have elements to think that Bion understood that the use of psychoanalytic theories reveals similarities to individual mental functioning, in which ideas often serve to avoid contact with reality – and not the other way around.

Do we share this vision?

In my observation, Bion's epistemological and methodological proposals in *Transformations* permeate the psychoanalytic thinking among us at the Brazilian Psychoanalytic Society of São Paulo. When colleagues who are not interested in the theory of *Transformations* discuss the way they work, it is possible to observe postulates from Bion's book incorporated into their work, for example, tolerance to uncertainties about their observations, interference by the observer in the act of observation, respect for the quest to be what one is, inevitable transformations in the act of representing what was experienced, and an important presence of the hallucinatory dimension. Supervisions offer a clear opportunity to observe these facts. In contrast, fruitful discussions about the theory of transformations are rare among colleagues who are knowledgeable on this subject.

Can we take these facts as signs of *empowerment by failure*? By failing to grasp Bion's formulations rationally, we put in motion other means to transform our experience. We *discover* by ourselves psychoanalytic problems that emerge out of the dimension of knowing, similarly to showing how to dance, instead of explaining how to do it. The ideas in *Transformations* are not presented as hypotheses of a theoretical system; they simply emerge as part of the mental apparatus of the analyst.

Do we share this experience?

In *Transformations*, Bion invites us to follow a significant change in course, to give up the monopoly of the symbolic and symbolizing aspects of mental life in exchange for accepting simultaneous contact with what has not yet been born and what will never be born to the representable dimension. This implies abandoning logical thinking and its basic premise of cause–effect relations in mental functioning, that is, the ways that we have been trained to think.

Although presented as an observational theory of the analytic act, the theory of transformations fundamentally changes the model of the mind, the understanding of the psychoanalytic process, the goal of psychoanalysis, and the analyst's way of being an analyst.

Do we share this understanding?

Models from emotional experiences

For me, *Transformations* is an intimidating book, a difficult to assimilate thinking system that points toward a concomitant love and hate for reality. Bion's study is an exercise of tolerance to frustration alternated with moments of wonder. No other book has enlightened me as much in terms of psychoanalytic work or has required so much emotional and intellectual effort. When I try to organize these ideas into a logical thinking system, I sympathize with Meltzer's exasperation when he mentioned that this book is the product of a disturbed mind.[1] However, when I approach the book as a stimulus to examine what I experience in my contacts with non-mentalized or dementalized situations, I am fascinated by the brilliance of the descriptions of mental functioning and Bion's level of abstraction, along with his ability to use models of refined knowledge referring to areas as diverse as geometry, poetry, history of philosophy, and epistemology. On the other hand, the book makes me appreciate my limitations and shortcomings.

I believe that much of the effect of *Transformations* comes from the particular method that Bion used to write the book. If we modeled the communication of ideas using logical thinking as the rays of a circle converging toward the center and giving it the shape of a thought, in *Transformations*, the direction of the ideas would be centrifugal, i.e., spreading thoughts. This leads to the unpleasant sensation that ideas escape us and that thoughts are always expanding into dimensions beyond our understanding. This would be comparable to micro-Big Bangs in almost every paragraph of the book.

The painful effort required to assimilate these ideas is comparable to that of someone becoming cross-eyed and seeing two objects instead of one. The sensation of visualizing two objects known to be one is curious and unpleasant. Bion's clinical approach lies in imagining the mind functioning not as a circle with a single center, but rather, as an ellipse with two centers, with a transitional area between the domains of each center, i.e., a form of mental functioning leading to an interaction between the vertex of the non-mentalized and the vertex of the developed mind – and not that of a polarization between the two, with the obfuscation of one or the other.

Would it be appropriate to consider *Transformations* the *pons asinorum*[2] in the development of Bion's thinking? Or in psychoanalysis? In the history of mathematics, Euclid's fifth proposition in *The Elements* was given the nickname of *pons asinorum* for being seen as a test of the student's ability to understand, as a bridge between the previous propositions, which are more empirically approachable, to the following propositions, which require increased abstraction and tolerance. Let us follow this analogy into different paths in Bion's entire work and in *Transformations*. The first three chapters of the book address the fundamental psychoanalytic theories (Freud and Klein) and examine them by conjugation with the theory of transformations. The last three chapters of the book deal with putting oneself in unison with reality. The six middle chapters are a true test of the reader's ability to abstract and tolerate frustrations by thoroughly examining the transformations in knowledge and minus knowledge. In other words, in order to reach the *other side of the river* (transformations into being), coming from classical psychoanalytical theories, the bridge would be the association of thinking and hallucinatory states.

In terms of Bion's entire body of work, *Transformations* is the bridge to a psychoanalysis that includes, in the field of psychoanalytic observation, areas that are not reducible to knowledge. This position radically changes the vision of the mind and goes far beyond the presentation of a theory of observation: it exposes the confines of the mental universe achieved by Bion, his personal and original vision of psychoanalysis.

This analogy to *pons asinorum* also contains the hope that, as happened with Euclid's propositions over time, greater familiarity with *Transformations* will make it a more accessible knowledge.

Transformations and the Bionization of Freud and Klein

Scholars of T. S. Eliot's work (1963) coined the neologism *Eliotization* to name one of the hallmarks of the poet's work. Eliot used to incorporate in his poetry excerpts from other authors, not as a reference, but as part of his own thoughts. Without any reference to the source, Eliot seemed to believe in the reader's culture and ability to identify the roots of the formulations that became part of his creation. I will use this model and the neologism *Bionization* to express a similar vision of the psychoanalytic field and *Transformations* as the most explicit example of this resource.

It is easy to identify Freud's and Klein's theories in Bion's theorizations. The most evident are the PS ↔ D formulation, projective identification as a normal mechanism in mental development, the idea of caesura, and Oedipus as a phylogenetic pre-conception. Other less obvious uses are worth pointing out to help create the perspective of psychoanalysis that we have become accustomed to relate to Bion. Details of this conjunction demand an extensive examination, as done by Cecil J. Rezze[3] based on his clinical experience. Here, I will limit myself to point out the most significant conceptual conjunctions.

1. One of the axes of psychoanalytic thinking – the theory of transference – is present in *Transformations* under the concept of transformations in rigid motion (Bion 1991, chapters I and II). However, this is not a new baptism for transference. There are significant differences in this new name that arise from privileging the notions of emotional experience, their inaccessibility as facts in themselves, and the processes involved in their transformations, such as the emphasis on the present experience – and not on the individual historical past.
2. The Kleinian theories of splitting and projective identification (theories that Bion recognized emphatically to have used differently from Klein) have a rich and rather singular fate in *Transformations*. In chapter III, Bion examines them initially as projective transformations, but when he reexamines them in chapter IV, a fine discrimination emerges between projective transformations and transformations in hallucinosis as previously undifferentiated. In chapter VIII, those transformations resulting from projective identifications are again examined, and new discrimination emerges, i.e., *transformations in −K (minus knowledge)*. These different treatments of the Kleinian concepts offer different perspectives by changes in the observational vertex.
3. The concept of the unconscious, another fundamental axis of psychoanalytic thinking, also receives a new approach, in which the polarization is no longer that of conscious and unconscious, but that of finite and infinite, starting from the recognition that the primitive mental phenomena could appear through *fistulas* between non-mentalized experiences (infinite) and the symbolic (finite) dimension, in which the non-mentalized experiences represent elements from infinite dimensions, involving countless factors (Bion, 1992, chapter IV, p. 313). This is an important change. If the classic psychoanalytic proposition is to leave aside conscious meanings and interpret unconscious ones by matching them with psychoanalytic theories, the proposition in *Transformations* involves the analyst's attention to transformations of emotional experiences happening in the analytical session that lead to the emergence of unconscious meanings that can be matched with mental states present in the analytic relationship.
4. The structural theory of personality was already *Bionized* in the theories of thinking, functions and α-function. The emphasis on instincts disappears when processes accessible in the analytic relationship under the form of intuitions are privileged. The adoption of an approach to the mind through identifiable functions in the analytic relationship – instead of through structures and conflicts between the structures – as well as the recognition that our observations as analysts are emotional experiences and intuitions,[4] and not instincts or drives. This modifies the parameters that analysts use to think about their experience.

Is *Transformations* the core of Bion's work?

I will work with the hypothesis that Bion's thinking became unique when he started to examine each experience by adopting simultaneous, non-excluding vertices. This epistemological proposal has been present since *Experiences in Groups*, but it is in *Transformations* that we find it fully present, owing to the apprehension of the mind by functional – not structural – standards, as well as by the development of the Grid[5] and the application of the theory of transformation in psychoanalysis.

A group of transformations[6] in mathematics can be seen as similar to constant conjunction in philosophy. In psychoanalysis, these concepts are present when two or more different mental states are associated, awaiting clarification of the identity element between both. The Grid and the theory of transformations are instruments that favor the clarification of this identity and the medium in which the transformation took place, i.e., thinking, hallucinosis, or being-at-one with reality.

A significant change occurs when Bion privileges the mental functioning of the analyst, who, in order to grasp the constant conjunction (the group of transformations), needs to abandon his logical form of thinking. When Freud identified the constant conjunction *childhood sexuality and neurosis*, he followed the prevailing path of scientific thought and established the causal relationship between both mental states, as well as their method of diagnosis, treatment, and interpretation of meanings. The analyst adopting the theory of transformations *thinks* differently: childhood sexuality and neurosis are associated elements in a group of transformations (constant conjunction), whose identity element will evolve from emotional experience or intuition emerging in the analytical situation. This identity element may – or may not – receive the analyst's attention. If it does, the final transformation will depend on the medium in which it is fostered. This point brushes upon the core of the theory of transformations and its potential to identify the origin (O), the media in which the transformation occurs (Tα), and the final form of the current transformation (Tβ). This momentous opportunity is due to changes in the mental functioning of the analyst, who is transferred from the dimension of *knowing about* to that of *being-at-one with reality*.

Another decisive change resulting from this positioning is the relativization of the clinical application of consensually accepted psychoanalytic theories, which are based on snapshots of mental functioning, favoring static models and scientific thinking. A second but no less significant change is the creation of the perspective of a multidimensional mind in different and concomitant movements.

It is worth considering that this perspective permeates Bion's remainder work.

I now propose an examination of the way Bion approaches the mind in *Transformations*, the height of his speculative formulations. In a new presentation, Bion incorporates what he has examined as learning from experience (the dimensions of knowing and not-knowing) and tackles what is non-representable but livable dimensions: thoughts without a thinker and existential experiences.

Some questions proper to the scientific dimension of psychoanalytic knowledge, which arise with this position, deserve attention.

Transformations can be seen as Bion's effort to harmonize psychoanalysis with 20th century scientific paradigms, e.g., a switch from a traditional model of the science of certainties, deriving from the study of sensorially apprehensible elements, to another of uncertainties, arising from the study of the atom and the universe. For that, Bion had to establish new epistemological parameters for psychoanalysis, which required new methodological formulations, interconnecting with (rather than replacing) the previous epistemological and methodological parameters. In physics, quantum theory does not replace Newton's laws of universal gravity. In clinical terms, this would be similar to the vertex of existence (being the reality) being different from the vertex of representations (knowing about reality), with both coexisting.

Bion sought support for these new formulations in mathematics, particularly in geometry, in the passage from the study of bodies to that of their movements. The mathematical developments of the 19th century – such as the theories of invariants, vectors, groups, and matrices – were topics studied by Bion (Sandler, 2005, entry "Transformation"). This suggests that he also had contact with the theory of groups of transformations[7] by Marius Sophus Lie (1870), which enabled the calculation of different movements of a body in Euclidean space and their algebraic representation. Another significant convergence is that the psychoanalytic theory of transformations allows the identification of the invariants in the formulations of the authors, to classify different views of psychoanalysis, as done with the geometries by Felix Klein, in 1872, using Lie's theory.

In this last sense, *Transformations* can be read as presenting in its first three chapters the examination – by the theory of groups of transformations – of Freudian transformations (transformations in rigid motion) and Kleinian transformations (projective transformations), organizing concepts and experiences related to neurotic and psychotic functioning, respectively. Chapters IV to IX present a detailed examination of the conjunction of the theory of thinking with the theory of transformations. The examination of transformations in knowledge (K) and transformations in hallucinosis can be seen as an extension of the discrimination between realistic projective identification and excessive projective identification, the latter being the original meaning of this concept, as a defense of a *status quo* in the personality. The transformations in hallucinosis are based on the latter, while the transformations in thinking are founded on realistic projective identification. The last three chapters of the book transcend yet another psychoanalytic caesura, with the examination of the transformations in being, a dimension proper *to exist* and no longer *to represent*. Using the same imperfect criterion of naming the type of transformation with the name of the author who formulated the theories highlighting the invariants, we could name the transformations in being-at-one with reality as *Bionian transformations*, for the importance that they will acquire in Bion's thinking until the last days of his life.

Although the models that gained most prominence in *Transformations* are mathematical ones, we must consider that the psychoanalytic theory of transformations also relies on philosophy, on Hume's concept of constant conjunction (Sandler, 2005, entry "Constant conjunction"), and on the Kantian examination of the process of knowledge. Substantial overlap exists between these formulations, suggesting the presence of a new *Bionization*. The sequence proposed by Bion, of recognizing the existence of emotional experiences that are not accessible in their ultimate reality (O) but only in their phenomenal counterpart (T) with its processes of transformation (Tα) and its final result (Tβ), bears much resemblance to Kant's description of the sequence of stages between something that is unknowable and something that is representable by understanding: primary and secondary qualities of the object, phenomena and its representations, and concept (Kant, 1781).

If we also recall that the model in which transformations are introduced to us in the book – that of the poppy-field painting – and that Bion resorts to artistic models throughout the book, we have to recognize the presence of an aesthetic dimension in his thinking. Thus, we have identified a tripod that Bion used to present the psychoanalytical theory of transformations (the scientific, the clinical and the aesthetic points of view).

Ending with the epigraph

The book *Transformations* emerges as the epistemologically most important book in Bion's work, as it substantiates the points of change to a new understanding of mental functioning.

The fate of this theory of psychic transformations can be followed in the sequence of the development of Bion's ideas: the theory disappears as a theoretical reference, which gives the impression of having been a failure in the eyes of the author himself. However, a simple examination will identify, in the texts that follow it, the presence and development of the epistemological changes brought with the theory of transformations. What Bion actually abandons is mathematics as the model for a precise psychoanalytic language. In other words, the rings are gone, but the fingers remain; the theoretical jargon *disappears,* but the psychoanalytic being *emerges*, as in the successful assimilation of a transplanted organ.

We return, thus, to the epigraph of the present chapter. The psychoanalytic thinking that comes with *Transformations* translates into changes not only in psychoanalytic knowledge but mainly in the psychoanalyst, as highlighted by the statements of each of the two analysts (Bion and Hanna Segal).

Notes

1 Meltzer (1998): "I think, both from the literary point of view and from the personal point of view, at that time, that he was in a very disturbed state of mind." See also Meltzer (1978, p. 71): "Is Bion patient B in disguise?"
2 *Cogitations*, pp. 111, 206 and 207.

3   See Rezze 1991, 1994, 1995, 1997, 1999, 2003.
4   "... impulses, emotions, and instincts (I do not distinguish these terms because there is no distinction that is sufficiently precise)." *Transformations*, Chapter V, p. 67.
5   The analyst's need to examine thoroughly the analysand's thoughts led Bion to create an instrument to identify their different uses and degrees of abstraction. With the Grid, it is possible to accompany and make notes on the transformations of a thought, so it is not surprising that in its original presentation ("The Grid," 1963 (Bion, 1997)) appear the basic lines of what came to be developed in *Transformations*.
6   "For my purposes, it is convenient to consider psychoanalysis as belonging to the group of transformations," chapter I.
7   "Group of transformations: A group of transformations is an algebraic structure that is obtained by an associative operation for which there is an identity element. Each associated element has an inverse (the second element) that along with the given element provides the identity element." Reference: *Encyclopedia Britannica*, entry "Geometry," location 1.4.

References

Bion, W. R. (1991) *Transformations: From Learning to Growth* (London: Maresfield Library).
Bion, W. R. (1997) "The Grid," presented at the British Psycho-Analytical Society on October 2, 1963, in *Taming Wild Thoughts* (London: Karnac Books).
Bion, W. R. (1992) *Cogitations* (London: Karnac Books).
Eliot, T. S. (1963) *Collected Poems 1909–1962* (London: Faber & Faber).
Freud, S. (1957) "Some character-types met with in psycho-analytic work," in *Standard Edition*, XIV (London: Hogarth Press). Originally published in 1916.
Kant, I. (1781) "Part I: Transcendental elementary theory, transcendental aesthetics," in *Critique of Pure Reason*.
Meltzer, D. (1978) *The Kleinian Development*, vol. III: *The Clinical Significance of the Work of Bion* (Strath Tey: Clunie Press).
Meltzer, D. (1998) Seminar conducted at the Brazilian Psychoanalytical Society of São Paulo, October 8, 1998. Presenter: C. J. Rezze.
Rezze, C. J. (1991) "*A comunicação do analista: clínica e pressupostos teóricos.*" Presented at a scientific meeting at the SBPSP on December 7, 1991.
Rezze, C. J. (1994) "*Transferência: tentativa de rastreamento em Freud, Klein e Bion.*" Presented at a scientific meeting at the SBPSP on August 3, 1994.
Rezze, C. J. (1995) "*Transformações na prática clínica e relação com inconsciente, sexualidade, recalcamento e transferência.*" Presented at a scientific meeting at the SBPSP on August 30, 1995.
Rezze, C. J. (1997) "*A fresta.*" Presented at a scientific meeting of the Psychoanalytic Nucleus of Curitiba on November 14, 1997.
Rezze, C. J. (1999) "*O sonho, o quase-sonho e o não-sonho.*" Presented at a scientific meeting at the SBPSP on April 29, 1999.
Rezze, C. J. (2003) "*Contribuição sobre 'Bernardo' e apreciação de André Green.*" Presented at a scientific meeting at the SBPSP on March 19, 2003.
Sandler, P. C. (2005) *The Language of Bion: A Dictionary of Concepts* (London: Karnac).
Segal, H. (1981) "Clinical contributions by Bion: memorial meeting for Dr. Wilfred Bion," *International Review of Psycho-Analysis*, 8, 3–14.

Chapter 13

Interpretation

Limits and ruptures of a concept and a practice

Júlio Frochtengarten

In this brief exposition, I wish initiate a discussion on *interpretation*, which has been deemed the quintessential instrument of our work in psychoanalysis. One might pointedly ask what might be driving me to this. Has this instrument lost its strength and effectiveness? Or have the patients changed and the new pathologies require an adaptation of the instrument or, perhaps, even a new instrument? Or has psychoanalysis changed and its prime instrument must be rethought? True to my clinical tradition, I will end the essay by presenting a session as an illustration of the ideas discussed.

I believe that, if anything has changed, it is us, the psychoanalysts, and how we understand both psychoanalysis and its method, and, consequently, our patients. Therefore, any discussion on interpretation will have to include what we think, today, about psychoanalysis, its goals and the instruments to achieve them, as well as a reflection on its methods or modus operandi.

I ascribe these changes to the contributions of Bion's work, which drew attention to our work as people involved in the analytical field, rather than merely analysts as "instruments" of inquiry. Thus, he drew attention to the investigative, emotional and intuitive dimension of the analytical method, which can lead to expansions beyond what is already known and established.

Interpretation emerged in psychoanalysis in association with the first concept of *transference*, whereby Freud claimed that patients substituted the figure of the doctor for important figures and models of their child sexuality. These substitutions had the nature of obstacles and it fell upon interpretation to establish, through words, the relationships between parental figures and the figure of the doctor, and between the past and the present.

It should be mentioned that transference as an obstacle is at the very heart of analysis, which is the recall of traumatic events. Thus, transference was seen as both inevitable and undesirable, although Freud heralded at the same time its usefulness in enabling the patient to reach the goal of recollection.

Resistances, however, are acted upon and thus became very powerful forces against analysis itself, particularly the so-called negative transferences and the unconscious positive ones. In this evolutionary moment, it was understood that there was an opposition between the actual relationship with the doctor –from which the patient had been ousted – and the transferential relationship.

Yet Freud realized that, for the patient, an acted-upon transferential relationship is also real. And, in this circumstance, the patient ceases collaborating, puts aside the intent of being healed, becomes indifferent to arguments and logic, and does not remember childhood relationships, even while reproducing them in the timelessness of the unconscious and its hallucinatory potential. Transference, being at the service of the compulsion to repeat, places a huge burden upon the analyst in terms of eliciting recollections.

It is amidst these adversities that the analyst must undertake the work of interpretation. Perhaps here, for the first time, as the analyst's instrument par excellence, interpretation comes up against a limitation and loses part of its strength, because it takes place in a different register than that of the forces that lead the patient to repetition. The long-suffering analyst is forever in the midst of this struggle between the intellectual and the instinctual, between understanding and action.

Perhaps because of the difficulties he encountered with the much sought-after elaboration (working-through), Freud mentions an "art of interpretation" in his essay "Remembering, repeating and working-through" (1958).

After 1920, with *Beyond the Pleasure Principle* (Freud, 1955), the "repetition-compulsion," hitherto a clinical phenomenon, is conceptualized as an inherent characteristic of the instincts. This, however, leads to a predicament with regard to the concept of interpretation. That which is compulsively repeated, being linked to death instincts, does not become part of the associative chains and, therefore, there is an entire area that cannot be reached by interpretation. Conceptually, therefore, the analyst's work encounters a new limitation. In clinical practice, however, things are different and analyses can progress and patients can benefit from them (which is surely a relief for analysts), for it is highly likely that the life and death instincts will emerge fused together.

Some of these problems were resolved by the stipulations introduced by Freud in the second topic: parts arising out of the id are unconscious, but not repressed; the ego itself has an unconscious part; and there may be original masochism (i.e., not secondary to sadism). Psychoanalysis will begin to tread hook, line and sinker into the realm of the psychoses, And the analyst's instrument will have to undergo, in practice and in theory, corresponding modifications to remain effective in these areas of destructiveness, non-inclusion, repetition-compulsion and negative therapeutic reaction.

These areas can be addressed through positive transference. This, however, depends on two factors mentioned by Freud in *Beyond the Pleasure Principle*: the relative strength of psychoanalysis vis-à-vis the changes that the ego has already suffered; and the relative strength of the life and the death instincts.

As can be seen, interpretation ceased to be a mere instrument to reestablish associative chains or fill gaps in memory. How can the analyst's work proceed from this moment on?

In "Constructions in analysis," Freud suggests that, in addition to interpretation, analysts use another instrument: *construction*, which is what an analyst places before a patient when the patient lacks memories. A construction is a conjecture awaiting examination, and "only the further course of the analysis enables us to decide whether our constructions are correct or unserviceable" (Freud, 1964, p. 265). He says that even if the construction does not give rise to a recollection, the results are similar. This means not only that changes in the patient are not triggered by knowledge, but also that the analyst participates in this process, even if no longer as the one who unveils and reveals. Thus, although the term *interpretation* continued to be used, its meaning was drastically changed.

When Klein (1951) stated that object relations exist from early life, she was also pointing to the existence of a precariously functioning primitive ego. The ensuing and inevitable counterpart of this assertion is that objects are mixtures of reality and fantasy, that they are loved and hated, external and internal, persecutory and idealized, because they are the result of splits, projections and denials, as well as of fluctuating oral, anal and phallic patterns. These objects, as well as the various modes of relationship with them, are actualized in the transference, as the analyst plays out aspects of the father and of the mother distorted by projections and introjections. According to Klein's conceptualization, the primitive dimension of the mind (including the primitive elements of the Oedipus complex and of the superego, as well as the central role of destruction and of sadism) places the analyst in a situation in which transference is absolute. Similarly, the work of interpretation now differs from that of the Freudian model, whereby transference was pre-established from the past to the present. Thus, interpretation must become more comprehensive and comprise all the elements of the total situation – including the fear of death (which, for Klein, exists as something represented), sadism, destructiveness – in order to enable integration and symbolization. In Klein's model, unlike the Freudian, this possibility is open to the analyst, because "when persecutory and depressive anxiety and guilt diminish, there is less urge to repeat [...] early patterns" (Klein, 1951, p. 438). This creates enormous difficulties for analysts, who have to deal with primitive dimensions of the mind – always a cause of much anguish – and, possibly, do things that are more akin to constructions than to interpretations. Likewise, analysts must also be capable of distinguishing, within the emotional (and total) experience they are living, what might be representations from what might be symbolic equations. Furthermore, they have to find the right language to reach these early areas of development.

Analysts were well aware of the difficulties of not being neutral observers. Thus, analysts that follow the Kleinian tradition propose to make use of their own feelings during a session to identify the feelings of the analysand that are projected "within" themselves (as action, not as communication). In this manner, they postulate using countertransference as a work tool. It should be stressed that this proposition – that analysts must discriminate between their own feelings and those that are aroused by the analysand – suggests that analyzed analysts have ample access to their unconscious, including access to the destructive forces derived from their own death instinct. According to this outlook, analysis would have enabled them to include these destructive forces into the mnemic chains, which, as we've said, is largely in line with Kleinian theory. Despite presupposing an ideal analyst, and this procedure being "easier said than done" (Segal, 1981, p. 86), the fact remains that these ideas allowed the analysts' emotions during the session to find their place in the theory, greatly reducing their suffering.

If we dispense with the postulation of an ideal analyst, how can we continue working in psychoanalysis? We have all grown accustomed to considering the bond with patients as essentially verbal. Thus, when we begin to realize that we are emotionally involved, we also become aware that we do not merely observe, examine and interpret, and that our mental state is indeed affected while listening to the patient. Accordingly, the quality of observation that is possible in psychoanalysis has to be rethought.[1] I believe this is the road taken by Bion's models and theories, especially after his theory of transformations (Bion, 1984), in which, although retaining many Kleinian concepts, he emphatically includes the person of the analyst. If, on the one hand, this disorganizes the entire previous conceptual edifice, and consequently significantly increases our turmoil, on the other hand it creates a continent for flesh-and-blood analysts, who are unavoidably affected by their patients in a session. Finally, I think that Bion's theory eventually contributed to an objective construction of subjectivity.

By bringing the concept of *transformations* to psychoanalysis, Bion also notes that analysts necessarily observe their emotional experience with patients from their own biased viewpoint. Furthermore, echoing Kant, he points out that any apprehension analysts may have results from a transformation that takes place in their own mind, and is never the thing-in-itself. When conveying their transformations to the patient, analysts disrupt the field created by the patient, and a new cycle of transformations begins to occur, determining everything that will ensue.[2] If we accept and embody this proposal, both of us, patient and analyst, each according to their emotions, will assess with greater or lesser precision the events taking place in the room. It is possible that therein lies the essence of the work of analysis. Moreover, each one of our verbal interventions – either when seeking words to express ourselves or when conveying them to the patient – disrupts the central characteristic of that moment.

We are in constant tension between certainties and doubts concerning what we know about the emotional experience we live with our patients: if, on the one hand, some interpretation – including, therefore, our subjectivity – is always being made, on the other we never know for sure how much of this knowledge was shaped by personal thoughts and feelings, since subjectivity cannot be quantified and detached from the object. Submitting our formulations to be verified, proven or validated by subsequent experiences also does not increase our assurance. To work in this constant tension requires humbleness and recognition of the limits of our knowledge about the other, a difficult condition to maintain due to our incipient omnipotence and omniscience. The pain of this limitation often leads us to see ourselves as analysts endowed with neutrality, who act as if our unconscious was preserved and kept out of the relationship with the other. In the moments when we can neither contain the experiences that we liven or learn from them, we end up replacing psychoanalysis with interpretations derived from psychoanalytic theories. Yet, this is not a conscious choice: it is dependent on our own analysis, our personal educational background, our theoretical choices and also on our internal disposition and abilities, which are variable, pliable and malleable from moment to moment.

In our relationship with the patient, we are whole, with a conscious and an unconscious mind, socializing and suffering mutual interference. If we manage to maintain ourselves in this condition, we continue to use the theories – transformed by training and learning – but in the stage of preconceptions. In this stage, theories are the backdrop that allows the juxtaposition of intuition and all that takes place in analysis; that guides observation and allows expansion and enrichment, resulting in unsaturated formulations.[3] Only when we are truly in this state can we examine ourselves (and, perhaps, examine the other), perceive and recognize the typical modes of our mental workings.

At the core of the relationship with patients there is always an emotion – of either love, hate or knowledge. And it is in this emotional environment that attainable thinking gradually takes place, focusing on emotions and creating meanings so that that experience becomes significant. In my understanding, therefore, analysis advances from emotion to thought – not thought with an adaptive or developmental function, but rather dream-thinking. Conceptually, this process takes place through an α-function that establishes a *contact-barrier* that selectively separates and unites conscious and unconscious elements, and gives rise to oneiric thoughts. To put it another way: the analyst is the bearer of new ideas or, at least, provides continence so that the patient can establish relationships and produce new thoughts, abstractions and generalizations juxtaposed to the emotional experiences he or she lives. In this manner, there is a thickening or densification of the experience, because contact with elements that exist but have not yet been thought is conducive to symbolic formation and the integration of dispersed thoughts.

As an analyst, I am in the field, embedded into it. This is a source of great difficulties, because, at the same time, I must observe what I am going through and, if possible, express myself about things related to the emotions I experience with the patient. Instead of interpreting the patient's states of mind, I keep score and formulate some conjectures and metaphors whose power to catalyze mental expansion will likewise depend on the other's possibilities. This manner of working evinces the investigative dimension of the analytical method; not the investigation itself, but an investigation that is a template and intends to promote learning from lived emotional experiences, thus opening up new possibilities for the individual's future. As a result, an alternative dimension also emerges: *not* learning from experience, actively attacking knowledge, the area of non-representation and of the negative bonds of love, hate and knowledge[4] (which have been examined by many other authors). Learning and growth are functions of internal objects, of their oneiric possibilities. And a real analyst, with an emotional knowledge connection,[5] contributes to this task. For us to consider this flesh-and-bones analyst, we must take our limitations into account, either because the patient affects our state of mind or because our own analysis was not – and could not have been – complete. This creates a kind of shelter for our difficulties. As a result, we can benefit from learning the limits of interpretation.

Over the one hundred years of the history of psychoanalysis, we have gone from analysts who have a model of mental development – implicit or explicit – for themselves and their patients, to analysts who contribute to attainable growth and who investigate and expand the field they investigate (as Bion wrote). Coming across all the unknowns and all that we don't know and, at the same time, also coming across a profusion of theories in psychoanalysis are both sources of great suffering for all of us. However, if we are aware of this suffering, we can use ignorance itself to guide our work of investigation, following possible expansions and growths, unlike what happens when there is a very strong attachment to developmental models or theories. I am aware that all these assertions also derive from a theory, but one that has been useful for me in clinical practice, as it supports my observation in psychoanalysis.

***

True to my clinical tradition, I think it would be useful at this point to present a session as an illustration of what was said above.

The session I will refer to was the first one after a twenty-day break due to my vacation. In the two weeks prior to this interruption, the patient, who had been unemployed, started a new job and, for this reason and because of scheduling issues, session times had not yet been defined.

The patient arrives and is five minutes late. She seems a little flustered. As she lies down, she tells me that she had made arrangements at work so as to be able to come in at one of the time slots I had proposed, which seems to me an attempt to properly match the schedules I had offered her. She then remains in silence, which I interrupt after a few minutes to say that she seems to be more at ease there at work than here with me. I make this intervention with the purpose of breaking up an atmosphere that seems to me of intense anguish, opening up the possibility of conversation.

And, indeed, this makes it easier for the patient to start communicating verbally. What ensues is a communication made with great difficulty: her voice seems contained, she speaks so softly that some words are cut off, and I realize I am missing some of them, even though I can follow their overall meaning. (Incidentally, this muffled and subdued way of expressing herself will continue almost to the end of the session.) Amidst great anguish, she says that she had always heard, about herself, that she was easy to get along with; no one had ever told her – as they had been doing these last few days – that she was a difficult person to deal with. She says the work environment is also problematic and is convinced that, if it were today, she would not have been hired – they even told her that she is not leading people or taking the initiatives that she ought to. She adds that when she gets home, all she wants to do is to stay in her room with the doors closed. And that she has not had sex with her boyfriend for a month, and that he would be right to do what she was convinced he would do, namely, cancel the upcoming wedding … In short, the emotional climate is one of complaints against herself, her performance, her ability to relate to others. And while she seems to agree that "that's just how I am," there is an effort to tell me what she feels. I am there, closely following her story and the emotions that accompany it, but I am unable to bring myself to offer something new. I just make some points and notes, and draw her attention to this opportunity she has of talking about her feelings.

I notice that this prompts her to continue talking. She is still distressed, but the whining tone of complaint has abated or gone away. Perhaps some unfolding and elaboration of her present experience is taking place, as she tells me that she has always used alcohol to help her socialize, but that she is not even drinking anymore at the moment. Then again, she no longer opens her mouth when she is with friends and finds them drunkards and boring. My impression that she is actually elaborating her experiences is strengthened when she says that she's always undergone analysis out of habit, "It is a custom at home, my father, my mother, brothers have always done it and they told me to do it." This time, however, it's different, she felt the need to come. She is expressing a new feeling, because throughout our work I've witnessed her enormous difficulties to express and manifest her need for help – mine or anyone else's. I am now hopeful of being useful to her, because, as the previous emotional climate dissipates, something important and rare is happening there, at that very moment, with her. A gateway to communicate with the patient seems to open up, because what were grievances against herself became, over the course of the emotional experience of the session, a possibility of elaboration and interlocution with the analyst. This is what I try to talk to her about. I also think about possibly contacting the interruption in analysis, because despite the present difficulties, all this comes gushing out (although I say nothing about these last thoughts of mine).

After a few minutes of silence and feeling more serene, she remembers, as an association, a recent conversation in which her father told her about having had dinner with someone important, "some president of I don't know what." At that dinner, the father said that he and his daughter were very similar, that they both faced up to things. And then she asks me: "How can I now tell everyone that I seem to be like that, but that's not how I always am?" She also associates this with the sickly and serious condition of her mother, who may die. She says she sometimes fears that people are hiding an even more serious illness from both of them. The patient says that in the last few days she has even wanted to kill herself, or to let herself die. One day, driving on a riverside expressway, she felt very sleepy and thought about parking the car for a while, but went on, thinking that she might die in an accident. Moments later, she did park the car and waited until she got better to continue driving. I experience concern about suicide, which soon clears up and turns into compassion: we are having a very emotionally charged conversation, but it is a conversation about feelings, thoughts and imaginations, about being with living things. So I feel my concern dispelling even more and I point out that, at that moment, she is also looking for better ways to deal with the person she is and with the life she has.

It's now the end of the session, but she still adds that she was always seen as a tractor, a person who got what she wanted because she went after it and wouldn't give up until she attained her goal. Only now does she realize that this might not be a compliment, or a quality, but rather a lie.

Considering the session as a whole, it seems to me that there were no interpretations, at least in the classic sense of the term. The interventions were attempts to communicate what I was going through and to draw the patient's attention to what she herself was going through. Some of these interventions broke up the atmosphere created by the patient and that permeated the session, perhaps without her realizing it. Others contributed to enhance an already existing emotional atmosphere, enabling the emergence of new mental phenomena – feelings, emotions, ideas, imaginations, dreams ... Thus, as all this was taking place, configurations hitherto unknown (because they had not been experienced) emerged in the verbal and experiential relationship with the analyst, as well as gradations of meanings and new articulations between thoughts. This movement expanded continence to the emotions, to the possibilities of representations and to the field of attainable communication, which may bring new possibilities to her life and to how she lives it.

Notes

1 As Eva Rosenfeld, one of the psychoanalysts analyzed by Freud, stated to Paul Roazen (1977, p. 216) "Freud stood on the pier and 'fished' for the mother relationship, but still standing on the pier, whereas we are 'at sea' with our patients."
2 "... we have to remember that what we observe is not nature in itself, but nature exposed to our method of questioning" (Heisenberg, 1971, p. 57).
3 Category D4 in the grid developed by Bion.
4 −L, −H, −K links (Bion).
5 K link.

References

Bion, W. R. (1984) *Transformations* (London: Karnac).
Freud, S. (1955) *Beyond the Pleasure Principle*, in *Standard Edition*, XVIII (London: Hogarth Press). Originally published in 1920.
Freud, S. (1958) "Remembering, repeating and working-through," in *The Case of Schreber, Papers on Technique and Other Works, Standard Edition*, XII (London: Hogarth Press). Originally published in 1914.
Freud, S. (1964) "Constructions in analysis," in *Moses and Monotheism, An Outline of Psycho-Analysis and Other Works, Standard Edition*, XXIII (London: Hogarth Press). Originally published in 1939.

Heisenberg, W. (1971) *Physics and Philosophy: The Revolution in Modern Science* (London: George Allen & Unwin). Originally published in 1958.

Klein, M. (1951) "The origins of transference," *International Journal of Psycho-Analysis*, 33: 433–438.

Roazen, P. (1977) *How Freud Worked: First-Hand Accounts of Patients* (Northvale, NJ: Jason Aronson).

Segal, H. (1981) "Countertransference," in *The Work of Hanna Segal: A Kleinian Approach to Clinical Practice* (Northvale, NJ and London: Jason Aronson). Originally published in 1977.

Chapter 14

The "squabble" (*prise de bec*) between Beckett and Bion

The "experimental" insight in the glaring darkness

Luiz Carlos U. Junqueira Filho

> What is that which always is without ever becoming?
> And what is that which is always becoming but never is?
>
> (Plato, *Timaeus*, §27)

I. Introduction

Two facts inspired me in writing this work. First of all, the casual encounter in the Tavistock Clinic (London) during 1934–1935 between Samuel Beckett and Wilfred Bion. At 28 years old, Beckett, a young student from Trinity College (Dublin), was depressed, confused and disabled by several psychosomatic disturbances such as furunculosis, dyspnea and tachycardia; his nights were sleepless, or he awakened with frantic nightmares to the point of avoiding sleeping out of fear of dreaming.[1] Geoffrey Thompson, his doctor and friend, convinced he was near to a nervous breakdown, sent him to Tavistock in search of analysis where he was received by Bion who, at 39 years old, was beginning his psychotherapeutic training, after his studies in modern history at Oxford and graduation in medicine.

The few pieces of information we have concerning this epsode are found in Deirdre Bair's biography of Beckett (1978, mainly ch. 8), and I had my attention drawn to the fact he gave an account of his sessions saying, with irony, he had undertaken 134 "squabbles" – *prises de bec* – with Bion. According to Didier Anzieu (1997), this curious French expression used by Beckett, besides suggesting the patronymic "Becquet" of his Huguenot ancestors who emigrated to England, etymologically invokes the ironic or defamatory term. In another work, Anzieu (1992, p. 44) imagines a presumptive remark from Bion, concerning Beckett's tricks: "Il me donne la becquée et, quand je vais pour le prendre, il me flanque un coup de bec" ("He offers me a bit, but, when I hurry to catch it, he strikes me with his beak").

It is important to stress that in those times neither was Beckett the great writer who would be awarded the Nobel Prize in 1969, nor was Bion the great psychoanalyst who at the end of his life produced the trilogy *A Memoir of the Future*, a sort of oneiric illustration of his whole work. Nevertheless, if we trust Bion's conviction of the great importance of pre- and post-natal experiences in the development of adult psychism, we can also trust that both were already involved with the endeavor of organizing their primitive anxieties, in order to ensure mature and creative lives. If we consider the highly original works they both produced, we may assume that in the exciting atmosphere of these encounters a sort of emotional laboratory emerged, where transgression and boldness could continuously produce "experimental insights." Let us understand by experimental the interaction between two schizoid personalities possessing a "modernist Gestalt" (Simon, 1988, p. 22) prone to "experience, play, transgress, amplify limits, to formulate and enact all the implication of their ideas."

The second fact was the opportunity I had to see *Film*, the only cinema script created by Beckett, exhibited at the New York Film Festival in 1965. The conceptual coordinate used by him was inspired by the Irish idealistic philosopher George Berkeley for whom "esse est percipi" ("to exist is to be perceived"): in that sense, even if we suppress all our external perception (animal, human or even divine) looking for non-existence, we continue at the mercy of self-perceptions that warrant existence. Therefore, the only way to escape "being perceived" would be to appeal to the radical solution of *not-being*.

For psychoanalysts, perhaps the most interesting questions raised by *Film* are: a) to contrast our external vision (something that we could call *outsight*) attuned to grasp a sense of reality, with our internal vision (the *insight* of our technical glossary), moulded to apprehend psychical reality; and b) to grant us assistance in understanding the psychical implications of Bion's binocular vision.

That is why I felt it very useful to work out the dialectic being ↔ not-being, arising from the convergent, although antonymous contributions of both works in question. Beckett, as we know, is the "poet of feebleness" (Souza Andrade, 2001), of nothingness, of the unqualified, of depersonalization, of deconstruction; Bion is the one that invokes the "no-thing" as an object that induces the subject to think it or evacuate it – and in the extreme case, Bion (1965, ch. 7) describes the "supreme non-existent object," the one that abhors any speck of existence.

II. Outsight and insight

Film begins and ends with the closing of an eye, an explicit reference to the famous image of an eye severed by a blade in Buñuel and Dali's *Un Chien Andalou*, which could symbolize external vision apt to be sensorially stricken: this vision of "the face eye" that prevails in Beckett's characters is necessarily opinionative and, therefore, vulnerable to schizo-paranoid anxieties. Psychoanalytical insight, however, is attached to interior vision produced by "the mind's eye" mentioned by Shakespeare, always prone to grasp perception from the depressive position or in Bion's terms, to be at one with the object through reverie observing it from the inside of the object.

Grotstein (2007) named his last book *A Beam of Intense Darkness*, an allusion to Freud's famous suggestion, that the analyst should blind himself artificially in order to better apprehend psychic reality. He stresses that Bion had, in a given moment, translated this passage of Freud's in a letter to Lou Andreas Salomé as: "When we conduct an analysis we need to produce *a beam of intense darkness*, in order that something obscured by a glaring illumination could glitter even more in darkness."

I introduced the oxymoron "glaring darkness" in this chapter's title to stress that Bion as well as Beckett employed this expressive device when approaching their investigations. In fact, Webb and Sells (1997) produced a comparative study between the apophatic language of neoplatonic mystics and the statements of Lacan and Bion, suggesting that psychic knowledge can tread upon a road coming from "not-knowing" to "knowing." The meaning, in such cases arises through the tension between a positive proposal (cataphasis) and another that negates it (apophasis). In the same sense, Souza Andrade (2001, p. 69) mentions Moran's reflections concerning his meeting with Molloy, resulting in its self-cancellation using epanortosis; a stylistic figure that recaptures narrative flow in order to reinterpret it in the opposite sense.

"To emit a beam of intense darkness" is not a prescription available to the will but a suggestion that, if we come inside the "chamber of maiden thoughts" (Keats, letter to Reynolds, March 5, 1818) of the analysand free from the illusory illumination provided by memory, desire and knowledge of the analyst, than we can grasp the analysand's "wild thoughts" (Bion, 1997) framed in an infra- or ultra-sensorial specter.

Some artists use the pictorial technique to introduce a sense illusion named *trompe-l'oeil*: the principle underlying this procedure is to explore areas of self-deceipt in the observer, exactly as happens in cases of prestidigitation. Instead of the eye being deceived, the eye here lets itself be deceived. Being aware how much vision is seduced by the obvious, the artist and the magician disguise the trick diverting the attention of the spectator from the place where it occurs.

Considering that the human psyche is vulnerable to endless kinds of self-deceipt, the analyst should instruct himself in this twilight game that constitutes metapsychology in its essence. In fact, metapsychology, in my understanding, is the ensemble of economic operations used by the psychism, trying to represent emotions through "aesthetic tricks." We hope, thus, that the analyst casting on the stage of the session a beam of intense darkness could track conversely the script created by the playwright analysand, in order to recognize the "mental illusion" of the main character of the analysis: himself.

Bion (1991, p. 271) offers us a dialogue between P.A. (Psychoanalyst) and Paul (Saint Paul):

P.A.: The "penetrating shaft of darkness" is what I would like to use to illuminate what Freud calls obscure areas of the mind.
PAUL: "Be shelled eyes with double dark," as Gerard Manley Hopkins calls it, "and find the uncreated light."

III. Monocular vision → Binocular vision

In *Film*, we spectators are dragged by the camera, that is we thumb a ride in a monocular vision. The character appointed in the script as "O" (curiously the same sign used by Bion in *Transformations* to designate *ultimate truth*) was also confined to monocularity.[2] Reference to binocular vision is widespread through the film: the *pince-nez*, two holes in the rocker, both buttons to bind the document file, both eyes in the print hanging on the wall, and so forth. The character, cinematographically, is "split" into object (to be persecuted) and eye (which persecutes): until the end of the film, we can't be sure whether the perception persecutor is an external agent or the self. In order to maintain this condition, the character is always seen from behind or at most from a lateral angle of 45°, granting him an "immunity zone" (Beckett's expression) to protect him from the anxiety of being perceived.[3]

In his literary work, Beckett is perfectly conscious of these questions, approaching them in several ways. Let us see, as example, the recognition by Molloy, of the limitations of monocularity:

> And of my two eyes only one is functioning more or less correctly. I misjudged the distance separating me from the other world, and often I stretched out my hand for what was far beyond my reach, and often I knocked against obstacles scarcely visible on the horizon.
>
> But I was like that even when I had my two eyes, it seems to me, but perhaps not, for it is long since that era of my life, and my recollection of it is more than imperfect.

In sequence, Lousse uses the binocular vision Mother ↔ woman to spy on Molloy, reversing the sense of the primary scene and justifying Beckett's caustic description of mothers as "uniparous whores"[4] (or would-be monopanoptical beings centered on tirelessly watching husbands and sons, as was his own mother?):

> Lousse herself I saw but little, she seldom showed herself, to me, out of tact perhaps, fearing to alarm me. But I think she spied on me a great deal, hiding behind the bushes or the curtains, or skulking in the shadows of a first-floor room, with a spy-glass perhaps. For had she not said she desired above all to see me, both coming and going and rooted to the spot. And to get a good view you need the keyhole, the little chink among the leaves and so on, whatever prevents you from being seen and from seeing more than a little at a time. No? I don't know. Yes, she inspected me, little by little, and even in my very going to bed, my sleeping and my getting up, in the mornings that I went to bed.

A little further, binocular vision is singularized in its more operative characteristic, how to fuse separate images into a single one:

However that may be, I see a young woman coming towards me and stopping from time to time to look back at her companions. Huddled together like sheep they watch her recede, urging her on, and laughing no doubt, I seem to hear laughter, far away. Then it is her back I see, as she goes away, now it is towards me she looks back, but without stopping. But perhaps I am merging two times in one, and two women, one coming towards me, shyly, urged on by the cries and laughter of her companions, and the other going away from me, unhesitatingly. For those who came towards me I saw coming from afar, most of the time, that is one of the advantages of the seaside.

As his basic dramatic structure, Beckett uses the interaction between pairs of characters representing complementary or antagonistic psychic functions:[5] this is the case of Mercier and Camier, Vladimir and Estragon, Pozzo and Lucky, Nagg and Nell, Hamm and Clov. Hamm, for example, is settled in the tyrannical center of a constellation where, due to his blindness, he functions as a star without its own light, his existence being dependent on Clov's diligent work, always scrutinizing the world in search of lights to illuminate his boss:

HAMM: Did you ever see my eyes?
CLOV: No.
HAMM: Did you never have the curiosity, while I was sleeping, to take off my glasses and look at my eyes?
CLOV: Pulling back the lids? [Pause] No.
HAMM: One of these days I'll show them to you. [Pause] It seems they have gone all white. [Pause] What time is it?
CLOV: The same as usual.
HAMM: [gestures towards window at right] Have you looked?
CLOV: Yes.
HAMM: Well?
CLOV: Zero.

(Beckett, 1957)

The more Hamm prompts Clov to scrutinize the world through monocular vision using an eyeglass to be positioned at the window, the more the final result is null; the more his anxieties exact the vision of sea waves, seagulls, in short, of the world horizon, Clov accumulates a string of zeros, making clear that the misunderstanding not only prevented the formation of binocular vision, but also projected Hamm's blindness into the environment. As pointed out by Souza Andrade (2001, p. 15), introducing his *Endgame* (from which the above quotation was extracted), the sado-masochistic relationship between Hamm (evoking hammer) and Clov (in association to *clou*, nail in French) posits a sterile debate between two points of view (vertices, in Bion's terms) that never meet.

Christopher Ricks (1990, p. 61) in his brilliant analysis of Beckett's "dying words" that frame his "feebleness syntaxis," warn us with a beautiful instance of what I would call a monocular word in describing the world. He quotes the passage in which Hamm calls peremptorily for a single word to abridge the world Clov is viewing from the window:

HAMM: What is the whole?
CLOV: What is the meaning of whole? In a single word? Is this you want to know? Let's wait a bit [turns the eyeglass outside, looks, turns the eyeglass down, and says to Hamm]: *corpsed*.

If we track the semantic meaning of *corpse*, we are informed that, as a transitive verb it represents the act of killing, of producing a deceased but, as a theatrical slang it means to "upset an actor during his performance after some mistake." Kenneth Branagh, the English actor, amplifies the term to the ungovernable laugh that takes the artist during the performance, throwing him apart from the original script. This is something related to the Greek *hamartia* used in the Iliad (Brandão, 1986, p. 72), in the sense of missing the target, missing the path, to commit a fault, to stumble by thoughtlessness; to Beckett, therefore, the monocular synthetic word for human precariousness would be "to jump the track."

A fair example of "binocular word" has been given by Beckett inspired by Joyce's expressive neologisms: dissatisfied with the word "doubt" to signify extreme states of uncertainty, he created the expression *in twinsome twinminds*, which evokes, with a rare power of aesthetic synthesis, the image of the "meeting of two divided twin minds."

Several Beckett scholars, including Ricks (1990, pp. 47–48) have drawn our attention to a *sui generis* aspect of his biography, the need, after his move to Paris, to produce a binocular work, that is, in French and English, almost simultaneously. French took possession of Beckett being a language that enabled him to express with simplicity the flow of feelings that embedded him when under the tropism of the black sun of death. A good manner to follow this "binocular word" would be to observe the poetic construction forged to express the extinction of "this."

imagine si ceci – just think if all this

un jour ceci – one day all this

un beau jour – one fine day

imagine – just think

si un jour – if one day

un beau jour ceci – one fine day all this

cessait – stopped

imagine – just think

Faced with this example, we understand how the French has a fluidity and harmony absent in English. The physiology of binocular vision according to Bicas (2004) teaches us that this vision occurs by the superposition of both visual fields in a strict area of optimization: beyond and below this level, we have diplopia and confusion, demanding a cortical suppression to block them. But normal binocular vision is useful, enabling us to have simultaneous perception and stereoscopic vision.

In that sense could we perhaps say that for Beckett the French poetic version was the creature of a binocular vision that lent the French aesthetic form instead of the uncolored fragmentation of the English, granting an essentially Beckettian aesthetic: after all, wouldn't *ceci cessait* be prettier and more elegant than *all this stopped*?

Bion (1962, p. 54), as we know, introduced in psychoanalysis the concept of binocular vision, when trying to solve the contradictions implicit in the theory of consciousness as the sense organ of psychic quality, as proposed by Freud, suggesting that the proliferation of α-elements creates a contact-barrier that establishes, concomitantly, the separation of conscious and unconscious qualities,[6] Bion gave us access to the genesis of two crucial functions of psychic functioning: *correlation* and *self-observation*. By that same motive, he warns us that "the impartial register of psychic quality of the self becomes jeopardized because the vision of one part by the other is, so to speak, 'monocular'."

After this statement, Bion felt he had a powerful device for observing emotional development, drawing him to advise an absolute necessity, during the analysis, to help the patient make use of this binocular vision to integrate his pre- and post-natal existences, his endo- with his exoskeleton, his infra- with his ultra-sensory perceptions, in short, his soma and his psyche. As a matter of fact, he offers a good model to understand the double transit amid these areas, illustrating how a somato-psychotic disintegration gives way to a psychosomatic integration. Using the pictures drawn by Picasso (1956/2003) on a glass canvas and also a vertex of observation, the painter and the filmmaker who was handling the movie in front of him, it is possible to go along with the specular inversion of the image, and thus to echo the permanent conversion between sense and the psychic in our human outlook on the world.

IV. Being ↔ Un-being

The nostalgia of old words never ceased to awe Beckett. We could understand this feeling as an expression of his certitude of being born with a clear message to the world able in that moment only to be whined, because unable to be spoken. Yes, hearing Beckett elaborate his complaint about the simple subject of *nothing*, it is difficult not to believe that this alert cry was already present/absent at his birth:

> The expression that there is nothing to express, nothing with which to express, nothing from which to express, no power to express, no desire to express, together with the obligation to express.
>
> (Beckett, 1983)
>
> I can't go on like this. (Opening words of Estragon in *Waiting for Godot*)
> (Beckett 1952)
>
>
> Not being deceived is the best that could happen to me, the best I could have done, being deceived, wishing not to be, knowing I was, and not deceiving myself or not being deceived. (*L'innommable*)
>
> (Beckett, 1953)
>
> To know nothing is nothing, not to want to know anything likewise, but to be beyond knowing anything, that is when peace enters in, to the soul of the uncurious seeker. (*Molloy*)
>
> (Beckett, 1951a)

It is possible to suppose that Beckett's reference to "being deceived" was attached to being born without being consulted or to the fact of having had an incomplete birth.[7] His skeptical vision concerning birth is well represented in the neologism *wombtomb*, clearly inspired by Joyce and which abridges Vladimir's astonishment in the face of the unavoidable path that projects person from the uterus to a tomb. That is why, inspired by Sébastien Chamfort whom he considered a twin-soul, Beckett arrived at this sharp precept: "Life is a disease that falling asleep softens each sixteen hours in a palliative manner: death is the cure." After reading Bion's reflection (1991, p. 414), would we not believe he and Beckett were also twin-souls?

> Death is not a disease any more than birth. Disease is constantly conjoined to both; so is life – and human beings are liable to think one causes the other.

Paul Sheehan (2000), discussing Beckett's *Texts for Nothing* (1967), warns us that the "vacuity of inexistence" would be the frivolous and unreachable desire of "had never existed," trying to enforce ourselves to the more modest "do not already exist" of non-existence. Beckett was always under a pattern of "expectant threat": in the same way that Malone proclaims his end which never happens, as if he "forgot dying," Beckett himself seems to execrate existence but, in the end, transforms his suffering into the raw material of his work and "in a curious combination of Descartes and Schopenhauer, he subverts the maxim: 'I cry, therefore I exist'" (Souza Andrade, 2001, p. 47).

It is interesting to note that all throughout their works, Bion and Beckett never explicitly mentioned each other, perhaps out of discretion or even cryptomnesia but, in fact, they explored the same subjects with incredible similarity. I will mention an evident example: on several occasions, questioned about the key to understanding his work, Beckett answered with two statements: "Zero is more real than nothing" and "Where you are worth nothing, you should want nothing."

The full sentence is: "Not the numb peace of their own suspension (from the senses), but the positive peace that comes, when the somethings give way, or simply add up to the Nothing, from this Nothing, which in his guffaw of the Abderite[8] said that the naught is more real."

Bion (1965, ch. 11), in line with Plato, Kant, Berkeley, Freud and Klein, was convinced that "a curtain of illusion separates us from reality," which thence is unknown and unknowable. He uses the sign "O" (evoking the mathematical zero) to designate the ultimate reality of any object, embracing: a) Platonic forms and phenomena that evoke them; b) Godhead, "God" and "His" incarnations, and c) ultimate reality or truth. His postulate is that "reality" does not lend itself to being known, but only "to being," contrasting with transformations that "deal with phenomena and are dealt with by being known, loved or hated – (K, L, or H)." Therefore, he desires a transitive verb "to exist or to be" to be used only with the term "reality." We can only "be at one with O" or "being O."

As we conclude from these explanations, zero is a fundamental concept for both of them, even recognizing that to Bion it was an arrival point, whereas to Beckett it sounded like a starting point.

The second statement dear to Beckett was extracted from Arnold Geulincx' aphorism in the wake of Descartes, formulated in Latin: *Ubi nihil vales, ubi nihil velis*. It is noteworthy here the strategic use of the word *nihil* that, with its nihilistic aura, draws us to the universe of destitution, of meaninglessness, associated with helplessness and lack of desire or passion, both linked to "nothing" (Stevens, 2005, p. 2). In this case the unavoidable correlation is with Bion's advice that the analyst should positively rid himself of memory, desire and knowledge, in order to disentangle the threads of sensoriality that could weave the web of the illusion curtain, hampering the psychoanalytical pair's production of a transformation in O.

Let us briefly contrast man's existential outlooks according to our authors. In *Terra bionensis*, the inhabitant is invited to be a "skillful administrator of psychic pain," confronting him to face suffering "if possible, through science or, after that, by any other method available, including religion" as Bion once said. Besides that, he is warned that the fear of death is linked to the will to live: then, if fear is split off, the same will take place with vitality, enthusiasm and creativity, leaving the person in a condition of annihilating voidness. That is why he is oriented to be open to the multiplicity of vertices (Bion, 1970, ch. 8) as the only formula to act while keeping thoughts of pain in mind, instead of trying to evacuate pain by acting it out.

Bion's characters, in spite of not showing their perplexity concerning their existence in the same manner as those of Beckett, however, suffer in intimacy with their own conflicts, approaching them from different vertices.

PRIEST: You are being extremely self-contradictory in claiming that it is a science *and* is true. It must have a point of reference outside itself. You cannot believe in Truth any more than you can "believe in God." God is –
ROLAND: – or is not.
P.A.: No. "God is, or is not" is only a human formulation in conformity with human principles of thinking. It has nothing to do with the reality. The only "reality" we *know about* is the various hopes, dreams, phantasies, memories and desires which are a part of us. The other reality exists, is, whether we like it or not. A child may want to punish a table for hunting him when he suffers a contusion. But he may desire to punish himself for "suffering" a contusion. He may ultimately be compelled to believe that, in addition to these facts, there is a table that is neither good nor bad, like it or not, forgive it or punish it. We may decide to punish our god, or to punish ourselves for believing in "it" or "him" or "her." It will not affect the reality which will continue to be real no matter how unsearchable, un-knowable, or in which degree its being/not-being is beyond the grasp of human capacity. After all, we do not know much about the world we live in, or the minds we have.

Bion's outstanding contribution concerning the mechanisms underlying the change of vertices, sprung mainly from his experience with psychotics who showed him two powerful resources to handle "catastrophic change" (Bion, 1970, ch. 12) involved in emotional development: *reversible perspective and binocular vision*. Even when these devices fail, as occurs most of the time in psychotic collapses, the psyche tries still to reorganize itself using a wide range of mental symptoms, the only and important exceptions being what Bion named the "supreme non-existent object" (Bion, 1965, p. 102). This object is violent, greedy, envious, ruthless, murderous and predatory, without respect for the truth, people or things. Its operative model should be what Pirandello might have called *a character in search of an author*. Clinically the psyche involved in this condition appears to entertain the phantasy of such a self-contradictory object, obliged to exist sufficiently to feel that he does not exist: the problem is simplified by a rule that "a thing can never be, unless it both is and is not."

A special prominence should be attached to some personalities, described by Bion (1959), lodging an internal object that attacks any link between objects, threatening primary narcissism, granting reality to non-self-objects. In these cases, the analyst's interpretations can be so highly fragmented that the patient fears sleeping and, during this period of unconsciousness, suffering an outflow of his mind, submerging in a state of mindlessness.[9] Everything happens as if the self threatened to be obfuscated by the presence of a powerful non-self, intent on ridding itself of this "nameless dread" (Bion 1962, p. 116) by a process of self-annihilation: it is not the origin of the anxiety but its perception that is attacked.

In *Transformations* (1965, p. 151), Bion associates the presence or absence of an object, its existence or non-existence, to the "design" we could extract from it, using the geometry of points and lines: but to the non-existent object, the reaction is depression. On the other hand, the state of the object, if intact or fragmented, if total or partial object, which depends on its arithmetic condition, whether it composes a unity or fractions of unity: in the case of fractionalization, the subject reacts by mobilizing persecutory anxieties.

In *Terra beckettensis*, in its turn, newborns are hastily vaccinated against potency, success and hope. In 1956, Beckett, granting an interview to the *New York Times* declared: "I handle with impotence, ignorance. It seems there is a kind of aesthetic axiom that expression is achievement. I think that nowadays he who pays attention in his experience finds an un-expert, an un-canner, who cannot. The other kind of artist, the Apolline is completely strange to me."[10] On another occasion, he said:

> The Kafkian hero is lost, but is not spiritually precarious; my people, however, are crumbling. At the end of my work nothing lasts, except what remains to be named. In my last book, *L'innommable*, we find a complete disintegration. Nothing about "I," about "have," about "be." Nothing nominative, nothing accusative, no verbs. No way to get through. The last thing I wrote – *Textes pour rien* – was an attempt to escape from disintegration, but failed.
>
> (quoted in Souza Andrade, 2001, p. 186)

In *Dream of Fair to Middling Women* (Beckett, 1983), the character Belacqua, borrowed from Dante, spends several hours in bed curled up, alone in the dark, thinking of the best way to nullify his existence or imagining the book he would write to "state silences more competently than ever a better man spangled the butterflies of vertigo."

The description of the "dark zone" of Murphy's mind illustrates the chaotic interior space in which Beckett's characters plunge in unavoidable manner:

> A flux of forms, a perpetual coming together and falling asunder of forms, nothing but forms becoming and crumbling into the fragments of a new becoming, without love or hate, or any intelligible principle of change. Here there was nothing but commotion and pure forms of commotion. Here he was not free, but a mote in the dark of absolute freedom. He did not move, he was a point in the ceaseless unconditioned generation and passing away of line.
>
> (Beckett, 1938, pp. 65–66)

Stevens (2005, p.18), comparing the notion of nothingness in Bion and *Murphy*, says that "as the links with other humans are experienced as filled with cruelty and dread, he is led to an idealization of a state of no-feelings, no-connections, no-thoughts, and to a need to find an inanimate container (the chair), a nonseeing and nonfeeling mirror (Mr. Endon), and finally to his own mind."

V. Epilogue

In short, Bion's work labels him as the great star of *negative capability* in psychoanalysis, while Beckett's work credits him as the great defender of *positive incapability*.

An important issue to be stressed is that, in a cursory reading, both works apparently ignored sexuality, but to my understanding, this is not true: perhaps it would be more adequate to think that, being aware of helpless human endeavors to fight death, the supreme life absence, they painted fertility in sombre shades, as if a mere secondary condition.

The few references of Beckett's to sexuality spring out of human degradation, as in his opening poem "Whoroscope" (1930), or in such mechanical devitalizations as exposed in *Malone Dies* (Beckett, 1951b), in which Macmann "strives in order that his genitals would penetrate his mate as one that tries to put a pillow inside a pillowcase, folding it and pushing with his fingers."

In Bion's epistemological period, sexuality is almost condensed in the configuration container–contained ($♀♂$), but, in his trilogy *A Memoir of the Future*, it undergoes successive incarnations in real-life episodes as, for example, when Alice's blood throbs from her physical contact with Rosemary.

Film allows us to follow the progressive restriction of vision (binocular vision → monocular vision → zero vision) and, in parallel, an escalation of negativization of social conditions, of sexuality, of memory, of identity and of mental and body functions. As the self is no more perceived and no more perceives, it starts vanishing, and its survival is only possible by checking pulse palpitations: blood is reduced to a mere vital sign.

Bion as well as Beckett potentialize their world views from essential existential questionings: "How to think the unthinkable, how to name the unnamable, how to know the unknowable, how to deal with O, the ultimate reality?", they could cry being at one. Their ingenious formulations teach us that to exist is in agreement with inexistence, that thing is linked to no-thing, that positiveness springs from negativeness.

Beckett, like Schopenhauer, pursues the "paradise lost of non-existence" and proclaims with pride that his work, in contrast to Joyce's *work in progress*, is content with a humble *work in regress*. Bion, like Milton, looks for the potency of form in the "formless and void infinite."

Notes

1 Decades later, Bion mentioned the psychotic anxiety of only being able to dream in the analyst's presence.
2 In English, an eye-covering is designated as a *film*, suggesting an interesting word-play with *Film*, as if part and whole had become unified.
3 Beckett, it seems, had offered Chaplin the role but, fortunately, it was finally given to Buster Keaton, better suited to interpret a persecuted personality.

4 There is an intrinsic logic in this lethal attack on woman's procreative capacity, if we think that, for Beckett, to be born is to live in a vale of tears. To a post-Kleinian like Bion, the capacity to elaborate frustration enables the person to build a mind in the present "Vale of Soul Making" (Keats, letter to George Keats, May 1919).
5 In the digital era in which we live, the basic configuration is essentially binary, with the important distinction that binary is zero plus one, and not one plus two.
6 It is highly probable that Bion was inspired by William Blake concerning the concepts of "binocular vision" and "beta-element," although he never quoted him explicitly on these issues. Williams and Waddell (1991, p. 71), mentioning Blake's "mind's eye," explain that "if man doesn't clean the doors of perception, he gets imprisoned by the walls of a cavern, bounded by meaningless sense-impressions." This cleansing of perception is effected through the spiritual dynamism of contrary passions which endows man with a hierarchy of two-, three- and four-fold vision.
7 Beckett stated that his "life insight" occurred during Jung's conference at the Tavistock, which he attended at Bion's insistence, where he equated his personal catastrophe to the fact of having been born only "partially."
8 The reference is to Democritus of Abdera who used an arithmetic term to represent naughtness, but who believed that an addition to something else could generate "something": hence the conclusion that "Naught is more real than nothing." Sheehan (2000) mentions this passage as "The long silent guffaw of the knowing Non-Existers."
9 This sort of "mental liquefaction" is very similar to some of Beckett's descriptions.
10 This formulation is totally attuned with "negative capability" as mentioned by Bion (1970, p. 125).

References

Anzieu, D. (1992) *Beckett et le Psychanalyste* (Thise/Besançon: L'Aire/Archimbaud).
Anzieu, D. (1997) *Crear/Destruir*, ch. 10: "Beckett y Bion" (Madrid: Biblioteca Nueva).
Bair, D. (1978) *Samuel Beckett: A Biography* (New York: Touchstone).
Beckett, S. (1938) *Murphy* (London: Routledge).
Beckett, S. (1951a) *Molloy* (Paris: Minuit).
Beckett, S. (1951b) *Malone meurt* (Paris: Minuit).
Beckett, S. (1952) *En attendant Godot* (Paris: Minuit).
Beckett, S. (1953) *L'innommable* (Paris: Minuit).
Beckett, S. (1957) *Fin de Partie, suivi de Acte sans Paroles* (Paris: Minuit).
Beckett, S. (1967) *Stories and Texts for Nothing* (New York: Grove).
Beckett, S. (1983) *Disjecta: Miscellaneous Writings and a Dramatic Fragment* (London: Calder).
Bicas, H. (2004) "Fisiologia da visão binocular," *Arquivos Brasileiros de Oftalmologia*, 67 (1), 172–180.
Bion, W. R. (1959) "Attacks on linking," *International Journal of Psycho-Analysis*, 40 (5–6), 308–315.
Bion, W. R. (1962) *Learning from Experience* (London: Heinemann).
Bion, W. R. (1965) *Transformations* (London: Heinemann).
Bion, W. R. (1970) *Attention and Interpretation* (London: Heinemann).
Bion, W. R. (1991) *A Memoir of the Future* (London: Karnac Books).
Brandão, J. (1986) *Mitologia Grega*, 1 (Petrópolis: Vozes).
Grotstein, J. (2007) *A Beam of Intense Darkness: Wilfred Bion's Legacy to Psychoanalysis* (London: Karnac Books).

Picasso, P. (1956/2003) *The Mystery of Picasso*. The Milestone Collection (DVD).

Ricks, C. (1990) *Beckett's Dying Words* (Oxford: Oxford University Press).

Sheehan, P. (2000) "Nothing is more real: experiencing theory in the *Texts for Nothing*," *Journal of Beckett Studies*, 10, 89–104.

Simon, B. (1988) "The imaginary twins: the case of Beckett and Bion," *International Review of Psycho-Analysis*, 15, 331–352.

Souza Andrade, F. (2001) *Samuel Beckett: O Silêncio Possível* (São Paulo: Ateliê Ed.).

Stevens, V. (2005) "Nothingness, no-thing, and nothing in the work of Wilfred Bion and in Samuel Beckett's *Murphy*," *Psychoanalytical Review*, 92 (4), 607–635.

Webb, R. and Sells, A. (1997) "Lacan and Bion: psychoanalysis and the mystical language of unsaying," *Journal of Melanie Klein and Object Relations*, 15 (2), 243–264.

Williams, M. H. and Waddel, M. (1991) *The Chamber of Maiden Thought* (London: Tavistock/Routledge).

Chapter 15

Caesura and mental pain

Luiz Tenório Oliveira Lima

I. Nine points for reflection (excerpts from Bion's essay "Caesura" (1989))

1. In the physical sciences the human being is dealing with a physical material: psychoanalysts are concerned with characters, personalities, thoughts, ideas and feelings.

   - But whatever the discipline there is a primitive, fundamental, unalterable and basic line – the truth [which both serves as the basis of and limits the work of scientists, religious persons and artists].[1]
   - Since we are dealing with human characters we are also concerned with lies, deceptions, evasions, fictions, phantasies, visions, hallucinations. (pp. 41–42)

2. I can imagine that there may be ideas which cannot be more powerfully expressed because they are buried in the future which has not happened, or buried in the past which is forgotten, and which can hardly be said to belong to what we call "thought." (p. 43)

3. When the analyst is not sure what it is that is obtruding he is in the position of having an intuition without any corresponding concept – that intuition might be called "blind." Any concept, for example projective identification, is empty when it has no content.

   [Between intuition and interpretation – the conceptual formulation (the transitive idea).]

   The analyst's role, in other words, is one which inevitably involves the use of transitive ideas or ideas in transit. The analysand, likewise, is attempting through his free associations to formulate an experience of which he is aware. (pp. 43–44)

4. Can any method of communication be sufficiently "penetrating" to pass that caesura in the direction from post-natal conscious thought back to the pre-mental in which thoughts and ideas have their counterpart in "times" or "levels" of mind where they are not thoughts or ideas? (p. 45)

   [The penetration in coitus as a pictorial image.]

The analyst is restricted to what is available to him from his experience of his own life on the one hand, and to what he considers to be the facts which are unfolding in his presence on the other. (p. 46)

5(a) The ability of the analysand to take advantage of the possibility of success which has opened out is a symptom of the penetration from the situation which Freud describes as intra-uterine, to the situation which is conscious and post-caesural. I do not suggest that the event is related to the dramatic episode of birth itself, but rather that that dramatic situation, if borne in mind, is easier to use as a model to understand far less dramatic occasions which occur over and over again when the patient is challenged to move from one state of mind to another. (p. 47–48)

5(b) Like birth, the caesura of marriage is dramatic; it may obscure the fact that the events at the time of marriage and after are influenced by events which take place long before the marriage. (p.49)

I quote from Yeats's poem on this precise dilemma, "Solomon and the Witch":

For though love has a spider's eye
To find out some appropriate pain,
Aye, though all passion's in the glance,
For every nerve, and tests a lover
With cruelties of Choice and Chance;
And when at last that murder's over
Maybe the bride-bed brings despair,
For each an imagined image brings
And finds a real image there.

[...] for theoretical purposes, events which are in the *womb of time* eventually show themselves in the conscious life of the person concerned who then has to act in the situation which has now become actual. (p. 49, italics added)

6   Some patients repeatedly state that they have some particular experience and then give the reason why – making it part and parcel of their formulation. This continued repetition suggests a state of mind which is proper to a person who only lives in a causal world. (p. 51)

7   The important thing is not that a patient is a borderline psychotic, or a psychotic, or a neurotic, but that he is a total character *minus* ... (p. 52)

8   In the psychoanalytic experience we are concerned both with the translation in the direction of what we do not know into something which we do know or which we can communicate, and also from what we do know and can communicate to what we do not know and are not aware of because it is unconscious and which may even be pre-natal, or pre-birth of a psyche or a mental life, but is part of a physical life in which at some stage a physical impulse is immediately translated into a physical action. (p. 53–54)

9 So ...? Investigate the caesura; not the analyst; not the analysand; not the unconscious; not the conscious; not sanity [rationality]; not insanity. But the caesura, the link, the synapse, the (counter-)transference, the transitive–intransitive mood. (p. 56)

II. A dream, a session and some notes

"I had a strange dream," says the patient as he lies down on the couch.

He continues: "I was in a 'caravel,' which recalled, from within, the wooden windows of an old 'train.' Something 'medieval,' ancient. Lots of people were moving about in that setting. Preparations were underway that suggested many of them would be hanged there."

And: "I found it strange that so many gallows were being built in the various rooms. I saw the nooses being hung, with those telltale knots."

- People moved to and fro, talking on cell phones and using palmtops; they seemed serene and happy.
- There was no authority in charge.

He continues: "I was concerned with avoiding the hanging of so many people. I didn't know who to turn to. I was looking for someone, but found no one, and yet I felt calm."

"Despite all the commotion with the hangings, the atmosphere was not heavy."

The analyst thought of a situation in a modern company – the patient is an executive in a large corporation.

The patient proceeds with several associations. The day before the dream, he had gone to a smaller town where the company he works for has a branch. He mentions the recent layoffs and the reshuffling of the board.

Going back to the account of the dream, he says that, in the dream, he kept watching everyone's movements and the many gallows being assembled by workers. He says: "We are all in the same boat." And goes on to mentions two other lines of associations that I summarize as follows:

1 A conversation the day before with one of the company directors who has cancer and is undergoing chemotherapy. It was a painful conversation. He thinks: "We are all in the same boat in the face of death."
2 On the same day, while driving in traffic, he heard on the radio the news of the birth centenary of French writer Simone de Beauvoir. This news triggered in his mind memories of youthful readings of numerous books: *Nausea*, by Jean-Paul Sartre; *The Second Sex*, by Simone herself; and Camus' novel *The Plague*. He then remembered the religion classes in high school, when he

came into contact with these authors and with the work of the thinker Teilhard de Chardin. There, contrary to what one might expect in a Catholic school, according to him, he became skeptical and materialistic.

Brief comments by the analyst:

- The boat of the dream as his company and his analysis – an ongoing navigation that alludes to anguishes from the present moment and the distant past.
- The boat as "the boat of life," death, the passage of time (past and future). The current present as the future of the youthful past.

[These notes and the nine points extracted from Bion's essay "Caesura" were intended to stimulate a discussion group organized by the author during the 2008 conference "Psychoanalysis: Bion: Transformations and Developments."

I hope that, with the publication of these notes, readers will be encouraged to think through these issues as they relate to their own clinical experience.]

Note

1 The author's comments appear in square brackets throughout the text.

Reference

Bion, W. R. (1989) *Two Papers: The Grid and Caesura* (London: Karnac Books). Originally published in 1977. See also *Complete Works*, vol. X (London: Karnac Books), pp. 33–49.

Chapter 16

Apprehending psychoanalysis with Bion

Odilon de Mello Franco Filho

The initial warning

This chapter is not a text properly. Perhaps it could be considered a *pre-text*. Or it might also be interpreted as a *pretext* to establish communication as we reflect on Bion.

I set forth two distinct *blocks* of ideas on this chapter's chosen theme. In Block 1 (one), I align some personal considerations on Bion and on how we have transformed his work by appropriating it in our clinical routines. In Block 2 (two), I will yield the floor to the author himself, highlighting some ideas I gathered from his book *Cogitations* (Bion, 1994), originally published in 1992.

With this method, I endeavor to establish some sort of creative interactivity, not only with myself and with Bion, but also with the reader. It is worth bearing in mind that, in his writings, Bion emphasized that they did not exist to convey truths, but to encourage readers to think for themselves. It is by exercising our creativity and freedom of thought that reading Bion becomes more fruitful, and I hope our work method is aligned with what we value in Bion's ideas and can be the driving force of our interaction, enabling interpretations, creative reflections and freedom of ideas.

Block 1 – Bion: identification or imitation

This proposal will be discussed from two perspectives: Bion as an author and as a clinician.

Bion as an author

Bion is not an easy-to-read author, at least for us from a Latin culture, as if this reason would minimize the problem. Engaging ourselves with his writings requires, above all, a certain degree of psychoanalytic clinical experience, as he himself cautioned. Reading Bion presumes that we are at least somewhat familiar with the central characteristics of the numerous authors he cites, for we find quotes from writers, philosophers, mystics, scientists and, of course, other

DOI: 10.4324/9781003171584-16

psychoanalysts. His style is, likewise, not straightforward, as he deviates from the usual canons of communication we are used to in the literature of our field. In fact, we can even say that multiple styles are present in Bion's writings, depending on the subject he is dealing with or the stage of his psychoanalytic production. Some passages, for instance, resemble daydreams that are no easy task to follow.

Our effort to "understand" what Bion's writings communicate can lead to discouraging results. He himself suggests that we let ourselves be carried away as we read the text, without seeking to "unravel" or "untangle" it, nor attempting to see it as a complete and organized piece founded on academic logic. He is actually even more radical, inviting us to "forget" the text so as to give room to our own transformations, which may arise even at the level of dreams. In his 1975 paper "Caesura" (Bion, 1977) this recommendation is explicitly made.

Given these characteristics of his writing, Bion clearly does not want to be taken as a model of a writer, at least not in my reflective reading. Failure to take this into account can lead to bizarre distortions, as when, wishing to testify to his or her adherence to Bion's ideas, an analyst attempts to mimic his style (or lack thereof), producing highly sophisticated texts, full of literary and philosophical quotations, and indefectible quasi-mathematical notation systems mimicking Bion's. We are thus in the realm of imitation, not of healthy identification. It is worth remembering that, when quoting meaningful authors, Bion was not emulating them, but rather using them as a source of inspiration within a culture he was familiar with by education and experience.

Finally, a Bion introduced as *hermetic* becomes easy prey to a form of mysticism that would be a disservice both to his work and to his image.

This item about Bion as an author might be sewn up with the following question: "Bion, author of what?" Personally, I believe he was the author of a scant number of theories – the notions of *reverie* and α-*function* would be some examples. I see his greatest contribution, as an author, in the fact that he raises issues pertinent to the analyst's attitude towards his object of study. Bion seems more interested in questioning the methods by which we try to understand the analytical situation than in arriving at propositions about, for instance, the origins of fantasies or the "reasons" for the Oedipus complex. In this sense, Bion does not intend to establish another psychoanalytic school to compete with the existing ones to understand increasingly regressive mechanisms. His goal seems to have been simply to help analysts refine their manner of "seeing" when faced with a psychoanalytic object. In the sphere of epistemological concerns, what he says can be of interest to analysts from different schools. Bion does not encourage competition between these schools. He merely makes recommendations on how the analyst may "organize" his or her experience in the setting according to frames of reference based on rigorous attitudes of observation. In this regard, his text "Caesura" is a prime example of this rigor and may nurture the ideas and thoughts of any psychoanalytic group, regardless of their current designation among us. Bion is not a Bionian.

Bion as a clinician

In his writings, Bion mentions many of his clinical experiences, and even recalls the interpretations that occurred to him each time. I believe, however, that it is not from these quotations that we will derive the most realistic portrayal of his clinical practice. For me, the most striking source of information about his possible manner of working are his reflections on clinical material of the so-called "Supervisions," many of which came to us through actual recordings. I believe that, in order to get to know Bion, it is essential to read his "Seminars." In the aforementioned recordings, we are able to discern now humbly he speaks about the analyst's role and "power," and about the limitations of the analytical method. (He once asked, "What can we expect from a method in which the analyst can only intervene through the spoken word?") At the same time, we note his respect and attendant "compassion" for the patient.

When queried or interviewed, Bion systematically avoided giving full and definitive answers; sometimes he even strayed from certain issues. As I see it, however, he did not do this out of nonchalance, but on purpose, so as to not be thrust into the role of a "guru" proffering words of salvation. Perhaps he wanted to avoid the mythicization of his person, sensing that to mythicize is just one stage prior to fantasies of cannibalization.

Another thing that stands out in his interventions is that he *never* explicitly quotes the concepts and theories he laid down in his books. As I recall from the supervisions I listened to, there is no record of him ever mentioning directly topics such as *a-function*, *reverie*, *β-elements*, *LHK links*, *bizarre elements* or *grids*, among others. Yet, all these notions are there, albeit in colloquial language, at the core of his observations. They are not repeated as formal concepts, but are part of references and intuitions that, being deeply ever-present, did not have to be named with a technical or academic vocabulary. In short, Bion did not have to imitate himself!

Although working with intuitions and thrusting himself *passionately* into the relationship with the analysand, Bion never assumed a "no holds barred" attitude, as if what the person feels is the only criterion of truth and the only source of interpretation. Whenever he spoke, even spontaneously, his words were stripped of the mannerisms that intend to convey the impression that the analyst entitled to say to the patient everything that goes on in his or her mind.

This is the Bion that was formed in me, the Bion that led me to *apprehend* psychoanalysis – in the writings he authored, in the recordings of his seminars, in the direct contact that I had the opportunity to have with him, and in my personal analysis. By holding him in such high esteem, I hope I am not mimicking him somehow in my daily life or in this essay.

Block 2 – Bion in his own words

Below are some verbatim quotes from Bion's book *Cogitations* (1994), which I hope will inspire reflections and discussions.

1. I assume that the permanently therapeutic effect of a psycho-analysis, if any, depends on the extent to which the analysand has been able to use the experience to see one aspect of his life, namely himself as he is. It is the function of the psycho-analyst to use the experience of such facilities for contact as the patient is able to extend to him, to elucidate the truth about the patient's personality and mental characteristics, and to exhibit them to the patient in a way that makes it possible for him to entertain a reasonable conviction that the statements (propositions) made about himself represent facts.
2. It follows that a psycho-analysis is a joint activity of analysand and analyst to determine the truth; that being so, the two are engaged – no matter how imperfectly – on what is in intention a scientific activity. (p. 114)
3. The cause is that fact which is selected to give coherence to elements whose relationship to each other is either not perceived, or else seen to be such that it is irrelevant or inimical to the scientific deductive system of the beholder. In particular, the hypotheses that act as premises to the system, together with the beholder's common sense and the elements for which a cause is to be found, are brought together so that time is shown to link the elements to each other and not to separate them. It is intended to refute or deny the idea or possibility that time separates one element from another, just as in other contexts it may be desired to find a fact that demonstrates the coherence of elements that otherwise might be supposed to be separated rather than linked by space.
4. It is not, therefore, that there are many different opinions as to the cause of a certain event, but many different scientific deductive systems and therefore many different elements that can be selected as the intersection of the class, "cause," and the class, "effect." (p. 171)
5. The cause and the selected fact are alike in that they are both ideas that have the power of being associated with an emotional experience that at one moment gives rise to a sense of creative synthesis and awareness of still unsynthesized discrete objects. Every emotional experience of knowledge gained is at the same time an emotional experience of ignorance uni-lluminated. […]
6. The selected fact relates to synthesis of objects felt to be contemporaneous or without any time component. The selected fact thus differs from the cause that relates to the synthesis of objects scattered in time and therefore with a time component. (p. 275)
7. Ultimately, a science stands or falls in proportion as it is a valid technique for discovery, and not by virtue of the "knowledge" gained. This last is always subject to supersession; indeed, supersession of findings by new findings is the criterion by which vitality of the subject is judged. (p. 190)
8. The positive and negative therapeutic reactions are in essence the same; they are therapeutic reactions intended to take attention away from psycho-analysis. Like the insistence on "cure" as an objective for taking up analysis, they

are objectives for continuing or stopping; they are "covers," rationalizations, "reasons" operating in a role as slave to ... what? The passions? Or some unknown such as hatred of doubt? (p. 301)

9   Anxiety arises because one knows that analysands come with an idea of cure, and one knows it is almost certain that they will not get, and cannot get, what they call "cure." Almost – but not quite. But even supposing one can lead them to something better – a very large supposition – even that is far from certain. What then? Is it possible simply to say, "Try it?" Much analysis, and even more psychotherapy, is ludicrously omnipotent and optimistic. (p. 311)

References

Bion, W. R. (1977) *Two Papers. The Grid and Caesura* (London: Karnac Books).
Bion, W. R. (1994) *Cogitations* (London: Karnac Books). New extended edition.

Chapter 17

Extensions into the realm of minus

Paulo Cesar Sandler

> "Certainty" is a part of life as is "uncertainty." We cannot avoid either; they are opposite poles of the same feeling. I do not know what name to give to the "same feeling" – that is, the feeling of which they are opposite poles. Perhaps if I were a poet or philosopher I could. It does not help that I am thought to be a psychoanalyst because that is my profession.
>
> (Bion, 1979, pp. 511–513)

> The first problem is to see what can be done to increase scientific rigor by establishing the nature of minus K (−K), minus L (−L) and minus H (−H). I shall start by considering the mechanics of thinking.
>
> (Bion, 1963, p. 51)

> One thought alone occupies us; we cannot think of two things at the same time. This is lucky for us according to the world, not according to God.
>
> (Pascal, 1657)

Among Bion's main clinical observations in psychoanalysis, it would be fair to emphasize his study of the peculiarities that typify the processes of knowledge in the psychotic personality (Bion, 1957a), to form broader theoretical concepts in his explorations about the "mechanics of thinking" (Bion, 1961; Sandler, 1997g). Both are direct derivations of Freud's three interlinked theories, namely, (i) of instincts, (ii) of mental functioning and (iii) about internal objects (Freud, 1911a, 1915). Bion focuses our capacity to make links "between objects considered to be in relationship with each other" (Bion, 1962, p. 42; Sandler, 2005, p. 406) under three modes (or transformations) of those objects: (i) materialized things, (ii) other people, (iii) transient events.

Bion's first theory of links consists of a model depicting three basic links between people and things through quasi-mathematical signs: L = love; H = hate; K = knowledge. In its most primitive form: the baby–breast relationship that materializes into the basic human instincts – life, death and epistemophilic (Freud, 1909, 1920; Sandler, 1997d, p. 71; 2005).

We, human beings, have a double-tracked capacity: to make and to unmake those links; Bion called the latter "minus," borrowing from Gottlob Frege's theory of numbers, designating it with a quasi-mathematical notation: "−".

DOI: 10.4324/9781003171584-17

This chapter is an attempt to build an expansion of the concept minus, derived from clinical practice.

My experience shows two presentational modes to the realm of minus: either as a purely destructive action in analytic sessions or as a constitutive action that subsumes the whole analytic situation.

The range of application of theories

My first attempt to cope with phenomenal manifestations of the instincts of hate and love or death and life (Freud, 1920) in the analytic setting, from 1974 to 1981, was conducive to impasse-creating situations in the actual session, imperiling the analytical relationship: most patients misapprehend the psychoanalytic assessment – a scientific description of facts – as if it were endowed with judgmental values.

Patients felt that harboring the emotional experience of hating was morally bad – as if they were criminals as soon as they felt it. Analysis would be unconsciously equated to a judgment in a court room; the analyst is seen as if he or she is the judge. Klein observed false depression in the patients who cannot put up with depressive phenomena and color them with feelings of persecution, expressing coarse self-recriminations and blind guilt. They find the depressive position unbearable, deny and project it onto the analyst (Klein, 1946a, 1957). The judgment is internal: they feel alone, helpless, submitted to a harsh, murderous superego. Unwittingly or not, the analyst would stimulate the false depression when couching interpretations in the words hate and love – furnishing a confusion-producing container to his or her own unanalyzed psychotic traits.

Whereas with other patients the realization of guilt about their own aggressive feelings was conducive to the enjoyment of an experience of freedom to move toward the depressive position, accompanied with less fear of moving back to its tandem companion – a renewed paranoid-schizoid experience.

In the first case, patients just feel persecuted: not therapeutic, it is ensued by a new bout of omniscience and omnipotence. Atonement proves to be impossible. There emerges an intra-session impasse: a quasi-impossibility to experience what Bion called "becoming O."

"O"

A quasi-mathematical sign to represent the ultimate reality: the very first initial stimulus (internal or external) to put the psychic apparatus into function (Bion, 1965, p. 15; Sandler, 2005, pp. 527, 795). Becoming O can be seen as the final product of a transient and relative lack of (at least) three seminal mechanisms of defense of the ego – denial, projective identification and rationalization (Freud, 1919a; 1937, pp. 235–240; 1938a; 1938b), which I see as the untruth carriers. This lack allows for the emergence of an insight – a needed factor to become O, an "endo-psychic" event dealing with the three systems of the psychic apparatus:

conscious, pre-conscious and unconscious, via a contact-barrier (Bion, 1962, p. 64). Patients immobilized in the paranoid-schizoid position remain unable to "become O." There are renewed attempts to restore transference neurosis (Freud, 1912), and this mindset increases tendencies to escalate toxic dependency: a mark of personal irresponsibility. The mounting experience from 1974 to 1981 indicated that I was facing a problem refractory to being dealt with by existing psychoanalytic theories I knew:

> The problem, psycho-analytically, is easier to grasp if O represents ultimate reality, good and evil. Becoming O would then seem to be easier to associate with cure than becoming ultimate good or ultimate evil by splitting. Moreover, health may be more easily associated with being passive, vis-à-vis ultimate good and evil, rather than with being active. ... The interpretation should be such that the transition from knowing about reality to becoming real is furthered. ... Any interpretation may be accepted in K but rejected in O; acceptance in O means that acceptance of an interpretation enabling the patient to "know" that part of himself to which attention has been drawn is felt to involve "being" or "becoming" that person. For many interpretations this price is paid. But some are felt to involve too high a price, notably those which the patient regards as involving him in "going mad" or committing murder of himself or someone else, or becoming "responsible" and therefore guilty.
>
> (Bion, 1965, pp. 148–149, 153–154, 164)

Contradictions, paradoxes and the two principles of mental functioning

I suggested elsewhere that the ability to tolerate paradoxes can be seen as an added "rule" together with the realization of Oedipus and of the existence of free associations, as established by Freud, in order to evaluate if work is psychoanalysis or not (Sandler, 2013b, p. 99): "Foul is fair, fair is foul," warned the Witches, but Macbeth could not realize it, debasing the observation into sadism. Goethe, who translated Shakespeare into German, seemed not to be fooled by the presence of paradoxes:

FAUST: How are you named?
MEPHISTOPHELES: A slight question for one who so disdains the Word, is so distant from appearance: one whom only the vital depths have stirred.
FAUST: We usually gather from your names/ The nature of you gentlemen: it's plain/ What you are, we all too clearly recognize/ One who's called Liar, Ruin, Lord of the Flies./ Well, what are you then?
MEPHISTOPHELES: Part of the Power that would always wish Evil, and always works the Good.

(Goethe, 1834, I: iii)

A transdisciplinary study published elsewhere examines, from the psychoanalytic vertex furnished by the work of Melanie Klein, the cycles of progresses and the ensuing reactive regresses in the history of ideas in western civilization, as a spur to further advancements or not. Progresses and regresses form a paradox; the very same action can contain both. My hypothesis is that the cycles reverberate, in science and art, the tandem movement between the paranoid-schizoid and depressive positions; in Bion's quasi-mathematic notation, PS↔D (Klein, 1946a): another paradox to be coped with by analysts and any one of us human beings. In that research, I suggested differentiating two kinds of relationship between pairs of opposites as they emerge in analytic sessions (Sandler, 1997c, p. 191; 2000a, p. 126; 2003, p. 62; 2006; 2011a, p. 7; 2018): either as contradictions or paradoxes. This is not a philosophical or rhetorical discrimination as it may seem, due to its empirical origin in the clinical practice of psychoanalysis (Bacon, 1620; Bion, 1962, p. 77; 1975, p. 92; Sandler, 2001c; 2005, p. 415; 2015b; 2015c).

Contradiction: a verbal formulation derived from the Latin expression *contra dictum*, involving two oppositestatements, expressing a war-mindset. One statement "triumphs" over the other, in a parasitical relationship between the two (Bion, 1970, p. 95). Contradictions admit resolution in terms of right or wrong and are the aftermath of the triumph of desire – one among the sensuous counterparts of the prevalence of the principle of pleasure–unpleasure (Freud, 1911a). Contradictions are amenable to being understood and temporarily resolved according to formal (Euclidean) logics, through the exercising of "pure reason" (Kant, 1781). This happens when one finds a gullible audience prone to be influenced by one endowed with authoritarian rationalization, who denies doubt (Freud, 1911b, p. 49; 1925): a powerful psychic mechanism to build paranoid psychoses, which offers to its beholder feelings of blissful, triumphant states of mind. The beholder phantasizes "ownership" of absolute truth. Contradictions are conducive to states of inanimate, static immobility, under the aegis of an intrapsychic (hallucinated) defusing of life and death instincts (Freud, 1920).

The earliest experience that provides emotional maturation seems to experience the no-breast: the experience of having real contact with a real breast that never fulfills the pre-conception of the breast (Bion, 1961, p. 117). One must not confuse the first realization of a breast, that is, the matching of a pre-conception with a real breast, with the fulfillment of the desired, pre-conceived breast. The sense of fulfillment must not be regarded as if it were the fulfillment of desire – a common misinterpretation that echoes the earlier confusion between the fulfillment of instincts and the fulfillment of desire (Freud, 1915). The realization is the finding of something *and* some no-thing in reality. The finding of a real breast is paradoxically fulfilling – as a realization – *and* simultaneously unfulfilling, due to its transitoriness. With the exception of hallucinatory states, the real breast cannot be the exact, one hundred percent fitting to what can analogically be seen as the blueprint of the baby's pre-conception of the breast. The breast that the baby finds *never is* the desired breast, which may be found only in hallucination, precluding the inception of the principle of reality – depicted in many myths as Paradise

Regained, the Golden Calf, etc. Too many times, the real breast is not even the needed breast.

One who sets their conscious thought to resolve contradictions is one who feels they have found an all-fulfilling, ideal breast.

Paradoxes

A homeostatic balance between the psychotic and non-psychotic personality allows for tolerance of frustration, providing a development in the thought processes: one learns from experience through tolerating the existence of gaps (lack, the no-thing), given by experiences of unfulfillment of desire. Repeated surrenders to reality testing (Freud, 1915, p. 114; 1924a; 1924b) promote changes in the way that some personalities deal with contradictions: one may evolve from the reductionist contradictions to cope with paradoxes (Winnicott, 1969). Which do not admit resolution but tolerance. The term paradox (παράδοξο) is composed of the prefix *para* and the suffix *doxa* – knowledge. There are two sets of knowledge running parallel. They are the stuff that real life is made of: a factor in the development of common sense and the tolerance of doubt (Locke, 1690; Bion, 1959). Paradoxes are antithetical pairs which relate through symbiosis and lead to a synthesis.

A basic invariance of human life – the difference, the most basic form of sexual reproduction in mammals – can be tolerated. Paradoxes constitute the basic ethos of living systems which evolved from opposing pairs to creative couples.

In the realm of sensuously apprehensible phenomena one may resort to the biological vertex: a materialized form is married couples and their outcome: the progeny. From a musical vertex: the counterpoint. From the psychoanalytical vertex: the exercising of an "analytically trained intuition" to achieve interpretations, and with a little bit of luck, a transient insight in order to become O (Bernstein, 1950; Bion, 1965, p. 18; Sandler, 2000b, p. 48).

The ancient Greeks' advancements in the toleration of doubt and of paradoxes correspond, in my hypothesis advanced in the transdisciplinary research quoted above, to a moment of working through the depressive position, both in the individual work of these authors *and* in its social counterpart, the Academy: the scientific and artistic establishment founded by Plato and his contemporaries. He described a respectful recognizance of alterity, or otherness, prefiguring psychoanalysis: the method of the maieutic (μαιευτική), introduced by his master Socrates, which was a development of the exercising of dialectics (διαλεκτική), meaning, two truthful languages about the same object – a paradox, in other terms. I suggest that maieutic formulates verbally the description of a phenomenal, materialized manifestation of a whole with a hole: "a thing and no-thing." It is the first manifestation of tolerance of paradoxes, the transient, sensuously apprehensible counterpart of "a thing and no-thing" – in itself, ultimately unknown, but intuitable and usable.

The realm of minus and the negative

Bion's work, like Freud's, is a development of earlier contributions from previous theorists of science, with a seminal difference in its nature: both draw their theories from practical psychoanalysis, which takes into account emotional experiences and not cerebral, logical reasonings. My summarized definition of Bion's contribution about minus is: minus is like a non-concrete, immaterial realm that complements, as a matter of necessity, the positive "sense-able" realm of materialized reality.

At almost the same time that Socrates developed the maieutic, it struck the negative of it – in the form of mischievous denial, performed by the Sophists' destructive contribution. Under my hypothesis, it was a return to a paranoid-schizoid position. Based in Euclidean logical deduction, they degenerated Socrates' method into a special kind of war-like rationalistic rhetoric to destroy an opponent (Plato, c.380 BCE, pp. 551–552). A set of rationalized statements would triumph over the other. Such a degeneration reached its apex in rhetoric – once a primitive science – during the Roman empire; a decay, disguised as a development, institutionalized in Europe by the "sacred" rhetoric issued by the Apostolic branch of the Roman Catholic Church, by the work of many, from which I emphasize St. Paul, St. Thomas Aquinas and René Descartes, who profited from split parts of Aristotle's work (Sandler, 1997b, pp. 75–83). One and a half millennia later, the Lutheran Reformation questioned this use of rhetoric, opening the gates to a more encompassing rescue of Socrates' and Plato's non-warring dialectic. It can be seen in the work of some thinkers from which I select for now Baruch Spinoza, Immanuel Kant and G. W. F. Hegel. They unearthed Plato's numinous realm, which cannot be apprehended by the sensuous apparatus and contains the ultimate truth – which is paradoxically ultimately unknown. Kant defined the noumena as a negative: a "limit-concept" that frames the limits of knowledge obtained by "pure reason," better understood by psychoanalysis under the name of rationalizations (Kant, 1781, p. 160; Sandler, 2000a, pp. 43–56; Freud, 1911b). Kant realized the limits of rationalized knowledge when he faced irresolvable "antinomies" of "pure reason" – paradoxes, in other terms. Inspired by Kant, Hegel made a further step in human approaches to paradoxes, in his pregnant hints about "philosophy of mind" (*Geist*) (Hegel, 1817–20). From the integration of two sets of statements, called thesis and antithesis, he saw the possibility to create a third immaterial entity, hitherto uncreated and thus unknown. I suppose that this creative movement is given either when the "thesis" or the "antithesis" functions as the negative, vis-à-vis the other, producing the transcendent synthesis: a "third" element. It is a product of both poles of the antinomies that is neither of its forebears but resembles them; the concept of "movement" is a primary achievement of the Enlightenment (Sandler 1997e, p. 216).

Gottleb Frege (1950) is responsible for another step in our approach to paradoxes, showing that the realm of minus, or negative, or "no-" contemplates the "possibilities of impossibility." In its propositional content, the negative cannot be put on the same level of what I suppose to be the "realm of plus," or "yes," or "positive," or, in a mathematical formulation, "$_+$," which is affirmative and occupies a materialized position in space-time (Sandler, 2011a, p. 13–35; 2013a, pp. 66, 93).

The realm of minus indicates "what is not"; in the theory of science it is an anti-positivism. Thus it cannot have the properties assigned to what would be countered, in a bi-univocal sense, the "what is." It is ineffable. At the end of his life, dispensing with his previous technical terminology, but with common-sense, conversational formulations, Bion offered a developed mode to express the realm of minus in the decisive moment of any given session of psychoanalysis – in which an insight may emerge:

BION: I don't understand.
MYSELF: Perhaps I can illustrate by an example from something you do know. Imagine a piece of sculpture which is easier to comprehend if the structure is intended to act as a trap for light. The meaning is revealed by the pattern formed by the light thus trapped-not by the structure, the carved work itself. I suggest that if I could learn how to talk to you in such a way that my words "trapped" the meaning which they neither do nor could express, I could communicate it to you in a way that is not at present possible.
BION: Like the "rests" in a musical composition?
MYSELF: A musician would certainly not deny the importance of those parts of a composition in which no notes were sounding, but more has to be done than can be achieved in existent art and its well-established procedure of silences, pauses, blank spaces, rests. The "art" of conversation, as carried on as part of the conversational intercourse of psycho-analysis, requires and demands an extension into the realm of non-conversation.

[…]

BION: Is there anything new in this? You must often have heard, as I have, people say they don't know what you are talking about and that you are being deliberately obscure.
MYSELF: They are flattering me. I am suggesting an aim, an ambition, which, if I could achieve, would enable me to be deliberately and precisely obscure: in which I could use certain words which could activate precisely and instantaneously, in the mind of the listener, a thought or train of thought that came between him and the thoughts and ideas already accessible and available to him.

(Bion, 1975, pp. 189–191)

Pauses are as important as the "positive," sound-producing notes; they differentiate music from noise, making for what we know as rhythm, which conveys life's immaterialized pulse, its dynamic inner mystery that emerges in transient facts – which can be communicated, to good enough receivers. Bion resorted to Hopkins's theological poetry to emphasize that "lips shape nothing," and "eternal silence" is the only thing one "cares to hear." In shaping nothing, truth emerges (Hopkins, 1918). Parthenope Bion Talamo recommended paying "intense attention to nothing in particular." A biological formulation may constitute a model: the uterus, which has a virtual, negative space-time, with its collapsible walls.

In Freud's parlance: the patient's free associations and the analyst's free floating attention (Sandler, 2013c, pp. 109, 137). Free associations obtrude from the realm of minus.

My supposition is that the realm of minus is the true numinous realm of the unconscious: (*das Unbewußte*, in Freud's German) a concept endowed with practical utility to take care of individual beings, derived from empirical raw data obtained by clinical experience: "The domain of thought may be conceived of as a space occupied by no-things" (Bion, 1965, p. 106).

The unconscious system describes an immaterial and un-thought realm – but existent, intuitable and transiently usable. The *existence* of the "negative" underlies and overlies the materialized realm of reality, of its phenomenal transformations. Its *apprehension* is before and beyond the range encompassed by the sensuous apparatus. Freud dwelt on the unconscious system, coining the term "psychic reality," a different form of existence when compared with material reality, which is a term coined by Kant (Freud, 1900, pp. 613, 696). I suppose that it is the negative, immaterial counterpoint of materialized reality. Conversely, material reality is the positive, material counterpoint of immaterial psychic reality. Both are two forms of the same (monistic), ultimately unknowable "existence": the unknowable ultimate reality-in-itself.

Bion elicited the counterpunctual value of "minus" in his theory of thinking: the baby that tolerates the no-breast is capacitated to think the breast (Bion, 1962). The concrete absence is a pre-condition to the inception of thinking processes. In his last contribution, he furnished a model drawn from the theory of numbers, in which the negative numbers expanded the apprehension and use of the mathematical universe, until then limited to what mathematicians call the natural (positive) numbers (Bion, 1977).

Integration with Green's contributions

André Green, with Freud, Klein, Hanna Segal, Roger Money-Kyrle and Kurt Eissler are the only six analysts quoted by Bion (Sandler, 2005). In my conversations with André Green, first made public by himself (Green, 2003), he agreed with and appreciated my appraisal: since 1973 he alone has been reprising one of Bion's models of minus, in the form of "the work of the negative" (Green, 1973, 1975, 1986, 1999). This is an important part of Green's theory, matching Bion's theory about problems with the "contact-barrier" and its debasement into a "beta-screen." The definition of contact-barrier is couched in paradoxical terms: it is an active and living filter that regulates the relationship between the conscious and unconscious. It both links and separates the conscious and the unconscious and is a warning: most of our psychoanalytic work is concentrated in the preconscious system, taking into account the unconscious system is ultimately unknowable and the "once so powerful" conscious system (or consciousness) has the function of a sensuous organ (Freud, 1900, pp. 611–693; Bion, 1962, pp. 16–17; Sandler, 2001a; 2001b; 2005, pp. 125–164; 2018). Green discussed my idea that minus can be regarded as a raging generator of nothingness, first adumbrated by Bion in 1962. A phenomenal expression of it is war; from the psychoanalytical vertex, the cycle envy–greed. Green's "work of the negative" expanded our insights about the way in which patients feel a "negativation" of real facts; he agreed with my idea that negativation belongs to the realm of hallucinosis. He also observed patients who nourish a sensation of sheltering a "hole": a perverse negative object. There is an affective vacuum: such a hole is the stuff of nothingness: a paradoxical "no-stuff." Patients in such a state have an analysis featuring emptied, concrete wording, "full of sound and fury, signifying nothing" (Shakespeare, *Macbeth*). One cannot introject; one seems able only to "excorporate" (Green, 1997a; 1997b). I concluded that the "work of the negative" is a concretized manifestation of the prevalence of the minus realm, from an imbalance in relation to its "positive" counterparts. According to Green, the patient cannot stand the "double limit": one cannot transform messages from one's unconscious system in a way that they could be suitable to verbalization. I would add: suitable to be presented, intra-psychically, into pictographic imagery and thus cannot be represented in verbal forms. I suppose that Ferro described the inverse of this same process as the "narrative" counterparts of α-elements (Ferro, 2005). The paucity of pictographs enhances the feelings of nothingness. Binocular vision is unavailable to the concretized "primordial mind" which is capable only of monocular prejudices. I suppose it is the point of inception of "enforced splitting" (Bion, 1962, p. 10).

Dr. Green described minutely a clinical case where disturbances of thought resulted in a phobia of thinking (Green, 2000) – which precludes the obtrusion of free associations. Green thinks that the work of the negative is responsible for this deficiency. He had previously called its aftermath the "hole," meaning that these patients bypass the pre-conscious system. To my mind, Green developed Freud's concept of acting-out, defined in scattered parts of Freud's work, from 1896 to 1937. (The best review seems to be made by Fenichel, 1945.) He agreed with my idea that his patients acted out in the sessions "negativating," in the realm of speech, one of the poles in a dialectical pair. I concluded that a "negative action" (my term) is an expression of the "phobic position" (Sandler, 2018).

Dialectical pairs cannot be split in reality but only in hallucinosis, through rationalized misunderstandings – they are the weapons of politicians and of all liars whose social function can be seen in Bion's parable about liars (Bion, 1970, pp. 100–101; Sandler, 2015b, p. 21):

> The liars showed courage and resolution in their opposition to the scientists, who with their pernicious doctrines bid fair to strip every shred of self-deception from their dupes, leaving them without any of the natural protection necessary for the preservation of their mental health against the impact of truth. Some, knowing full well the risks that they ran, nevertheless laid down their lives in affirmations of lies so that the weak and doubtful would be convinced by the ardor of their conviction of the truth of even the most preposterous statements. It is not too much to say that the human race owes its salvation to that small band of gifted liars who were prepared even in the face of indubitable facts to maintain the truth of their falsehoods. Even death was denied and the most ingenious arguments were deduced to support obviously ridiculous statements that the dead lived on in bliss. These martyrs to untruth were often of humble origin whose very names have perished. But for them and the witness borne by their obvious sincerity the sanity of the race must have perished under the load placed on it. By laying down their lives they carry the morals of the world on their shoulders. Their lives and the lives of their followers were devoted to the elaboration of systems of great intricacy and beauty in which the logical structure was preserved by the exercise of a powerful intellect and faultless reasoning. By contrast, the feeble processes by which the scientists again and again attempted to support their hypotheses made it easy for the liars to show the hollowness of the pretensions of the upstarts and thus to delay, if not to prevent, the spread of doctrines whose effect could only have been to induce a sense of helplessness and unimportance in the liars and their beneficiaries.
>
> (Bion, 1970, pp. 100–101)

This too human social fact is reflected in the psychoanalytical movement as the tragedy of knowledge in psychoanalysis:

> This is due, in part, to the failure to grasp the nature of relativity, in particular the fact that it includes paradox. The restriction imposed by the limitation of thought to thoughts with thinkers implies the polarization "truth" and "falsehood," complicated further by morals.
>
> (Bion, 1975, p. 80)

I suppose that the realm of minus is the nest in which psychoanalysis is nurtured: "What we want to hear from our patient is not only what he knows and conceals from other people; he is to tell us too what he does *not* know" (Freud, 1938b, p. 174; Freud's emphasis). "Nothing is to be gained from telling the patient what he already knows" (Bion, 1965, p. 167). "The dominant feature of a session is the unknown personality and not what the analysand or analyst thinks he knows" (Bion, 1970, p. 87). We must discuss with our patients that which both of us do not know: "thoughts without a thinker" (Bion, 1962, pp. 83–86; 1963, p. 35).

The underlying, unspoken, immaterial, and non-sensuously apprehensible emotions demand that the analyst puts at the analysand's disposal his "analytically trained intuition" (Bion, 1965). It is a mutually fruitful "flash between two long nights" in which the analytic couple compresses all of its life experience, affects, passions and concern for truth. Is it the mental counterpart of the big-bang theory that tries to depict the great universe? When the negative realm obtrudes, it intermingles destruction with sublime creativity, entailing the mystery of life and death instincts. I strongly suppose that insights, in psychoanalytic sessions, are the progeny of this creative immaterial act (Sandler, 2011b, p. 68).

A strong predilection to intolerance of paradoxes

Negation together with rationalization are psychic mechanisms best observed by Freud (1925, 1911b) and Klein (1946a) as factors that fuel the thoughtlessness of pseudo-thought, when there is a prevalence of the psychotic personality under the disguise of the non-psychotic personality. To rationalize using just Euclidean logic is, in my experience, a serious menace against the very survival of the psychoanalytic movement. I suppose that rationalized practices under the beliefs of the positivist religion (Comte, 1896) are a main form of what may be called "minus-psychoanalysis" – which engineers false networks of causality, enhanced by the use of the narrative form (Bion, 1963, p. 46; 1965, pp. 97, 120), in order to institutionalize the delusion of predictions and of ad hoc "theorizing," typical of false science (Popper, 1959; Sandler and Costa, 2018). Rationalization "allows" for learning intellectually about analysis while remaining a virgin with regard to suffering the experience of analysis: this is the difference between "becoming" and "knowing about" (Freud, 1912, 1919b, 1926; Bion, 1965, p. 153). In analysis, this failure engenders a blindness to the dreamy nature of free associations and provokes a frozen clinging to manifest contents. It allows for taking the patient's utterances at face value. It is a denial of the paradox that symbols "mean something that is not themselves" (Gombrich, 1959).

Minus K

The K link has two paradoxical activities – constructive (K) and destructive (–K). The latter is a forceful, hateful and envious attempt to denude meanings, thus proving that to misunderstand is superior to understanding: "envy precludes a commensal relationship." Some patients are concerned to prove their superiority to the analyst "by defeating his attempts at interpretation. They can be shown to be misunderstanding the interpretations to demonstrate that an ability to misunderstand is superior to an ability to understand … there is a moral superiority and superiority in potency of UN-learning." The breast cannot be felt as a moderator of the dreadful and annihilating feelings; cannot allow a re-introjection; cannot be growth-stimulating.

I would add to Bion's observation: such a breast does not cease to be a breast; it is a minus breast in the −K domain. It is felt as "enviously to remove the good and valuable element in the fear of dying and force the worthless residue back into the infant." Paranoid violence of emotions affects the projective processes "so that far more than the fear of dying is projected." The denudation of meaning obtrudes when the process of denudation is seen from the vertex of K (knowledge). "The seriousness is best conveyed by saying that the will to live, that is necessary before there can be a fear of dying, is a part of the goodness that the envious breast has removed" (all quotations, Bion, 1962, pp. 96–97).

−K allowed the eliciting of a minus container–contained: $-♀♂$. It creates a sense of without-ness. Which differs from nothingness. In clinical practice it appears as "an envious assertion of moral superiority without any morals" (Bion, 1962, p. 97). The minus container–contained

> shows itself as a superior object asserting its superiority by finding fault with everything. The most important characteristic is its hatred of any new development in the personality as if the new development were a rival to be destroyed. The emergence therefore of any tendency to search for truth, to establish contact with reality and in short of be scientific ... is met by destructive attacks on the tendency and the reassertion of "moral" superiority ... in K; the climate is conducive to mental health. In −K neither group nor idea can survive partly because of the destruction incident to the stripping and partly because of the product of the stripping process.
> (Bion, 1962, p. 98)

The ultimate misunderstanding: a transient destruction of truth

−K is not lack of knowledge. It has a meaning which "is abstracted leaving a denuded representation" (Bion, 1962, p. 75). It is a fragmented knowledge under the aegis of the principle of pleasure–unpleasure. Its aftermath is a transient destruction of the apprehension of truth. −K is the medium of unlawful lawyers, politicians and propagandists, destined to convince people of all things that are not. −K uses pieces of truth devoid of truthful intentions. It is not intended to lead to accretions of knowledge, but rather to extinguish the evolution of knowledge. In today's parlance: "fake news."

Bion's observation of phenomena corresponding to −K opened up the path to his observations of hallucinosis which improved the formulation of −K as a link. Its function is the building of conscious, phenomenal, materialized appearances of the negative realm. −K transforms the immaterial invariants in a "raging inferno of greedy no-existence", in short, transformations in hallucinosis (Bion, 1965, p. 135). Those patients feel that there is a

> superiority of the method of hallucinosis over the analytic method. ... Hallucination may be more profitably seen as a dimension of the analytic

situation in which, together with the remaining "dimensions," these objects are sense-able (if we include analytic intuition or consciousness, taking a lead from Freud, as a sense-organ of psychic quality).

(Bion, 1965, p. 115)

Defining −L and −H

The apprehension of phenomena corresponding to the model of −L and −H sheds further light on unresolved issues in the psychoanalytic session, which I suppose are mishandled as if they were just manifestations of hate.

Bion defined precisely −K but left just a definitory warning hint about −L and −H. Namely, −L is not the same as hate; −H is not the same as love (Bion, 1963, p. 52).

My extension to Bion now is to define −L and −K strictly patterned within the confines of Bion's definition of −K. This statement embodies a disclaimer: I am not proposing anything new, but just an extension to make explicit something implicit in Bion's writings. Also, my definitions of −L and −H are made from their own vertexes, as an artificial division for the purpose of didactic communication. It is a mere preparation to apprehend both simultaneously in clinical practice, in which such a division *does not occur*. Analogically, −L and −H amount to two sides of the same coin. The difficulty is inherent in verbal formulations, for "psycho-analytical events cannot be stated directly, indubitably, or incorrigibly any more than can those of other scientific research" (Bion, 1970, p. 26).

Minus L is an attempt to prove that to un-love is superior to love. Does it bring with it hate? Yes and no. Hate is the most primitive form of love and a condition to love. In −L, Hate is *not* the primary impulse because in −L there is an added violence of feelings and emotions; hate is continuously not momentarily denied and projected; it cannot be even barely experienced.

−L, enslaved by the principle of pleasure–unpleasure, expresses itself as the climax of repeated attempts at evasion. It is conducive to the destruction of truth in the area of perception. Reality itself is not destroyed; what can be destroyed is the perception of it. "Truth is robust and shall prevail" (Bion, 1979, p. 499).

Freud observed difficulties in the apprehension of "the other," of the "not-me" in many works (for example, Freud, 1921). The individual vertex to apprehend the very first primeval "not-me" is the mother as an object of one's libidinal cathexis of love and hate. From then on, added complexities await the realization or not of the relationship of "me" and "not-me" (otherness, alterity). If violence of emotions and the genetic fetters of primary narcissism and primary envy are not too strong, and if a good enough mother linked through love to a father is available, mother helps the baby to perceive and to apprehend what father is all about (Winnicott, 1960; Bion, 1962, p. 68). Tolerance of paradoxes is called into action in those two steps of development. An added complexity depends on the sexual orientation of the baby that gives the form to Oedipus (♀ or ♂: genetic, not generic). In any case −L makes the inception of rivalry between father and mother. The next ontogenetical step is marked by reactive formation through the form of identification, or imitation (Philips, 1997). Octave Mannoni saw this path as a search for awareness about a human truth: helplessness (Mannoni, 1968, p. 19).

It is not just the quantity or intensity of hate that destroys the object, but the violence of love (Klein, 1932). My clinical experience shows that such a violence stems from intolerance of frustration (Bion, 1960a, p. 133; 1960c, p. 241). Hating hate turns hate into a forbidden sphere to the baby and precludes a good enough balance between life and death instincts for the rest of one's life. Sometimes chance intervenes to deal with the consequences of this situation. Violence of love overwhelms hate, and without hate, the precursor of love, love itself becomes impossible. −L aims to achieve an absolute denial of frustration, brushing aside the experience of real love, which demands renunciation of total pleasure and the integrative, binocular tolerance of a paradox, namely, that the object that is loved and the object that is hated are one and the same object.

Denial of hate or hating hate precludes the achievement of what Bion (inspired by Berlin, 1953) called "a sense of truth." This often overlooked but in my view seminal concept is a remarkable integration of Kant, Hegel, Freud and Klein:

> the counterpart of the common-sense view in private knowledge is the common emotional view: a sense of truth is experienced if the view of an object which is hated can be conjoined to a view of the same object when it is loved and the conjunction confirms that the object experienced by different emotions is the same object.
> (Bion, 1961, p. 119; Sandler, 2005, p. 731)

The alternative to suicide or homicide is −L, fueled by greed. If envy is something that "lay waiting, single-celled, to become malignant" (Bion, 1975, p. 10), −L is dependent on violent (narcissistic, paranoid-schizoid), mounting, ever-heightening and raging envious impulses. Love emotions are taken to their utter consequences. The defusing of life and death instincts is unavoidable: hate is denied and put into abeyance. In the mind of the beholder, it is felt as if it was extinguished.

In −L, love "out-loves" love – therefore, love is inhibited by love (Bion, 1960a, p. 125). In the long run love is felt to be extinguished by love; the aftermath is reduced to un-love; the lifetime of the individual is spent achieving the final extinction of love. The rivalry with the breast reaches its apex: there is the hallucinosis of self-generation, despisal and dismissal of the creative couple, associated with a murderous superego. In the realm of phenomena it is expressed by criminal psychopathic and sociopathic features, encircled by a quasi-perennial mania (Sandler, 1969; 2018).

Denudation being the chief feature of envy, this situation of quasi-absolute envy in −L is felt to remove the bad and worthless element in the fear of dying.

The same "forcing back into the infant" described in −K by Bion is made with such violence that the infant loves a worthless object. It cannot discriminate this worthless object from the worthy and yet-not-dead, alive object. Such a confusion seems to be the basis of idealization. It must be differentiated from hate and sadism, even though the latter can function as a tool in this confusion. The worthless residue is then an un-lovable one, felt as if it was loved. Due to its very nature, it cannot be loved without imperiling the ego; to un-love is the last resort to preserve life.

The effect of −L in the analytical setting is to build a non-analytical pair, which goes on resolutely to the path of idealization of the analyst, under the aegis of the principle of pleasure–unpleasure (Sandler, 2018). Collusion would be synonymous with a minus-analysis, in which there are sensuously apprehensible appearances indicating a happy and successful analysis – a situation that smells of "danger," as exemplified by Bion in "Evidence" (Bion, 1976). −Love begets an intra-session "society of mutual admiration" made by a group of two (Bion, 1975, p. 120).

In the denial of the pain involved in the un-loving part-object, there is a replacement of L with −L. Bion's observations about −K apply to −L: the un-loved object becomes object of something unnamed that is felt as love. The denudation of love obtrudes when the very process of denudation is seen from the vertex of L (love).

These processes are unconscious thus the un-loved breast is unknown and unknowing. The unknown and unknowing un-loved breast furthers the seriousness of the predicament that "is best conveyed by saying that the will to live, that is necessary before there can be a fear of dying, is a part of the goodness that the envious breast has removed" (Bion, 1962, pp. 96–97). There is no awareness, except indirectly, of the fear of dying. In some patients, it is possible to achieve a transient contact with it, at the risk of a renewed manic acting-out to deny it. The denied part gets the upper hand in the overt behavior of the individual.

There is *no* lack of love in −L, albeit it is perverted. −L denies the materialized part of the breast as a justification for greed and thus −L deprives the external breast that is offered of its realness, through a reverted enforced splitting (Bion, 1962, p. 10) that cannot follow its original path – the overvaluing of sensuous, materialized assets. The breast, like knowledge in −K, remains in a state that cannot be abstracted, but just in a hallucinated "all-fulfilling" concretized form that cannot face any test of reality (Bion, 1962, p. 75). Split off from material reality, it exists only in a tailored hallucination by self-styled "lover." To split off material from psychic reality impoverishes both forms (or transformations). If, and when denudation itself is considered by the beholder as if it is the last resort to preserve the object, the object itself is tuned into an un-loved one.

−L is expressed by narcissistic uses of love that lack loving intentions. Spoiling, pampering and seducing are presented as if they could express love. They are not intended to lead to accretions of love, but rather to immobilize a feeling of love into a materialized form. The result is a hallucinated or deluded sense of ownership over human beings, to concretize the pseudo-love. The concretization precludes movement which is the stuff of life (Sandler, 1997f, p. 177; 2013a, p. 73). It is not conducive to evolution, matching and creation. It is "homo-": nourished by the delusion of paranoid self-sufficiency.

Some patients are concerned to prove the superiority of hallucinosis to the analytic method in trying to turn the analytic session into an activity to extract love at all costs. The premature, thin, tenuous, instantaneously made transference is immersed in a sense of idealization (Bion, 1957a, 1957b). It means that the patient un-loves the analyst as he or she really *is*. The defeating of "the analyst's attempts at interpretation" as indicated in –K has a specific form: there is a "misunderstanding of the interpretations" that tends to turn interpretations into emotional statements conveying claims of mutual love under a monochromatic mode. The "moral superiority and superiority in potency" of UN-loving is easily demonstrated because real love is the most painful alternative. Real love requires abstinence and renunciation. –Love abhors abstinence. Real love implies eternal suffering under the shadow of a perspective of loss, which ever occurs, even in variable degrees, as an essential condition to propitiate renewed situations in which L will happen again, in unknown forms and with a hitherto unexperienced depth – they are yet unborn. –L imagines alleviation before a future loss and is against a progeny: its motto displaying moral superiority could be: why would one bring children into this damned, wretched, painful world? "This destructive activity is tinged with 'moral' qualities derived from the 'super'-ego quality of $-(\female\male)$" (Bion, 1962, p 98).

Minus H is a forceful attempt to prove that to un-hate is superior to hate. The same considerations about envy, which precludes anything other than a parasitic relationship, are valid here. The breast cannot be felt as a moderator of the dreadful and annihilating feelings; the breast that is felt as bad is, so to speak, "co-opted." It is turned into a false good breast. If the baby's envy is excessive, a minus-loving mother nourishes –H siblings.

–H is not lack of hate. It is the triumph of hate through an absolute splitting of love from hate. There is a "moral superiority and superiority in potency" of UN-hating. A greedy, violent love is the instinct that prevails, resulting in the defusing of instincts.

Clinical sources

The general formula is given by Bion in the clinical example of the milkman: "I am self-supporting because I can hallucinate a meal, time, an ejaculation and whatever else I need."

> Thanks to the patient's capacity for satisfying all his needs out from his own creations he is entirely independent of anyone or anything other than his products and therefore is beyond rivalry, envy, greed, meanness, love or hate; but the evidence of his senses belies his pre-determinations; he is not satisfied.
>
> (Bion, 1965, pp. 132, 137)

The non-motherly mother

Some females develop a basic insensitivity to callousness. A materialized form is given by mothers who abandon their babies. In my experience, to use this phrasing in a session risks degenerating into a situation of persecutory guilt that is not the manifestation of a real achievement of the depressive position – but rather a depression colored by paranoid feelings (Bion, 1959, p. 7). The analyst is seen as a judge with the qualities of a vengeful God. The whole situation in transference exemplifies the "power to arouse guilt" – which

> is essential and appropriate to the operation of projective identification in a relationship between infant and breast. This guilt is peculiar in that its association with primitive projective identification implies that the guilt is meaningless. The $-(♀♂)$ contrasts therefore with conscience in that it does not lend itself to constructive activity.
>
> (Bion, 1962, p. 98)

If the analyst makes part of the shared hallucinosis with the patient in this intrasession guilt-factory, there will be an unnecessary and potentially damaging enhancement of unnecessary painful, destructive guilt in the patient and in some instances, in the analyst too.

As in –H, hate is not the dominant instinct, the emotion

> to which attention is drawn should be obvious to the analyst, but unobserved by the patient; an emotion that is obvious to the patient is usually painfully obvious, and avoidance of unnecessary pain must be one aim in the exercise of analytic intuition. Since the analyst's capacity for intuition should enable him to demonstrate an emotion before it has become painfully obvious it would help if our search for the elements of emotions was directed to making intuitive deductions easier. ... Thus, if the hate that a patient is experiencing is a precursor of love its virtue as an element resides in its quality as a precursor of love and not in its being hate. And so for all other emotions.
>
> (Bion, 1963, p. 74)

Mothers are not analysts, but there is a kinship in the quality – if not the quantity – of the needed reverie in both (Bion, 1962, pp. 36–37; 1963, p. 19). If real life is the concern of real analysis, the avoidance of unnecessary pain in the analytic setting is equally necessary in the relationship of a mother and her baby. Through a reversion of perspective (Bion, 1963, p. 54) this kind of "unmotherly," psychically disabled mother abuses the child's capacity for self-containment due to her unsuccessful attempts to use her baby as a deposit for her own anxieties. Instead of a bidet-breast, one has a bidet-infant.

If such an un-motherly mother finds an omnipotent baby, intolerant of frustration, the baby "becomes" the breast in a shared hallucinosis of the unpaired couple. The child seems to demand no care at all; if the child cannot hate, or learns to un-hate, mother's deficiencies and distance are denied. From then on, they are felt as important just to elevate the child as if he or she could fill the functions of the breast. These children are condemned to precocity, fated to take impossible responsibilities, as a matter of survival. In my experience, it is a tremendous stimulus to phantasies of superiority leading to omnipotence, omniscience and to the development of autistic traits.

The following vignette comes from the opportunity of having undertaken, initially, the analysis of a mother of three, which lasted for seven years, and then, five years later, of her middle-born son, X, then a young man. The mother felt that analysis was good for her and told X to look for the same analyst. She advertised to relatives that X was her chosen son, because "he is undemanding, gives no trouble: never cries. I must wake him to have milk so I can do it as it pleases me." X became too attached to a baby-sitter. It was an open secret to relatives that her real preference was for the first-born – a daughter four years senior. Until the arrival of the last one, another boy, felt by her to be "the most beautiful baby she ever saw." She continued advertising that X was the chosen one: evidence that she hardly could hear her own statements. Once she stated a certainty: "It is better to not love anybody; if one loses one's love, one will suffer a lot." In analysis, it emerged a prototype of her relationship with X. She tried to manifest her conscious admiration toward the father's skills and gave an example: at six months, X slipped under his blanket at the crib and could not breathe anymore. As usual he did not cry. The father was watching TV in another room and suddenly rose up to look for X, only to find him cyanotic under the blanket – and saved him. By the way, X is identical to the father, the mother stating with admiration that at 10 years old, X's diminutive shoulders seemed fit to withstand the long sessions of crying, regretful, victimizing speeches she inflicted on him. "I cannot say this to my daughter; she cannot stand it." X is forced to tolerate her lamentations; but at the same time the boy also decides, albeit unwittingly, to do so due to his own psychic features, mainly phobic and paranoid. When the analyst meets X, he is impacted by X's likeness to the mother – not just in his physical appearance, due to genetics, but also his psychic tendencies and creations.

The mother resorted to lies and disguises in order to evade painful situations. One day a valued piece of china has been broken at home. On the same day, she secretly invites relatives to have tea. In the evening, the father comes home. She decides to hide the two facts from the father, who smells a rat (probably he was an intuitive observant) and becomes enraged at the lies, storming out in fury, slamming the door. The mother begs, "X, bring Dad back home! Father always threatens to leave home and will do this now, once and for all" leaving X suspicious, through side comments, that the father wanted to beat her; or perhaps had beaten her before. X takes his bicycle to go to the father's office to convince him to go back; the father tenderly welcomes the boy, realizing his predicament; explaining to his son that he left as a way to calm down; he would never beat his own wife. This is a repeated situation in X's latency and adolescent days. X's emotional experience enforces the thought, unconsciously accepted by him, that he is responsible for the mother's well-being and for keeping the marriage healthy – in a twisted Oedipal stimulus.

The mother becomes phobic and guilty after seeing the movie version by Alan Pakula of William Styron's *Sophie's Choice*, starring Meryl Streep. In light of –L, an observer could ask: who, in reality, was her chosen one?

The hypercritical hypocrite

Z, an otherwise good-humored, funny, intelligent and able person, dedicated his professional life to a caring activity. His conscious intention was sincere; he wished to be seen as a helpful person – betraying unconscious guilt. His ironic intelligence attracted attention and applause, as if he was a professional comedian doing stand-up. Loving sadistic acts is a well-known fact much used by totalitarian politicians, who explore the cycle greed–envy to get votes. He used much of his efforts to criticize everybody and anybody in any situation one may consider. No trivialities were left aside. He swiftly would turn to being hypercritical with friends who were supposed to be honored by his acid criticisms. Z is an example of a popular motto in Brazil: "Lose a friend but never lose a joke." His good humor and effortless ability to make friends was easily debased into mordacity and sarcasm. Z seemed to be immune to experience: he lost a great many of his friends but did not lose his paranoid feelings of superiority, enhanced by his availability to work and technical prowess. The non-psychotic personality gave the criticism rational credence. Once he was watching a movie made in the fifties. There appeared on the screen a huge Le Corbusier-inspired dwelling on the outskirts of Paris, destined for the working classes. It was an irrelevant part of a thriller, an entertaining pastime. He had amateurish knowledge of architecture which was no impediment to a critical appraisal of what he felt to be an inhuman, crime-provoking environment that provided opportunities for profit-seeking builders. "That building is fated to be a slum!" To prove his point, he cited Muslim disturbances made by people who now lived in that place, erected seventy years before as a novelty in impoverished post-WWII France. His comments were truthful and apt but devoid of real love or interest in either the Muslims' living conditions or social inequalities. Both served as containers for incensing himself and for his reasoning capacities. As a matter of consequence, he perversely damaged the life situation of leisurely watching a movie with his family. He could not enjoy the film; he used it to pester his wife and children. The whole comment was to prove how smart he was. People liked him but paradoxically avoided contact with him, as a way to self-protect from his comments. To be with him was an exhausting task, because he would do anything to extract unconditional proofs of love from friends – a psychotic trait. Malignant narcissism (Kohut, 1984) is a factor of –H. The will to live, necessary before there can be a fear of dying, becomes hallucinated because the goodness that the envious breast should remove is so feeble that in practice it amounts to nothing.

These patients feel that aggression and exploitation are superior to the use of the object (Winnicott, 1969), are much better and are symbolically equated to love; lack of capacity to love cannot be developed towards love, but rather to un-love.

The hypercritical hypocrite is able to mimic love. Sooner or later un-hate makes its appearance. In the long run there is neither love nor hate, but just a case of confused stupor and stuporous confusion. The infant tries to madden the breast – and if the breast should become mad, at least it could be felt to be alive and could be loved or not; and hated or not. This exploitative pattern, a projective identification of the exploitative breast, becomes a pattern throughout the person's life.

The person's demeanor and posture are, chameleon-like, of compliance and outward adaptation to a given social climate. Sometimes it borders on servility. It appears to the attentive eye as a false kindness. The person who chooses the −H relationship will ever insist that he or she is a superior being. They assert their superiority by finding fault in people who they are able to hate. Or to be able to complain when a given complaint is a realistic, self-defensive reaction. In the long run, neither hate nor love is left, in the same proportion that real love or realistic hate are denied existence.

In analysis, this patient abhors the K link and tries accordingly to provoke love and/or hate in the analyst. The disaster in this situation is that this patient cannot learn by experience from his or her acts of aggression; acrid criticisms are felt to merit being welcome, applauded and admired, but at the same time his acts are a desperate attempt to learn how to have real, rather than imitative, emotional experiences. How to have them when one keeps any real emotional experience at bay? The person becomes persecuted and increasingly isolated and tends to resort to hallucinosis. −K, −L and −H, when they prevail over K, L and H, as well as when K, L and H prevail over their negatives, form an apparatus that cannot be used to achieve conscious awareness of internal and external reality – which is dealt with as an undesired fragment and is fantastically expelled from the personality. The apparatus is felt as if it were an "expel-able" fragment. Its fate is to be lodged outside. Deprived of conscious awareness, the patient "achieves a state which is felt to be neither alive nor dead" (Bion, 1956, p. 38).

As far as my clinical experience goes, apprehending these facts in the light of −H and −L seems to be a useful extension to Klein's descriptions of attacks on the breast and Bion's descriptions of attacks on the perceptual apparatus up to its ejection, and the ensuing mental confusion about death and life. −H and −L create a proneness to deal with the animate with methods that could be more successful when applied to the inanimate.

The hypercritical hypocrite hates K and favors L, H, −L and −H, replacing the contact-barrier in a "living process." "Thanks to the beta-screen the psychotic patient has a capacity for evoking emotions in the analyst; his associations … evoke interpretations … which are less related to his need for psycho-analytic interpretation than to his need to produce an emotional involvement" (Bion, 1962, p. 24). The K link turns out to be impossible; the analytical approach limited to transformations in K is severely impaired.

−PS ↔ D and −♀♂

Bion adjoins to the definitions of minus and minus container–contained that of minus PS ↔ D: "disintegration, total loss, and depressive stupor, or, intense impaction and degenerate stuporous violence." The living movement symbolized by the double arrow is denied. Bion warns that the "descriptions of −♀♂ and −PS ↔ D are incomplete" (Bion, 1963, pp. 52–53), adding that he will use them "until further experience is forthcoming" and inviting, implicitly, future developments.

My suggestion is to apprehend minus container–contained (−♀♂) as the belief that infertility is superior to fertility: an imbalance between ♀♂ and −♀♂ results in attacking the "supreme creativity of the parental couple" (after Klein). Too much fertility would be prevalence of ♀♂. Too much infertility would be prevalence of −♀♂. They seem to have the same destructive outcome. Drawing an analogy from present-day societies, are both overpopulation and the destruction of the environment by nuclear bombs and plants, of the ozone layer and rainforests, which leads to the extinction of species, linked to "homo-" phantasies? I start from the supposition that it is psychoanalytically irrelevant if these "homo-" phantasies are coupled with sexual choices approved by the group or sub-groups within the encircling group. "Homo-" is defined here as a denial of human bisexuality and the negativation of the difference, which precludes the existence of a creative couple. Adherence to certain sexual choices is just a phenomenal form enslaved by the principle of pleasure and unpleasure. There is no moral judgment to state that "homo-" phantasies are un-creative from the biological vertex; human bisexuality determines that these phantasies exist in any human being. (−♀♂) is conducive to minus life. Minus life is not death. It is a sterile and solitary life.

Social aftermaths of contradictions and of the prevalence of the realm of minus

Sociologically, contradictions are fundamental to form the most primitive interpersonal relationship hitherto known – that of friend or foe. It favors uncreative, submissive pairs and abhors creative couples and progenies, through adoption of a set of moral values devoid of morality, applied just to the opponent. If the psychotic personality prevails, the splitting of the ego is successful in the realm of thought, corresponding to the only real effect of projective identification – otherwise, an unconscious phantasy (Klein, 1946b, p. 307). In hallucinosis, one's attacks on one's perception of the frustration are felt as successful. Self-righteousness, religiosity and totalitarian acting-out win the day.

The prevalence of the realm of minus can be found in the natural history of groups whose membership grows quantitatively, in which there is a tendency to replace the formation of truth-pursuing scientific meritocracies with authoritarian and bureaucratic political meritocracies (Young, 1958; Sandler, 2015a, p. 54). My experience with groups allows for the statements that the prevalence of scientific meritocracy is made under the supposition "that the personality of analyst and analysand can survive the loss of its protective coat of lies, subterfuge, evasion and hallucination and may even be fortified and enriched by the loss," while the tendency to empower predominantly the political meritocracy corresponds to Bion's observation that it "is an assumption strongly disputed by the psychotic and a fortiori by the group, which relies on psychotic mechanisms for its coherence and sense of well-being" (Bion, 1965, p. 129). The reasoning limited to contradiction is well suited to partisan activities, gathering members to be led by the self-righteous, most of them adepts of violence: judges, lawyers, teachers, police and undemocratic, idealist, totalitarian politicians who hallucinate that they know best.

As $-L$ is the enslaving of love to the principle of pleasure–unpleasure; I suppose that this is the primitive origin of the destroyers of beauty and truth. The person who hammered Michelangelo's *Pietà*, similar to the person who stained Da Vinci's *Mona Lisa*, did not hate art; he furnished an example tendering $-L$ to develop a parasitic link with art.

The idealistic revolutionary, a kind of inhuman human bred by the social movements Stalinism and Nazism (Buber-Neumann, 1967, p. 74; Bracher, 1969), spreads wholesale destruction not out of the social hate they entail, but from the violence of $-L$. In the former, towards the proletariat, in the latter towards "Aryans"; both preached the superiority of that pretended social class or race, respectively.

In regard to the emotional development of the apparatus of thinking, one achieves the ability to deal with differences with no single idea (or event, or thing, or personality, or group) overpowering or extinguishing a differing idea (or event, etc.): "Among the calamities of war may be jointly numbered the diminution of the love of truth, by the falsehoods which interest dictates and credulity encourages" (Dr. Johnson, 1758).

Does war, a social reality, have its origins in the realm of human thought processes? There seems to be an evolution from the primitive paranoid states, the warmonger's mind, that fantasize the ownership of the absolute truth, towards dealing with differences – in the form of democracy and, individually, in the achievement of a sense of truth.

Two modes of minus

My clinical practice shows that the terms "negative" and "minus" indicate the presence of at least two of the following counterparts in reality:

i **the destructive minus**: typical of the newborn, linked to the anxiety of annihilation as described by Klein (1932, 1952, 1957, 1963). In surviving babies, there is an envious and greedy prevalence of the psychotic personality that cannot tolerate the no-thing, disabling one's capacity to abstract the breast from its sensuously based concreteness. It is conducive to the greedy maintenance of minus, which dominates mental functioning. The personality that cannot tolerate the paradoxical realm of minus flows into a destructive, greedy prevalence of this very same realm. "Nothing" replaces the "no-thing"; "without-ness" replaces real lack of something. This human truth is reflected in innumerable myths – as for example, the myths of Saturn and Midas.

ii **the contrapuntal minus**, which obtrudes if and when a good enough development allows for the tolerance of the nature of the no-thing, that is inseparable from the thing. To live and to analyze – for "mystery is real life; real life is the concern of real analysis" – demand tolerance of the basic, paradoxical balance between what is "positive" – materialized, concrete, sensuously apprehensible things, events and people – and what is "negative" – the immaterial no-things that cannot be sensuously apprehensible, belonging to the realm of "ultra and infra-sensuous" (Bion, 1977, p. 307; 1975, p. 204, respectively). Like life, the contrapuntal minus, inhabiting our unconscious system, is perennially moving, like a flame; it is infinite as long as it lasts; it respects the principle of uncertainty (Heisenberg, 1958), embodying the mystery of what is ineffable; it is embedded in the ultimately unknowable "O."

References

Bacon, F. (1620). *Novum Organon: Aphorisms concerning the Interpretation of Nature and the Kingdom of Man*, in *The Great Books of the Western Hemisphere* (Chicago; Encyclopaedia Britannica).

Berlin, I. (1953) "The sense of reality," in *The Sense of Reality: Studies in Ideas and their History*, H. Hardy (ed.) (New York: Farrar, Straus and Giroux, 1996).

Bernstein, L. (1959) *The Joy of Music* (Pompton Plains: Amadeus Press, 2004).

Bion, W. R. (1956) "Development of schizophrenic thought," *International Journal of Psycho-Analysis*, 37: 344–346.

Bion, W. R. (1957a) "Differentiation of the psychotic and non-psychotic personalities," in *Second Thoughts* (London: Heinemann Medical Books, 1967).

Bion, W. R. (1957b) "Attacks on linking," in *Second Thoughts* (London: Heinemann Medical Books, 1967).

Bion, W. R. (1959) "Scientific method," in *Cogitations*, F. Bion (ed.) (London: Karnac Books, 1992).

Bion, W. R. (1960a) "Compassion and truth," in *Cogitations*, F. Bion (ed.) (London: Karnac Books, 1992).

Bion, W. R. (1960b) "Animism, destructive attacks and reality," in *Cogitations*, F. Bion (ed.) (London: Karnac Books, 1992).

Bion, W. R. (1960c) "Concern for truth and life," in *Cogitations*, F. Bion (ed.) (London: Karnac Books, 1992).

Bion, W. R. (1961) "A theory of thinking," in *Second Thoughts* (London: Heinemann Medical Books, 1967).

Bion, W. R. (1962) *Learning from Experience* (London: Heinemann Medical Books).

Bion, W. R. (1963) *Elements of Psycho-Analysis* (London: Heinemann Medical Books).

Bion, W. R. (1965) *Transformations* (London: Heinemann Medical Books).
Bion, W. R. (1970) *Attention and Interpretation* (London: Karnac, 1984).
Bion, W. R. (1975) *A Memoir of the Future*, vol. 1: *The Dream* (London: Karnac Books, 1990).
Bion, W. R. (1976) "Evidence," in *Clinical Seminars and Four Papers*, F. Bion (ed.) (Oxford: Fleetwood Press, 1978).
Bion, W. R. (1977) *A Memoir of the Future*, vol. 2: *The Past Presented* (London: Karnac Books, 1990).
Bion, W. R. (1979) *A Memoir of the Future*, vol. 3: *The Dawn of Oblivion* (London: Karnac Books, 1990).
Bracher, K. D. (1969) *The German Dictatorship: The Origins, Structure and Consequences of National Socialism*, translated by J. Steinberg (London: Penguin Books, 1991).
Buber-Neumann, M. (1967) *Révolution Mondiale: L'Histoire du Komintern (1919–1943) Racontée par l'un de ses Principaux Témoins*, translated by H. Savon (Paris: Casterman).
Comte, A. (1896) *The Positive Philosophy of Auguste Comte*, translated by H. Martineau (Ontario: Batoche Books, 2000). Reproduction of original edition (London: George Bell and Sons). Retrieved from: http://socserv2.socsci.mcmaster.ca/econ/ugcm/3ll3/comte/Philosophy1.pdf
Fenichel, O. (1945) "Neurotic acting out," in *The Collected Papers of Otto Fenichel* (New York: Norton, 1954).
Ferro, A. (2005) "Which reality in the psychoanalytic session?" *Psychoanalytic Quarterly*, 74: 421–442.
Frege, G. (1950) *The Foundations of Arithmetic*, translated by J. L. Austin (Oxford: Basil Blackwell).
Freud, S. (1900) *The Interpretation of Dreams*, in *Standard Edition*, IV–V (London: Hogarth Press).
Freud, S. (1909) "Analysis of a phobia in a five-year-old boy," in *Standard Edition*, X (London: Hogarth Press).
Freud, S. (1911a) "Formulations on the two principles of mental functioning," in *Standard Edition*, XVII (London: Hogarth Press).
Freud, S. (1911b) "Psycho-analytic notes on an autobiographical account of a case of paranoia," in *Standard Edition*, XI (London: Hogarth Press).
Freud, S. (1912) "Recommendations to physicians practising psycho-analysis," in *Standard Edition*, XII (London: Hogarth Press).
Freud, S. (1915) "Instincts and their vicissitudes," in *Standard Edition*, XIV (London: Hogarth Press).
Freud, S. (1919a) "On transience," in *Standard Edition*, XVII (London: Hogarth Press).
Freud, S. (1919b) "On the teaching of psycho-analysis in universities," in *Standard Edition*, XVII (London: Hogarth Press).
Freud, S. (1920) *Beyond the Pleasure Principle*, in *Standard Edition*, XVIII (London: Hogarth Press).
Freud, S. (1921) *Psychology of Groups and Analysis of the Ego*, in *Standard Edition*, XVIII (London: Hogarth Press).
Freud, S. (1924a) "Neurosis and psychosis," in *Standard Edition*, XIX (London: Hogarth Press).

Freud, S. (1924b) "The dissolution of the Oedipus complex," in *Standard Edition*, XIX (London: Hogarth Press).
Freud, S. (1925) "Negation," in *Standard Edition*, XIX (London: Hogarth Press).
Freud, S. (1926) "The question of lay analysis," in *Standard Edition*, XX (London: Hogarth Press).
Freud, S. (1937) "Analysis terminable and interminable," in *Standard Edition*, XXIII (London: Hogarth Press).
Freud, S. (1938a) "Splitting of the ego in the process of defense," in *Standard Edition*, XXIII (London: Hogarth Press).
Freud, S. (1938b) "An outline of psychoanalysis," in *Standard Edition*, XXIII (London: Hogarth Press).
Goethe, J. W. (1834). *Faust*, in *Goethes Werke: Jubiläumsausgabe*, vol. III (Frankfurt/Leipzig: Insel Verlag, 1998). Translated by A. S. Klyne. Retrieved from: www.iowagrandmaster.org/Books%20in%20pdf/Faust.pdf
Gombrich, E. (1959) *Art and Illusion* (London: Phaidon).
Green, A. (1973) "On negative capability," *International Journal of Psycho-Analysis*, 54: 115–119.
Green, A. (1975) "The analyst, symbolization and absence in the analytic setting," *Inernational Journal of Psycho-Analysis*, 56: 1–22.
Green, A. (1986) "Le travail du négatif," *Revue Française de Psychanalyse*, 50: 489–493.
Green, A. (1997a) "The intuition of the negative," in *Playing and Reality, International Journal of Psycho-Analysis*, 78: 1071–1084.
Green, A. (1997b) "The primordial mind and the work of the negative," in *W. R. Bion: Between Past and Future*, P. B. Talamo, F. Borgogno and S. Merciai (eds.) (London: Karnac Books, 2000).
Green, A. (1999) *The Work of the Negative* (London: Free Association Books).
Green, A. (2000) "The central phobic position," *International Journal of Psycho-Analysis*, 81: 429–451.
Green, A. (2003) *4 Questões para André Green / 4 Questions pour André Green*, bilingual edition (São Paulo: Departamento de Publicações da SBPSP).
Hegel, G. W. F. (1817–1820) *Philosophy of Mind*, translated by W. Wallace and A. V. Miller (Oxford: Oxford University Press, 1971).
Heisenberg, W. (1958) *Physics and Philosophy*, in *The Great Books of the Western Hemisphere* (Chicago: Encyclopaedia Britannica, 1994).
Hopkins, G. M. (1918) "The habit of perfection," in *The Works of Gerard Manley Hopkins* (Ware: Wordsworth Poetry Library).
Kant, I. (1781) *Critique of Pure Reason*, translated by M. Micklejohn, in *The Great Books of the Western Hemisphere* (Chicago: Encyclopaedia Britannica, 1994).
Klein, M. (1932) *The Psycho-Analysis of Children* (London: Hogarth Press and the Institute of Psycho-Analysis, 1959).
Klein, M. (1946a) "The Oedipus complex in the light of early anxieties," in *Contributions to Psycho-Analysis* (London: Hogarth Press and the Institute of Psycho-Analysis, 1950).
Klein, M. (1946b) "Notes on some schizoid mechanisms," in *Developments in Psycho-Analysis*. M. Klein, P. Heimann, S. Isaacs and J. Riviere (eds.) (London: Hogarth Press and the Institute of Psycho-Analysis, 1952).
Klein, M. (1952) "Some theoretical conclusions regarding the emotional life of the infant," in *Developments in Psycho-Analysis*. M. Klein, P. Heimann, S. Isaacs and J. Riviere (eds.) (London: Hogarth Press and the Institute of Psycho-Analysis, 1952).

Klein, M. (1957) *Envy and Gratitude* (London: Tavistock Publications).
Klein, M. (1963) "On the sense of loneliness," in *The Writings of Melanie Klein*. R. Money-Kyrle, B. Joseph, E. O'Shaughnessy and H. Segal (eds.) (London: Karnac Books and the Institute of Psycho-Analysis, 1996).
Kohut, H. (1984) *How Does Analysis Cure?* A. Goldberg and P. Stepansky (eds.) (Chicago: University of Chicago Press).
Locke, J. (1690) *An Essay concerning Human Understanding* (London).
Mannoni, O. (1968) *Freud: Introdução à Psicanálise* (Mem Martins: Publicações Europa-América).
Pascal, B. (1657) Pensées, translated by W. F. Trotter, in *The Great Books of the Western Hemisphere* (Chicago: Encyclopaedia Britannica, 1994).
Philips, F. J. (1997) *Psicanálise do Desconhecido* (São Paulo: Editora 34).
Plato (c.380 BCE) *The Sophist*, translated by B. Jowett, in *The Great Books of the Western Hemisphere* (Chicago: Encyclopaedia Britannica, 1994).
Popper, K. R. (1959) *The Logic of Scientific Discovery* (London: Hutchinson & Co.)
Sandler, J. (1969) "Delinquentes, personalidades psicopáticas?" *Revista Brasileira de Psicanálise*, I: 263–269.
Sandler, P. C. (1997a) "The apprehension of psychic reality: extensions of Bion's theory of alpha-function," *International Journal of Psycho-Analysis*, 78: 43–52.
Sandler, P. C. (1997b) "Questionamentos da transcendência em Platão," in *A Apreensão da Realidade Psíquica*, vol. I (Rio de Janeiro: Imago Editora).
Sandler, P. C. (1997c) "Paradoxos e contradições," in *A Apreensão da Realidade Psíquica*, vol. I (Rio de Janeiro: Imago Editora).
Sandler, P. C. (1997d) "Platão e a psicanálise," in *A Apreensão da Realidade Psíquica*, vol. I (Rio de Janeiro: Imago Editora).
Sandler, P. C. (1997e) "Indeterminismo," in *A Apreensão da Realidade Psíquica*, vol. I (Rio de Janeiro: Imago Editora).
Sandler, P. C. (1997f) "Psicanálise e iluminismo," in *A Apreensão da Realidade Psíquica*, vol. I (Rio de Janeiro: Imago Editora).
Sandler, P. C. (1997g) "What is thinking? An attempt at an integrated study of W. R. Bion's contributions to the processes of knowing," in W. R. Bion, *Between Past and Future*. P. B. Talamo, F. Borgogno and S. A. Merciai (eds.) (London: Karnac Books, 2000).
Sandler, P. C. (2000a) *As Origens da Psicanálise na Obra de Kant, A Apreensão da Realidade Psíquica*, vol. III (Rio de Janeiro: Imago Editora).
Sandler, P. C. (2000b) *Turbulência e Urgência, A Apreensão da Realidade Psíquica*, vol. IV (Rio de Janeiro: Imago Editora).
Sandler, P. C. (2001a) *Goethe e a Psicanálise, A Apreensão da Realidade Psíquica*, vol. V (Rio de Janeiro: Imago Editora).
Sandler, P. C. (2001b) "Le projet scientifique de Freud en danger un siécle plus tard?" *Revue Française de Psychanalyse*, numéro hors-série, 181–202.
Sandler, P. C. (2001c) "*Psycho-analysis, epistemology: friends, parents or strangers?*" Presented at the Congress of the IPA, Nice, July 2001, Official Panel on Epistemology.
Sandler, P. C. (2003) *Hegel e Klein: A Tolerância de Paradoxos* (Rio de Janeiro: Imago Editora).
Sandler, P. C. (2005) *The Language of Bion: A Dictionary of Concepts* (London: Routledge, 2019).

Sandler, P. C. (2006) "The origins of Bion's work," *International Journal of Psycho-Analysis*, 87: 180–201.

Sandler, P. C. (2011a) "The realm of minus and the negative," in *A Clinical Application of Bion's Concepts*, vol. II: *Analytic Function and the Function of the Analyst* (London: Routledge, 2020).

Sandler, P. C. (2011b) "Oedipus in the light of versus: from pair to couple," in *A Clinical Application of Bion's Concepts*, vol. II: *Analytic Function and the Function of the Analyst* (London: Routledge, 2020).

Sandler, P. C. (2013a) "Movement, matter, space and time," in *A Clinical Application of Bion's Concepts*, vol. III: *Verbal and Visual Approaches to Reality* (London: Routledge, 2020).

Sandler, P. C. (2013b) "A multi-dimension Grid," in *A Clinical Application of Bion's Concepts*, vol. III: *Verbal and Visual Approaches to Reality* (London: Routledge, 2020).

Sandler, P. C. (2013c) "Freie Einfälle: the verbal irruption of the unknown and free-floating attention: the personal factor," in *A Clinical Application of Bion's Concepts*, vol. III: *Verbal and Visual Approaches to Reality* (London: Routledge, 2020).

Sandler, P. C. (2015a) "Obscure, complicated and difficult?" in *An Introduction to "A Memoir of the Future" by W. R. Bion*, vol. I: *Authoritative not Authoritarian Psycho-Analysis* (London: Routledge, 2019).

Sandler, P. C. (2015b) "Commentary on *Transformations in Hallucinosis and the Receptivity of the Analyst*, by Civitarese," *International Journal of Psychoanalysis*, 96: 1139–1157.

Sandler, P. C. (2015c) "Fame: a mix of illusion, hallucination and delusion?" in *An Introduction to "A Memoir of the Future" by W. R. Bion*, vol. II: *A Matter of Fact or Facts of Matter?* (London: Routledge, 2019).

Sandler, P. C. (2018) "Wirkliche Psychoanalyse ist wirkliches Leben," *Jahrbuch der Psychoanalyse*, 76: 125–164.

Sandler, P. C. and Costa, G. P. (2018) *On Freud's "The Question of Lay Analysis"* (Abingdon: Routledge).

Winnicott, D. W. (1960) "The theory of the parent–infant relationship," *International Journal of Psycho-Analysis*, 41: 585–595.

Winnicott, D. W. (1969) "The use of an object," *International Journal of Psycho-Analysis*, 50: 711–716.

Young, M. (1958) *The Rise of Meritocracy* (New Brunswick: Transaction, 1994).

Chapter 18

From transference and countertransference to emotional experience in *Transformations*

Stela Maris Garcia Loureiro

Several psychoanalytical concepts are used in this paper, with the developments of the theoretical corpus in the Freud ↔ Klein ↔ Bion axes as backdrop. In particular, I will try to follow the evolution of the concepts of *transference* and its clinical repercussions, and, subsequently, of *countertransference*, eventually coming to Bion and his theory of *transformations*.

I. The evolving concept of transference

We know that the Freudian rationale for *transference* is based on concepts that, to preserve their internal coherence, must be correlated to the broader corpus of his theory. Thus, the notion of *transference* in Freud is permanently coupled with that of *repression* of child sexuality and its vicissitudes, and of *interpretation, unconscious* and *resistance*, among others (Freud, 1953a, 1953b, 1957a, 1957b, 1958a, 1961). *Transference* is, to be sure, the return of the repressed, which is acted out in the psychoanalytic relationship by re-editing past experiences in the figure of the analyst. The return of what has been repressed is also acted out in the symptoms of neurotic patients and in the dreams, parapraxes and jokes of daily life.

With Melanie Klein (1975a, 1975b), by establishing the notion of the *paranoid-schizoid position*, psychoanalytic observation leaves aside the notion of *repressed unconscious* and begins to address mechanisms related to phenomena hitherto foreign to analytical practice. This required the elaboration of new concepts, such as the notion of *inner world*, the theory of *object relations* and other basic concepts, including *projective identification* of the contents of the self onto the object. Klein's clinical practice brought to the foreground the notion of *inner world*, i.e., the field of emotional experiences constituted and organized from object relations, anxieties, fantasies and defenses. These are all structured according to another notion – a revolutionary one in the psychoanalytic frame of reference – that of *position*, substantiating the existence of both paranoid-schizoid and depressive positions. The classic Freudian concept of *transference* thus evolves into the notion of *projective identification*, formulated by Klein in 1946, an evolution that became possible through the perception of primitive aspects of the personality in the areas of the emotional development of children and of psychotic disorders. I highlight here the significance and operability of a microscopic view of mental functioning, particularly the *identificatory character* (self/object indiscrimination) of projective and introjective object relationships. Thus, the notion of transference in Klein comprises both projections and introjections in their identificatory dimension. The concept of *transference* as a total situation is developed (by Klein and Betty Joseph) as an attempt to expand the field of psychoanalytic observation and encompass all emotional experiences stemming from clinical practice, which was then being revamped.

Some Kleinians introduced the notion of "psychotic transference" in the case of schizophrenic patients, as they tried to apply the notion of projective identification to aspects of classical transference. We are today aware of their conceptual incongruity, although their perception did embrace an attempt to expand the field of neurotic phenomena so as to include psychotic phenomena.

Bion, however, on the basis of his clinical work, strove to articulate and expand the theoretical corpus of psychoanalysis towards "something" that might account for certain events related to ongoing emotional experiences, in terms of objectifying their vicissitudes and seeking out their operability beyond the transference/countertransference dynamics – a field he developed from his theory of thinking and during the elaboration of his epistemological trilogy.

Once again, we must stress the need for harmonious referential coherence if we wish to achieve the proper and requisite correlation of concepts. Thus, in order to integrate theoretical-clinical notions, it is important to discriminate within Bion's broader conceptual corpus.

Similarly, the notion of *countertransference* is an instrument of research for many analysts of the English school, who resort to their own emotional responses as a means of accessing the patient's unconscious. This is the cornerstone of the British controversies at the time of World War II, but even today the concept of countertransference enjoys widespread use, with all its attendant doubts and conceptual confusions.

The conceptual expansions described above, therefore, not only enabled the transition from classical *transference* to the notion of *projective identification* and the supposition of transference as a total situation, but also provided instruments to access mental functioning beyond neuroses. The notions of *inner world, object relations, early anxieties* and *paranoid-schizoid* and *depressive positions* redeemed the importance of our relationship with objects and of the entire field of emotional experiences in analytical work. But then arose the controversial issue of the use of countertransference, that is, of the psychoanalyst's implication and involvement in his or her clinical practice – a very far cry from one's desirable neutrality and emotional impartiality.

II. The evolving concept of countertransference

Freud was not very interested in the question of *countertransference* except to highlight its negative aspect and undesirability in analytical work: "We ought not to give up the neutrality towards the patient, which we have acquired through keeping the countertransference in check." (Freud, 1958b, p. 164)

In a prior text, "Recommendations to physicians practising psycho-analysis" (Freud, 1958c), we can identify his brilliant intuition as we apprehend that the patient's unconscious contents may be captured by the analyst in a singular manner: "[The doctor] *must turn his own unconscious like a receptive organ towards the transmitting unconscious of the patient.*" The telephone metaphor stands out:

> He must adjust himself to the patient as a telephone receiver is adjusted to the transmitting microphone. Just as the receiver converts back into sound-waves the electric oscillations in the telephone line which were set up by sound-waves, so the doctor's unconscious is able, from the derivatives of the unconscious which are communicated to him, to reconstruct that unconscious, which has determined the patient's free associations.
>
> (Freud, 1958c, p. 114)

Freud never proposed using countertransference in clinical work, although today we may admit that his observations above indicate an awareness of the variations of its use in analytical work in the future of psychoanalysis. He always insisted on the need to reduce countertransferential manifestations through the personal analysis of the analyst, who should maintain an attitude of abstinence and neutrality towards the patient. The analytical situation should be structured as a projective surface, in which only the *transference* of the patient would stand out:

> Other innovations in technique relate to the physician himself. We have become aware of the "counter-transference," which arises in him as a result of the patient's influence on his unconscious feelings, and we are almost inclined to insist that he shall recognize this counter-transference in himself and overcome it.
>
> (Freud, 1957b, p. 143)

Freud continues:

> We have noticed that no psycho-analyst goes further than his own complexes and internal resistances permit.
>
> (Freud, 1957b, p. 143)

> The doctor should be opaque to his patients and, like a mirror, should show them nothing but what is shown to him.
>
> (Freud, 1958c, p. 116)

While we notice in Freud a clear disavowal of the use of *countertransference* in clinical work, we also perceive in his theoretical corpus the roots of emotional experiences, albeit not conceptualized, which would eventually go beyond transference and countertransference: "I have had good reason for asserting that everyone possesses in his own unconscious an instrument with which he can interpret the utterances of the unconscious in other people" (Freud, 1958d, p. 322).

The dialogue between the analyst's unconscious and that of the analysand was based on the complementarity and correlation of free associations and evenly-suspended attention.

Melanie Klein was influenced not only by Freud, but also by her analysts, Ferenczi and Abraham, although each one adopted a different viewpoint with regard to the use of countertransference. However, like Freud, Klein considered countertransference an inappropriate and inconvenient factor that negatively interfered with the analytical relationship.

As psychoanalysis extended to new fields of clinical work, *countertransference* became an object of increasing interest. Thus, in the analysis of children and psychotics, the analyst's unconscious reactions gained prominence, and emotional reactions began to demand more attention.

Klein did not accept Paula Heimann's ideas regarding the use of the analyst's feelings and emotions as a source of information about the patient. Today, however, Kleinian analysts use the concept of *countertransference* in the broadest sense, i.e., as a mental state induced in the analyst as a result of the patient's verbal and non-verbal action, bringing to bear the fantasy of projective identification.

Bion, as a Kleinian, when working with groups in the 1950s, employed for the first time the notion of *projective identification* as a tool when using *countertransference*. Thus, initially, he was part of the current of Kleinian analysts who applied the notion of *projective identification in the countertransferential dimension* from his very first works on groups and also during his period of working with psychotics. To quote him:

> It is that in group treatment many interpretations, and amongst them the most important, have to be made on the strength of the analyst's own emotional reactions. It is my belief that these reactions are dependent on the fact that the analyst in the group is at the receiving end of what Melanie Klein has called projective identification.
>
> (Bion, 1961, p. 213)

In Roger Money-Kyrle's classic article "Normal countertransference and some of its deviations," we find the following observations:

> I will try to formulate what seems to be happening when the analysis is going well. I believe there is a fairly rapid oscillation between introjection and projection. As the patient speaks, the analyst will, as it were, become introjectively identified with him, and having understood him inside, will reproject him and interpret. [...] As long as the analyst understands them, this

satisfactory relationship – which I will call the "normal" one – persists. In particular, the analyst's counter-transference feelings will be confined to that sense of empathy with the patient on which his insight is based.

(Money-Kyrle, 2015, pp. 331–332)

Betty Joseph, in her "Transfer: the total situation," tells us:

Much of our understanding of the transference comes through our understanding of how our patients act on us to feel things for many varied reasons; how they try to draw us into their defensive systems; how they unconsciously act out with us in the transference, trying to get us to act out with them; how they convey aspects of their inner world built up from infancy – elaborated in childhood and adulthood, experiences often beyond the use of words, which we can often only capture through the feelings aroused in us, through our countertransference, used in the broad sense of the word.

(Joseph, 1985)

Bion agrees that the use of *countertransference* is an extremely useful technical resource. In his *Language and the Schizophrenic*, he states:

The analyst who essays, in our present state of ignorance, the treatment of [psychotic] patients, must be prepared to discover that for a considerable proportion of analytic time the only evidence on which an interpretation can be based is that which is afforded by the counter-transference.

(Bion, 1955, p. 77)

After this first phase of upholding the use of *countertransference*, Bion demonstrated his ability to reformulate his own ideas and changed his attitude towards the matter. He redeemed Freud's and Klein's notion that *countertransference, sensu stricto*, refers to the unconscious feelings of the analyst (and is thus unavailable to the analytical function) and is nothing more than the unanalyzed *transference* of the analyst vis-à-vis his or her patient – indicating, as Freud and Klein stressed, the need for the analyst to be reanalyzed.

In *A Memoir of the Future*, Bion emphasizes the unconscious character of *countertransference*:

Do not forget that "counter-transference" is by definition unconscious; it follows that I do not know the nature, in reality, of my counter-transference. I know theoretically, but that is only knowing about counter-transference – that is not knowing the "thing itself."

(Bion, 1979, p. 81)

In *Learning from Experience*, he uses the terms "container" and "contained," expanding Klein's notion of *projective identification*:

> Melanie Klein has described an aspect of projective identification concerned with the modification of infantile fears; the infant projects a part of its psyche, namely its bad feelings, into a good breast. Thence in due course they are removed and re-introjected. During their sojourn in the good breast they are felt to have been modified in such a way that the object that is re-introjected has become tolerable to the infant's psyche.
>
> From the above theory I shall abstract for use as a model the idea of a container into which an object is projected and the object that can be projected into the container: the latter I shall designate by the term "contained." The unsatisfactory nature of both terms points to the need for further abstraction.
>
> (Bion, 1962, p. 356)

The conceptual pair "container–contained" was progressively developed by Bion from a series of three articles he had written previously: "On arrogance" (1957), "Attacks on linking" (1959) and "A theory of thinking" (1962). In the latter, a seminal text, Bion expounds his theories on the nature of thought and on the ability to think, and expands the Kleinian concept of projective identification to more than an omnipotent fantasy, namely, as a primal communication method both in the primitive baby–mother relationship and in the analytical relationship. It is impossible to overemphasize the importance of the analyst's personality as the *receptor pole* of the patient's unconscious through the analyst's own emotions. This epistemological leap introduces a new logical framework in Bion's conceptualization, endowing psychoanalysis with extraordinary effectiveness, i.e., operationalizing the notion of *transformation of experiences through the process of containment* and its elaboration.

III. From containment to emotional experience in *Transformations*

Bion's theoretical and clinical evolvement had already allowed him to formulate his theory of thinking – learning from emotional experience, the elements of psychoanalysis and the theory of functions (α-function, α-elements and β-elements) – differentiating sensory reality from psychic reality and explaining the importance of the external object in the constitution of the subject and in infant development. These experiences take place through the function of maternal reverie, analogous to the analyst's dreaming in the analytical function, and eventually led to the elaboration of his observational theory in *Transformations*.

In this book, Bion emphasized that it was not one more theory on psychoanalysis, but rather, fundamentally, a contribution to the methods of observation in psychoanalysis. In other words, with the development of the theory of functions, Bion elaborated the notion of psychoanalytic elements and, consequently, the possibility that these elements, when surfacing in the clinical session, might be categorized in the Grid, contributing to enhance psychoanalysts' intuition.

Bion gauged that mental reality has two distinct qualities: sensory mental reality and psychic (non-sensorial) reality, and elaborated a basic frame of reference that would allow access to the mind: the α-function theory.

Thus, the elements of the sense world, called β-elements (stimuli from the sense organs, and emotions), must undergo a transformation process to access the life of the psyche. This is the task of the α-*function*, to process the sensory or β-elements into α-*elements*, thus opening up "sensory terminals" to psychic life.

This is a significant change of vertex that restores the importance of the external object in the structuring of the baby's personality through the function of maternal reverie – i.e., the activity of the α-function of the mother who welcomes the projections of β-elements she receives from her child, "detoxifies" them of their sensory elements and returns them to the child in a way that it can assimilate (Bion, 1962).

However, the watershed wrought by Bion in the evolution of psychoanalytic concepts and in the shifting of the analytical function's vertex is more clearly brought to light in his *Transformations*. This work aimed to be not one more theory of psychoanalysis, but basically a *theory of observation* of the mental phenomena of thought that come forth in sessions of analysis. The conceptual pair of *transformations* and *invariants* is immediately established, derived from the model of mathematics, giving rise to Bion's metapsychology, the metapsychology of "O" and its vicissitudes, loosely based on the Kantian concept of ultimate reality (and/or truth).

As Bion formulated his theory of *transformations*, initially discerned in observations of increasing complexity, he highlighted three significant features:

1 **Transformations in K.** These transformations produce knowledge, expand the mind and are identified as *transformations in K* (knowledge). Their expansion means growth and psychic development, and require that the analyst be capable not only of containment and discipline in observation (to preserve the analytical function), but also of freedom to exercise them, while the "demonic" aspects of the personality attack and seek to destroy the thinking capacity of the analyst–analysand duo. These transformations involve analytical work, the area covered by the field of the transformations in +K, which itself is comprised of operations that produce knowledge and take place according to the analyst's internal disposition, his or her negative capability (state of mind not saturated with memories, desires and understanding) and empathic availability towards the patient. *Transformations in knowledge always imply the analyst's capacity for containment, discipline in the observation of psychic phenomena, effort to preserve the analytical function and freedom to exercise it.*

2 **Transformations in −K.** These transformations are products of a repetition-compulsion mechanism, of destructive and envious aspects of the personality, and are indicated by the sign −K. All mental production associated with the more primitive aspects of the personality – whose stimuli were not processed

by the α-function (or, if they were, have been stripped of all sense and meaning) – will constitute distortions of perception. In ascending order of distortion, these are:

a   *Transformations in rigid motion*, which have come to be identified with Freudian transference and occur without major distortions of perception. They are often associated with the Oedipal nucleus and are, indeed, analogous to Freudian transference.

b   *Projective transformations*, which include the functioning of pathological projective identification and constitute the most distorted mode of perception, with erasure of limits and self–object relationships. They tend towards experiences of fusion and intense and violent identificatory processes, without contact-barriers. They are analogous to psychotic functioning in the dimension mentioned by Klein.

c   *Transformations in hallucinosis*, a concept formulated and developed by Bion corresponding to the highest degree of perception distortion. They produce false conceptions and false thoughts, resemble the psychiatric phenomena of hallucinations and deliria, and "sustain" themselves by means of intense and primitive emotions.

3   **Transformations in "O".** These derive from Bion's complex and profound abstraction, whereby "O" refers to formless infinite, ultimate reality, absolute truth, the thing in itself, that which cannot be known. Although outside the field of knowledge, "O" allows itself to "become" in the analytical field. And although unknowable, it can become the starting point for a specific experience of analytical interaction and ongoing unison between patient and analyst, prompting significant psychic changes in the patient. Then, when one reaches this state conducive to psychic growth and with the evolutions that can lead to transformations in K, one must reclaim the condition of *negative capability* (in the direction K → O), so that a new development cycle may begin. The concept of "O" speaks of something that cannot be known, that we cannot come to know, but nevertheless "is." The field of negativity provides us with the area of BEING and a meeting in unison between two people – patient and analyst.

Preceding the theory in *Transformations* (1965) and as part of his epistemological trilogy – together with *Learning from Experience* (1962) and *Elements of Psycho-Analysis* (1963) – Bion developed the notion of "psychoanalytic elements." These would be comparable to a molecule composed of multiple atoms, basic and simple elements that are constituted to form units of ideas and feelings emerging from the bond between analyst and analysand. They can be represented in the categories of the Grid. The psychoanalytic elements were further developed by Bion in his book *Elements of Psycho-Analysis*, but only by examining the whole of his work can we can extract their eight constitutive elements.

1   A dynamic *container–contained* relationship that interacts with Melanie Klein's concept of projective identification.
2   Oscillation of the paranoid-schizoid (PS) and depressive (DP) positions in both directions (PS ↔ DP). The concept of *selected fact*, used by the French mathematician Henri Poincaré, is stressed.
3   *L (love), H (hate)* and *K (knowledge)* links.
4   Relationship between *reason (R)* and *emotion (E)*.
5   Thought and idea.
6   Pain and suffering.
7   Relationship between narcissism and socialism.
8   Communication and language.

Grounded on the first elements of psychoanalysis – i.e., on the dynamic *container–contained* relationship interacting with the functioning of projective identification and the PS ↔ DP oscillations of the expression of *anxiety* – the field of emotional experience in the process of *transformation* eventually emerges, leading the patient to the possibility of learning from this experience and towards psychic growth.

In the analytical situation, under the vertex of learning from the ongoing emotional experience, an ability is developed to withstand the emotional turbulence in the PS (the analyst's attitude of patience) and attain the DP (the attitude of security) by formulating what one has lived and thought. When the elements of psychoanalysis are interrelated in the clinical space, they are articulated according to the *L, H* and *K* links, and the "mystery of the unknown" can be partly known by the analytical duo, within the clinical environment, through the constitution of *psychoanalytic objects*.

Another contribution of Bion would be the correlation with the notion of "caesura," the establishment of which seems to me essential due to his pertinent opposition to identifications.

Inquiries that will be the object of new reflections:

1   Considering that transference is an essential part of Freudian clinical work and is deemed essential to the analytical relationship, and that its counterpart, countertransference (the transference of the analyst to the patient) is an instrument unsuited to be used in clinical practice, how does one situate them in Bion's theory of transformations? *Transference* as a container of emotional experience? *Countertransference* as a resource available for the analyst to carry out his or her specific function?
2   As a result of these first inquiries, would the name that one gives to the phenomena that take place in the analysis room (e.g., *transferences* or *projective identification*) matter as much as the use one makes of them, so long as they promote psychic change?
3   In the dynamics of the *container–contained* relationship, is there a correlation with the notions of communicative and pathological projective identification?

4   Can *transferences* and *countertransferences* be categorized as emotional experiences in $+K$?
5   In the K → O evolution, what is the importance of negative capability?

Bion wrote: "Any attempt to cling to what he knows must be resisted for the sake of achieving a state of mind analogous to the paranoid-schizoid position" (Bion, 1970, p. 326).

These observations and their consequent achievements can help us to evolve from K → O, but to what extent can abandoning K lead us to the vertex of "O"?

References

Bion, W.R. (1955) "Language and the schizophrenic," in *Complete Works*, vol. IV (London: Karnac).
Bion, W.R. (1961) *Experiences in Groups and Other Papers*, in *Complete Works*, vol. IV (London: Karnac).
Bion, W.R. (1962) *Learning from Experience*, in *Complete Works*, vol. IV (London: Karnac).
Bion, W. R. (1963) *Elements of Psycho-Analysis*, in *Complete Works*, vol. V (London: Karnac).
Bion, W. R. (1965) *Transformations: Change from Learning to Growth*, in *Complete Works*, vol. V (London: Karnac).
Bion, W. R. (1970) *Attention and Interpretation*, in *Complete Works*, vol. VI (London: Karnac).
Bion, W. R. (1979) *A Memoir of the Future*, vol. III: The Dawn of Oblivion, in *Complete Works*, XIV (London: Karnac). See also London: Routledge, 2018.
Freud, S. (1953a) *The Interpretation of Dreams*, in *Complete Works*, IV–V (London: Hogarth Press). Originally published in 1900.
Freud, S. (1953b) *Three Essays on Sexuality and Other Works*, in *Complete Works*, VII (London: Hogarth Press). Originally published in 1905.
Freud, S. (1957a) "Instincts and their vicissitudes," in *Complete Works*, XIV (London: Hogarth Press). Originally published in 1915.
Freud, S. (1957b) "The future prospects of psycho-analytic therapy," in *Complete Works*, XI (London: Hogarth Press). Originally published in 1910.
Freud, S. (1958a) "Formulations on the two principles of mental functioning," in *Complete Works*, XII (London: Hogarth Press). Originally published in 1911.
Freud, S. (1958b) "Observations on transference-love," in *Complete Works*, XII (London: Hogarth Press). Originally published in 1915.
Freud, S. (1958c) "Recommendations to physicians practising psycho-analysis," in *Complete Works*, XII (London: Hogarth Press). Originally published in 1912.
Freud, S. (1958d) "The disposition to obsessional neurosis," in *Complete Works*, XII (London: Hogarth Press). Originally published in 1913.
Freud, S. (1961) *The Ego and the Id and Other Works*, in *Complete Works*, XIX (London: Hogarth Press). Originally published in 1923.
Joseph, B. (1985) "Transference: the total situation," *International Journal of Psychoanalysis*, 66: 447–454.

Klein, M. (1975a) "A contribution to the psychogenesis of manic-depressive states, " in *The Writings of Melanie Klein*, vol. 1: *Love, Guilt and Reparation & Other Works 1921–1945* (London: Hogarth Press). Originally published in 1935.

Klein, M. (1975b) "Notes on some schizoid mechanisms," in *The Writings of Melanie Klein*, vol. 3: *Envy and Gratitude & Other Works 1946–1963* (London: Hogarth Press). Originally published in 1946.

Money-Kyrle, R. (2015) "Normal counter-transference and some of its deviations," in *The Collected Papers of Roger Money-Kyrle*, ed. D. Meltzer (London: Karnac, 2015).

Appendix: The Grid

THE GRID

	Definitory hypothesis 1	Ψ 2	Notation 3	Attention 4	Inquiry 5	Action 6	...n
A β-elements	A1	A2				A6	
B α-elements	B1	B2	B3	B4	B5	B6	...Bn
C Dream-thoughts, dreams, myths	C1	C2	C3	C4	C5	C6	...Cn
D Pre-conception	D1	D2	D3	D4	D5	D6	...Dn
E Conception	E1	E2	E3	E4	E5	E6	...En
F Concept	F1	F2	F3	F4	F5	F6	...Fn
G Scientific deductive system		G2					
H Algebraic calculus							

Figure A.1 The Grid
Source: *Complete Works of W. R. Bion*, vol. X, pp. iii–vii (London: Karnac, 2014)

Index

Figures are indexed with italic page numbers

α-function 25n1, 29, 33, 85, 87, 89, 140
ability 23, 27–8, 31, 61–2, 73, 77, 80, 105–6, 116, 118, 154, 162, 165, 175–6, 179; analyst's 41; to dream 28; mental 74; reader's 106; student's 106
Abraham 174
absolute freedom 131
absolute splitting 159
adoptive mothers 21, 24
adrenal glands 9, 11
adversities 77, 113
aesthetic synthesis 126
alcohol 65–7, 118
alpha-elements 4–5, 7, 10
alpha-function 4–5, 12
analysis 2, 66, 114, 125; personal 89, 141, 173; real 160, 166; room 11, 14–15, 72, 74, 87, 93, 179; sessions 99
analyst-analysand 7–8, 27–8, 59–60, 73–5, 77–8, 80–2, 84–5, 88, 94–5, 98, 100–1, 114, 123, 135–7, 141–3; "analytically trained intuition" 154; relationship to attain a state of "at-one-ment." 9; thoughts led Bion to create an instrument to identify their different uses and degrees of abstraction 111n5
analyst/analysand: duo 177; duo in the analysis room 93, 177
analysts 5–9, 17–22, 25, 27–31, 34–42, 46–51, 53–4, 73–5, 77–8, 80–2, 84–5, 88–9, 91–3, 103–5, 107–8, 110–19, 135–8, 140–2, 158–61, 171–9; apprehension 115; attitude 140, 179; clinical 48; feelings and emotions 174–5; flesh-and-blood 115, 117; intuition 50;

Kleinian 174; language 46–7, 49, 51, 53–4; mind 20, 39, 46, 74; narratives 39; senior 44
analytical 12, 30, 163, 171; duo 29, 98, 100, 179; method 112, 116, 141; object 19, 22–3; relationships 18, 22, 91–4, 107, 145, 174, 176, 179; sessions 50, 84, 89, 103, 107; work 15, 44, 65, 72, 78, 99, 172–3, 177
Aquinas, St. Thomas 149
Arendt, Hannah 82
Aristotle 149
art 19, 73, 83, 147, 150, 165; critics 87; existing 150; "that is not in the present will never be" (Picasso) 84
Artigas, Vilanova 86
artists 87, 89, 123, 126, 131, 135
attitude 22–3, 61, 76, 78, 140, 173, 175, 179
authoritarian rationalization 74, 147, 164
authority 2, 6, 80, 137; of another person or group 75; in conformity with an establishment 81; outer 75; self-styled moral 79
autism 20, 40
autistic barriers 47–8
autistic encapsulations 28
Auto-Falante (2007) *86*
autonomy 42, 79–82
axes 35, 42, 107; Freud–Klein–Bion 91, 171; fundamental 107; horizontal 35, 38; vertical 10, 35, 38, 40

B (alpha-elements) 4
β-elements 92

Index

babies: adopted 17; beautiful 161; helpless 28; newborn 75, 77, 131, 165; omnipotent 160; primitive 176; surviving 165
The Bacchae 56, 64, 67
Bair, Deirdre 121
Beckett, Samuel 121–9, 131–3; description of mothers as "uniparous whores" 124; the great defender of positive incapability 132; potentializes his world view from essential existential questionings 132; reference to "being deceived" 128; and the "squabble" (prise de bec) with Wilfred Bion 121, 123, 125, 129, 131; and vision of "the face eye" prevailing in characters of 122; writes *Texts for Nothing* 128
beta-elements 4–5, 7, 10, 133
beta-screen 151, 163
Beyond the Pleasure Principle 12n2, 113, 147, 155–6, 158, 164–5
Bick, Esther 17, 20, 48
binocular vision 19, 124–5, 127, 130, 132–3, 152
biological mothers 21, 24
Bion Wilfred 6–12, 17–20, 22–5, 27–9, 33–8, 40–4, 46–51, 58–62, 73–5, 77–82, 92–4, 97–111, 121–5, 127–33, 138–41, 144–8, 150–60, 163–6, 171–2, 174–80; and the psychical implications the binocular vision of 122; asks how is the evidence of careful selection in accordance with psycho-analytic principles to be accounted for 99; associates the presence or absence of an object, its existence or non-existence, in *Transformations* 130; and catastrophic change 62; conceptualizations 4, 176; contribution to the theory of reversible perspectives 98, 149; definition of −K 156; definition of "minus" 149, 151; description of the state of mind called "reversible perspective" 98, 163; essay "Caesura" 135, 138; expounds his theories on the nature of thought and on the ability to think 176; highlights three types of emotional links that will apply α-function 47; and his term α-function coined for our cognitive perception of the inner and outer worlds 57; ideas of 103–4, 110, 139–40; indefectible quasi-mathematical notation systems mimicking 140; metapsychology 177; models and theories 115; observations 155, 158, 165; original and influential collection of papers *Second Thoughts* 44n6; ponders about the mental equivalents of embryonic remains 11; and psychic reality 60; restricts the term "thought" to the conjunction of a preconception with a frustration 9; self-analysis 24; and the "squabble" (prise de bec) with Samuel Beckett 121, 123, 125, 127, 129, 131; and the Tavistock Clinic 121, 133n7; theory of transformations 47–8, 109, 179; thinking of 17, 19, 21, 23, 106, 108–9; works of 5, 9, 18, 33–4, 104, 108, 110, 112, 140, 149, 156; writes *Four Papers* 10; writes *In Attention and Interpretation* 77; writes *Language and the Schizophrenic* 175; writes *Learning from Experience, A Theory of Thinking and Elements of Psychoanalysis* 85, 92; writes *Taming Wild Thoughts* 10, 38, 44; writes *The Italian Seminars* 10, 93
bisexuality 164
Blake, William 133
body 46–8, 51, 54, 61, 67, 109; adrenal 11; flaccid 51, 54; functions 132; lifeless 54; physical 11; puppet's 51; shapeless 51; upright 54
Bohr, Niels 97–8
Braga, João Carlos 103–11
Branagh, Kenneth 126
Brasiliano, Cícero José Campos 84–90
breast 9, 36–8, 62, 67, 147–8, 151, 154–5, 157–61, 163, 166; envious 155, 158, 162; exploitative 163; external 158; ideal 148; pre-conceived 147; psychosomatic 28; real 147–8; un-loved 158
Burkert, Walter 60, 68n2

Cadmus 63–4
caesura 18, 25, 29, 106, 135–8, 140, 179; body-mind 12; and mental pain 135, 137; psychoanalytic 109
catastrophe 29, 63, 133
catastrophic change 9, 19, 21, 25, 27, 29, 58, 60, 62, 65, 130
chemotherapy 137
childhood relationships 113
children 12, 66–7, 71, 74, 80, 88, 95, 159, 162, 174, 177; anxious, hyperkinetic and inattentive 24; attraction to the unknown being a natural process 101; bring about

change in the familial relationship 63; condemned to precocity, fated to take impossible responsibilities, as a matter of survival 161; emotional development of 171; projecting their greediness on babies 63; small 65; and the telling by parents of their adoption 78; young 63
civilization, Minoan-Mycenaean 69n7
clients 3–4, 6–8, 12, 35, 37–9, 41–4, 68, 81
clinical experiences 34–5, 90, 101, 107, 138–9, 141, 151, 157, 163
clinical repercussions 171
clinical situations 33, 41, 44, 56, 85, 87, 94
clinical vignettes 37
cocaine 65–7
compassion 23, 81, 119, 141
conception 19, 37–8, 41–2, 93; arising from the union of pre-conception and realization 36; of clinical practice 18; false 178; of projective identification 92; psychoanalytical 56
concepts 1, 4–5, 8–10, 20, 37, 41, 43–4, 49, 59–60, 62, 91–2, 96, 98–9, 107–10, 112–13, 135, 171–2, 178–9; basic 171; emerging 1; formal 141; fundamental 129; Kleinian 107, 115; new 8, 171; philosophical 12; psychoanalytical 171, 177; theoretical 101, 144
conflicts 20, 60, 98–9, 107, 129; permanent 101; strong 66; theoretical 91; unconscious 6
conjunction 9, 21, 109, 157; significant conceptual 107; theoretical 91, 94
conscience 28, 160
conscious awareness 18, 116, 163
consciousness 20, 23, 65, 127, 152, 156
container 21, 28, 47, 62, 91–2, 94, 162, 175–6, 179; Bion's conception of the 27; configuration 132; confusion-producing 145; dynamic 179; inanimate 131; minus 155, 164; primary 28; transformative 22
contemporary psychoanalysis 17, 19, 21, 23, 142, 150, 178
contradictions 20, 58, 99, 127, 146–8, 164–5
countertransference 5, 8, 18, 93, 114, 171–5, 179–80; normal 174
countertransferential dimensions 174
countertransferential manifestations 34, 173
creation 20, 56–8, 106, 108, 159, 161
creative synthesis 142
creativity 58, 63, 68–9, 95, 129, 139

criminals 35, 145
cures 18, 70–1, 73, 75, 77, 79, 81, 128, 142–3, 146

Da Vinci 165
de Camargo, Celso Antonio Vieira 56–69
de Lisonda, Alicia Beatriz Dorado 17–25
de Souza Marra, Evelise 91–5
death 29, 58–9, 71, 73, 75, 126, 128, 137–8, 144–5, 153, 163–4; drive 61, 91; fear of 114, 129; fighting 132; instincts 113, 115, 147, 154, 157; mental 29; ravaged by the anguish of 27; under the threat of 36
definitory hypothesis 35, 37–9, 41
Delcourt-Curvers, Marie 64
Democritus of Abdera 133n8
denudation (process of) 155, 157–8
depression 52, 65–6, 71–3, 77, 131, 160
Descartes, René 128–9, 149
descriptions 29, 35, 39, 56–8, 62, 64, 69, 91, 93, 97, 105; caustic 124; mythical 69; scientific 145
development 4–5, 7–11, 33–4, 39–40, 44, 61–2, 80, 82–3, 91–2, 100–1, 106, 108, 110, 148–9, 164; authentic 41; bodily 100; mathematical 109; mental 34, 41, 101, 106, 117; new 48, 155; physical 11; process 101; theoretical 33
dialectical pairs 152
dimensions 3, 8, 22, 35, 39, 43, 51, 102–5, 107–9, 116, 155–6; aesthetic 110; basal 8; countertransferential 174; hallucinatory 1, 8–9, 104; identificatory 7; intuitive 112; investigative 116; mystical 93; new 54, 63; primitive 114; psychic 20; relational 101; scientific 109; spectral 101; unconscious 8
disease 71–2, 75, 128
disorders 5, 24, 65; global 24; psychosomatic 100; psychotic 172; soma-psychotic 100
doctors 2, 23, 79, 95, 112–13, 121, 173
dream-thoughts 4–5, 12, 36, 38, 41–3, 47
drinking 65–6, 118
drowsiness 37–9
drugs 66, 82
dyspnea 121

ego 34, 40, 61, 100–1, 113, 145, 158, 164; bodily 61; conservation 60; functioning primitive 114

Eissler, Kurt 151
elements, psychoanalytic 176, 178
Elements of Psycho-Analysis 178
Eliot, T.S. 106
emotional 1, 3–9, 11–12, 27–9, 33, 39–41, 43–4, 46–50, 59–62, 64–5, 67–8, 88–9, 91–4, 100, 102–3, 107–8, 114–19, 162–3, 171–7, 179–80; development 24, 127, 130, 165, 171; experiences 1, 3–9, 11–12, 27–8, 33, 43–4, 47–8, 59–60, 64–5, 67–8, 88–9, 91–3, 107–8, 115–16, 142, 162–3, 171–3, 175–7, 179–80; impartiality 172; interferences 94; involvement 163; life 21, 49; turbulence 27, 29, 79, 100, 179
emotions 37, 39–41, 43, 46–7, 49–51, 53–4, 59, 62, 115–16, 118–19, 155–7, 160, 174, 176–7, 179; aesthetic 64; basic human 4, 48; language of 47, 50, 53; mother's 24; ongoing 50; paranoid violence of 155; patient's 73; primal 33; primitive 34, 178; primordial 36; strong 41, 44, 54, 94
emperors *see* Kublai Khan
enforced splitting 152, 158
Euripides 56, 64, 69
Eva, Antonio Carlos 14–17
evidence 23, 29, 36, 99, 158–9, 161, 175
evil 23, 59, 61, 146
evolution 9–10, 39, 43, 48, 88, 155, 159, 165, 171, 177–8, 180
existence 8–10, 36, 46, 49, 79–80, 96–7, 109–10, 122, 125, 129–31, 146, 148, 151, 163–4; autonomous 1; execrate 128; human 27
existential questionings 132
expectations 9, 36, 38, 76–7; analyst's 74; of finding one's biological mother 24; patient's 70; primeval 36; and values accepted by patients 74
experience 4–7, 11–12, 20–1, 29–30, 33, 46–50, 59–60, 65–8, 71–3, 92–5, 100, 103–5, 107–9, 114–16, 135–6, 145, 147–8, 160–5, 174–6, 178–9; of aesthetic fruition 47, 50, 54; analytical 5, 22–3, 28, 54, 62, 81, 92; atavistic 25; clinical 34–5, 90, 101, 107, 138–9, 141, 151, 157, 163; contemporary 12; emotional 1, 3–9, 11–12, 27–8, 33, 43–4, 47–8, 59–60, 64–5, 67–8, 88–9, 91–3, 107–8, 115–16, 142, 162–3, 171–3, 175–7, 179–80; existential 108; extreme 67; of internal and external relationships 60; intolerable unintegrated 48; learning 40–1; non-mentalized 107; ongoing emotional 4, 93–4, 172, 179; present 107, 118; primitive 18, 23; psycho-analytic 136; psychotic 39, 68
external objects 18–19, 48–9, 176–7
eyes 14, 22, 72, 74, 76, 110, 122–5

falsehoods 21, 91, 153, 165
falsifications 10, 38
family 51, 66–7, 70–1, 82, 87, 95, 162; adoptive 17; group 63; interviews 24; members 79; photos 24; problems 70; reunions 66; royal 63
The Family of Philip IV 87
fantasies 4, 18, 21, 48, 59–60, 67–8, 92, 114, 140–1, 171, 174
fathers 21, 24, 60–1, 63, 67, 79, 82, 93–4, 114, 118, 156–7, 161
fear 7, 28, 31, 41, 48, 76–7, 118, 121, 155, 157–8, 162; excessive 15; infantile 176; intense 29
Ferenczi 174
Ferro, A. 18, 20, 152
fertility 132, 164
fetal period 100
fetus 24
Filho, Claudio Castelo 70–83
Filho, Luiz Carlos U. Junqueira 121–33
Filho, Odilon de Mello Franco 139–43
films 30, 122, 124, 132, 162
formulations 36, 95, 106, 109–10, 115, 133, 136, 155; analyst's 36; biological 151; client's 4; conceptual 135; conversational 150; human 130; ingenious 132; mathematical 150; reactive 157; speculative 108; symbolic 116; theoretical 103; unsaturated 116; verbal 36, 147, 156
Foucault, Michel 87
Four Papers 10
freedom 131, 139, 145, 177
Frege, Gottlob 144
Freud, Sigmund 17–20, 58–61, 79, 81–2, 84, 91, 96–7, 99–100, 103–4, 112–14, 119, 123, 144–9, 151–4, 156, 171–4; and the concept of acting-out 152; concept of being wrecked by success 104; deals with the unconscious system, coining the term "psychic reality" 151; idea of the unconscious 73; and Melanie

Klein 1, 79, 93–4, 106, 129, 157, 175; proposal regarding sexuality 61; and the split 19–20, 44, 57, 68, 114, 124, 129, 152, 158; transference and the clinical work of 179n1; transference referring to the unconscious feelings of the analyst 175; transformations (in rigid motion) 109; writes about obscure areas of the mind 123; writes *Beyond the Pleasure Principle* 12n2, 113
Freud–Klein–Bion axes 91, 171
Frochtengarten, Júlio 112–19
frustration 9, 21, 67, 77, 100–1, 103, 105–6, 148, 157, 160, 164
functions 11, 15, 27–8, 33–4, 36, 39–41, 47, 57–8, 60–3, 80–1, 89, 99, 107, 116–17, 141–2, 176–9; analytical 18–20, 175–7; antagonistic psychic 125; capacity 40; developmental 116; exploratory 42; identifiable 107; linking 47; mental 20; performing administrative 84; social 152; speech 48; theory of 33, 176–7
furunculosis 121

Geulincx, Arnold 129
God 10, 22–3, 59, 61, 68–9, 129–30, 144
Goethe 146
grandparents 24
Green, André 29, 58, 151
Grid 4, 10, 29, 33–44, 68, 108, 111, 119, 176, 178, *182*; axis 35; exercises 29; importance as an instrument to develop the concept of knowledge 5; row A (beta-elements) 4
Grotstein, J. *50*, *123*
groups 6, 9, 59, 62, 74–5, 81, 101, 108–9, 155, 158, 164–5, 174; celebrations 66; encircling 164; primary 23; psychoanalytic 94, 140; social 60; supervisory 90; treatment of 174
guilt 25, 114, 145, 160

hallucinatory dimensions 1, 8–9, 104
hallucinatory states 106, 147
hallucinosis 6–8, 42, 44, 62, 64–5, 67, 92, 104, 107–9, 152, 155, 157, 159–60, 163–4
hate 47, 84, 101–2, 105, 116, 131, 144–5, 156–61, 163, 179; denial of 157; intensity of 157; realistic 163; social 165
Hegel, G.W.F. 149, 157
Heisenberg, Werner 97, 119, 166

helplessness 20–1, 77, 85, 103, 129, 153, 157
history 17, 20, 56, 60, 62, 95, 105–6, 117, 147; child's 24; modern 121; natural 164; transgenerational 25; unknown 17
Holy Spirit 10
human bisexuality 164
human fetus 24
human helplessness 20–1
human mind *see* mind
human souls 21
Hume, John 110
humility 21–2

identification 19–20, 109, 139–40, 157, 179
identity (personal) 65, 67
identity element (between two or more different mental states) 111
ideogrammatic expressions 62
image 10, 58, 69, 85–6, 122, 124, 126–7, 140; associated with language 57
impression 2–3, 6, 25, 34, 38, 40–1, 51, 75, 101, 110, 118; sensory 47; strong 84
imprisonment 39–40
In Attention and Interpretation 77
inability 63, 71, 97; to be a mother 22; body's 51; to think 29
infants 25, 36, 48, 50, 61–2, 155, 158, 160, 163; development 176; experiences 61; observation method 17; projects 176
infertility 164
innate pre-conceptions 38
instincts 60–1, 91, 107, 111, 113, 144–5, 147, 159; basic human 144; death 113, 115, 147, 154, 157; defusing of life 147, 157; dominant 160
instruments 5, 30, 34–5, 37, 40, 44, 108, 111–14, 172, 174, 179; analyst's 113; basic primary 28; new 112; quintessential 112
interpretation 35, 37, 39, 91–3, 97–8, 102, 112–17, 119, 139, 141, 146, 148, 154, 159, 174–5; analyst's 99, 130; art of 113; classic 54; couching 145; psychoanalytic 22–3, 35, 163
intimacy 56, 85, 94–5, 129
intolerance 73, 101, 154, 157
intra-sessions 158, 160
intuition 20, 39–40, 50, 96, 104, 107–8, 116, 135, 141, 160, 176
investigation 5, 15, 35, 85, 96–7, 116–17, 123; process 84; psychoanalytic 5, 61; qualitative 85

The Italian Seminars 10, 93

jokes of daily life 162, 171
Joseph, Betty 172, 175
Joyce, James 126, 132
judgment 79, 145; automatic 28; moral 164

Kant, Immanuel 35, 96, 110, 115, 129, 147, 149, 151, 157; concept of ultimate reality 177; describes the sequence of stages between something that is unknowable and something that is representable by understanding 110; examines the process of knowledge 110
Keaton, Buster 132n3
Keats, George 123, 133n4
Kiefer, Anselm 89
Kirschbaum, Isaias 96–102
Klee, Paul 89
Klein, Melanie 17, 62, 91, 101, 147, 151, 171, 174, 176, 179; death 17; descriptions of attacks on the breast 163; metapsychology 18; notion of projective identification 175; notion that countertransference, sensu stricto, refers to the unconscious feelings of the analyst 175; points to the existence of a precariously functioning primitive ego 114; states that object relations exist from early life 114
Kleinian 67, 172, 174; concept of projective identification 176; theories 62, 103–4, 107, 115; traditions 114; transformations (projective transformations) 109
knowledge 4–10, 43–4, 46–7, 49–50, 53, 60–2, 92, 102–3, 114–16, 142, 144, 148–9, 153, 155, 177–9; accessible 106; acquired 4; developing 6; fragmented 155; intuitive 60; new 88; private 157; psychic 123; psychoanalytic 109–10; rational 54, 149; refined 105; transformations in 7–8, 10, 93, 106, 109, 177
Korbivcher, Celia Fix 46–55
Kublai Khan 84

language 10, 28, 46–7, 50, 53, 57, 81, 126, 175, 179; of achievement 9, 50, 55, 79; apophatic 123; colloquial 10, 141; literary 57; metaphorical 28; modern Western 57; non-verbal 50; psychoanalytic 110; scientific 24; truthful 148; verbal 14, 50, 85

Language and the Schizophrenic 175
Las Meninas 87
learning 1, 3–5, 7–9, 11–12, 24–5, 33, 35, 37, 39–41, 43, 47–9, 92–3, 116–17, 175–6, 178–9; experience 40–1; memorized 40
Learning from Experience, A Theory of Thinking and Elements of Psychoanalysis 85, 92
Lima, Luiz Tenório Oliveira 135–8
Longman, José 83
loss 15, 21–2, 29, 31, 67, 95, 159, 165; momentary 65; significant 15; total 164; traumatic 94
Loureiro, Stela Maris Garcia 171–80
love 4, 23–4, 47, 101–2, 116, 131, 136, 144–5, 156–9, 161–3, 165; concomitant 105; drive following the direction of the ego 101; emotions 157; extracting 159; falling in 61; mimicking 163; mutual 159; out-loves 157; precursor of 157, 160; provoking 163; real 157, 159, 162–3; submissive 6; violence overwhelming hate 157; violent 159
lovers 63, 69, 136, 158
loving intentions 158

Mannoni, Octave 157
Marco Polo 84
medication 76, 82
Meltzer, D. 20, 110n1
A Memoir of the Future (trilogy) 18, 23–5, 83, 121, 132, 172, 175, 178
memory 9, 15, 20, 33–4, 40, 88, 91, 113–14, 123, 129–30, 132
Meninas 88–9
mental 22, 24, 28, 60, 67, 177; activities 8, 21; death 29; detoxification 28; disasters 29, 41; evolution 39; growth 21, 29, 33, 47, 94; inanition 73; life 3, 9, 28, 36, 40, 65, 67, 105, 136; liquefaction 133; nutrition 28; pain 100–1, 135, 137; phenomena 48, 107, 119, 177; states 15, 48, 50, 54, 100, 103, 107–8, 115, 174
mind: degenerate 81; and the hallucinatory facet of the human 63; multidimensional 108; transformations improving perspective on the human 103
Minoan-Mycenaean civilization 69n7
Minus (notation) 10, 144–5, 147, 149–57, 159, 161, 163–6; breast 155; container-contained 155, 164; contrapuntal 166;

destructive 165; knowledge 61, 106–7; psychoanalysis 154; total character 136
models 5–6, 9, 14–15, 19–20, 60–1, 84, 87, 96–8, 101, 103, 105–6, 110, 112, 151, 176–7; aesthetic 88; analog 27; artistic 110; conceptual 101; developmental 117; inspirational 19; medical 27, 75, 95; multidimensional 1; myth-based 60; neurotic/psychotic 18; operative 130; relational 100; static 108; structural 1; theoretical-psychoanalytical 15; traditional 109
modes 6, 50, 97–8, 114, 116, 144, 150, 165
Mona Lisa 165
Money-Kyrle, Roger 151, 174–5
morals 153, 155
mothers 21–2, 24, 50, 60–4, 67, 69, 71, 79, 82, 93–4, 118, 124, 156–7, 160–2; adoptive 21, 24; and the baby-relationship 176; biological 21, 24; communication 50; mature 21; young 71
movies 127, 162
Muslims 162
mystical dimensions 93
mystics 9, 62, 139; neoplatonic 123; nihilistic 62
myths 4–5, 22, 27, 35–6, 38–9, 43, 56, 58–61, 63, 65, 68, 101–2; indigenous 58; innumerable 166; of Oedipus 56, 60–1; personal 35, 59; in psychoanalysis 56–7, 59, 61, 63, 65, 67

narcissism 101, 179
"negative capability" (concept) 55
neuroses 5, 18, 60, 78, 96, 108, 146, 172
neurotic situations 67, 109, 136
New York Times 131
newborn babies 75, 77, 131, 165
Nobel Prize 97, 121
non-psychotic: personality 148, 154, 162; portions of the mind 98

observations 3, 5, 20, 22, 34–5, 43, 87–8, 94, 97, 101, 104, 106–7, 140–1, 173–4, 176–7; analyst's 7, 18, 87; clinical 20, 101, 144; psychoanalytic 106, 171–2
Oedipal 35, 80, 162, 178; condition 80; myth 35; nucleus 178; stimulus 162
Oedipus 6, 12, 31, 36, 56, 58, 60–3, 106, 114, 140, 146; blindness 62; dissuading 35n2; myth 58, 60, 62, 67–8; myth 67; tragedy 78

Oedipus at Colonus 60
Oedipus Rex 60
omnipotence 20, 115, 145, 161
omniscience 20, 115, 145, 161
opposite sex 79

pain 18–19, 21, 23, 43, 53, 64, 66–8, 70–3, 94–5, 129, 136; evacuating 129; psychic 129; unnecessary 160; *see also* mental pain
paintings 87, 89, 110
Pakula, Alan 162
palindrome 53
panic syndromes 27, 29, 31, 75–7
paradoxes 99, 101, 146–9, 153–4, 156–7
paradoxical 46, 49, 152, 166; activities 154; balance 166; combination 104; terms 151
paranoid-schizoid 65, 106, 145–7, 149, 157, 164, 171–2, 179–80
parents 58, 60–1, 63, 65, 67, 75–6, 78–9; adoptive 78; catastrophic changes in the 25; real 61; requesting interviews 24; seeking psychoanalytic help 24
passion 20, 22–3, 35, 39, 43, 102, 129, 133, 136, 143, 154
passive sex 67
passive sexual intercourse 67
patients 7, 17–18, 21–3, 28–9, 36–7, 46–51, 53–4, 65–7, 70–83, 98–102, 112–19, 136–7, 141–2, 145–6, 151–5, 158–60, 163, 172–9; adopted 17; autonomy 81; bypassing 152; collaborative 74; disturbed 40; influence of 173; life 73, 83; lying 20; misapprehending 145; neurotic 98, 171; observed 152; prospective 80; schizophrenic 172
Paul (St Paul) 25, 123
Pentheus 64, 67, 69
perception 40–1, 44, 76, 80, 89, 92, 130, 133, 156, 164, 171–2, 178; cognitive 57; cultural 60; distortions of 178; endopsychic 59; external 122; realistic 72; ultra-sensory 127
personal 19–20, 23–4, 28–30, 35, 40–1, 47–9, 61–8, 78, 100–2, 106–7, 109–10, 115–16, 122, 132–3, 139–42, 148, 153–5, 162–6, 176–7; analysis 89, 141, 173; catastrophe 133; communication 47; educational background 116; impoverishment 68; irresponsibility 146; problems 3

personality 28–9, 48–9, 61, 63, 68, 98, 101–2, 107, 109, 130, 163, 165–6, 177; analyst's 19, 176; attack 177; baby's 177; child's 78; client's 6; growth 104; human 62, 64; non-psychotic 148, 154, 162; persecuted 132; schizoid 122; unknown 153
perspective 14, 29, 43, 56, 59, 72, 80, 99–100, 103, 107–8, 159–60; changes 43; new 23, 33; reversed 98–9
phantasies 130, 135, 161, 164
phenomena 8, 27, 35, 39, 48–9, 96–8, 129, 148, 155–7, 171, 179; clinical 113; depressive 145; macroscopic 96; neurotic 172; observed 96, 98; psychiatric 178; psychic 85, 100, 102, 177; unintegrated 48
Philips, Frank 90n2, 90
phylogenetic pre-conceptions 106
physicians 12, 173
Picasso, Pablo 84, 87–9, 127
Picasso Museum 84, 87
the place of the real external object in the construction of the psyche *19*
Plato 121, 129, 148–9
Pope Julius II 30
pre-conceptions 36n4, 36, 38–9, 41–2, 106, 147; innate 38
pre-verbal infants 50
predictability 96
profound drowsiness 37–9
projections 40–1, 91–2, 114, 172, 174, 177
projective identification 6–7, 24, 34, 92, 106–7, 135, 160, 163–4, 171, 174–6, 179; excessive 109; notion of 171–2, 174; pathological 178–9; powerful 41; primitive 160; realistic 109
projective transformations 6–7, 48, 53, 92, 107, 109, 178
PS *see* paranoid-schizoid
psychiatrists 82
psychic 12, 19, 62, 97, 127, 177; apparatus 145; changes 53, 58, 178–9; development 99–100, 177; life 25, 59–60, 65, 177; mechanisms 147, 154; quality 4–5, 34, 127, 156
psychic reality 56, 58–60, 63, 65, 80, 151, 176; apprehending 123; immaterial 151; modifying 100; possible 25
psycho-analysts 142, 173
psychoanalysis 1, 17–20, 33–4, 40, 44, 48–50, 62, 76–85, 89, 96–7, 101–3, 105–9, 111–13, 115, 117, 146–7, 149–50, 153, 172–4, 176–7; addressing 96; apprehending 139, 141; contemporary 17, 19, 21, 23, 142, 150, 178; developing 96; elements of 33, 35, 37–9, 43–4, 92, 99, 176, 179; endowing 176; knowing about 49; modern 54; myths in 56–7, 59, 61, 63, 65, 67; prefiguring 148; replacing 116
psychoanalysts 23–4, 59–61, 73, 75, 78, 81–3, 94, 97–100, 102–3, 110, 112, 119, 121–3
psychoanalytic 4–5, 15, 17–20, 22–4, 33–5, 37–9, 43–4, 49, 67–8, 73, 75–6, 81–4, 93–6, 99, 101–10, 139–40, 145–8, 152–4, 171–2, 176–9; assessment 24, 145; games 37–8, 44; ideas 1; intuition 51, 68; objects 18, 22, 35, 37, 39, 43, 96, 101–2, 140, 179; practice 35, 75; principles 99; process 24, 99, 105; relationships 4, 15, 171; respectability 49; sessions 59, 87, 154, 156; theories 20, 68, 73, 81, 99, 103–4, 106–8, 116, 146; thinking 17, 95, 104, 107, 110; vertex 73, 75, 82, 147–8, 152
psychology 12, 54, 59
psychotic 18, 28, 39–41, 67, 74, 109, 130, 136, 165, 174–5, 178; anxiety 132; borderline 136; disorders 172; mechanisms 165; patients 163; personality 40–1, 144, 154, 164–5; phenomena 172; processes 34; situations 5; traits 162; transference 172

quality 23, 35, 39, 64, 84–5, 88–9, 96, 115, 119, 160; moral 159; of presence in sessions 87; psychic 4–5, 34, 127, 156; super-ego 159; unconscious 127
quasi-mathematical signs 144–5
quasi-perennial mania 157

reactions 1, 7, 37, 43, 52, 70, 76–7, 79, 82, 85, 142, 174; client's 7; emotional 174; natural 76; negative therapeutic 113, 142; patient's 43, 100; self-defensive 163; therapeutic 142; unconscious 174; violent 52, 82
recognition 44, 103, 107, 115, 124; establishment's 83; obscure 59
regressive mechanisms 140
relationships 3–4, 6, 14, 17–19, 42–3, 47–9, 61–2, 87–8, 92–3, 95, 112–14, 116, 141–2, 160–1, 179; analytical 18,

22, 91–4, 107, 145, 174, 176, 179; causal 108; commensal 154; experiential 119; external 60; familial 66; idealized 65; individual's 101; intense 35; parasitical 147, 159; psychoanalytic 4, 15, 171; sado-masochistic 125; sexual 67; transferential 91, 113
relatives 70, 161
religion 75, 129; classes of 137; persons 135; positivist 154; preaching 80
religions, modern 59
religious orders 79
repercussions 79, 171
representations 18, 47, 58, 92, 109–10, 114, 119; acquired 46; algebraic 109; denuded 155; mental 49; pictorial 62; symbolic 47
resistance 64, 91, 112, 171; to the analyst's attempts at interpretation 7; natural 68
resources 28, 75, 77, 79, 83, 104, 106, 179; inner 28; powerful 130; technical 175; unevolved 79
reverie 4, 20, 27–8, 33–4, 36, 47, 61, 122, 140–1, 160; grandparental 25; maternal 19, 25, 176–7; parental 25
reversible perspectives (theory) 98–9, 101, 130
revolutions 49, 62, 165, 171
Rezze, Cecil José 1–12, 33–44
rhetoric 149
Ricks, Christopher 125–6
rigid motion transformations 6–7, 44, 48, 92, 94, 107, 109, 178
risks 63, 153, 158
Roazen, Paul 119
Roman Catholic Church 149
Rosenfeld, Eva 119

sadism 113–14, 146, 158
sadness 21, 72, 77
Salomé, Lou Andreas 123
Sandler, Paulo Cesar 144–66
Sapienza, Antonio 27–31
Sapienza University, Rome 101
Sartre, Jean-Paul 137
SBPSP *see* Sociedade Brasileira de Psicanálise de São Paulo
schizophrenia 40–1
schools 17, 24, 85, 95, 140
science 18–19, 59, 96, 109, 129–30, 142, 147, 149–50; false 154; primitive 149; Western 96

scientific activity 96–7, 142
scientific deductive system 37, 39, 142
scientific dimensions 109
scientific research 101, 104, 156
scientists 96–7, 135, 139, 153
Second Thoughts 44n6
Segal, Hanna 103, 110, 115, 151
self 4, 11, 17, 28–9, 66, 124, 127, 130, 132, 171–2, 178; annihilation 130; containment 160; deception 153; destruction 23; devitalized 28; knowledge 18, 100; observation 127; respect 23, 81; righteousness 164–5
seminars 37, 141
sensations 38, 61, 87, 105, 152; bodily 37; and corporeal manifestations 50; which have not acquired representation 46
sense-impressions 5, 12, 22, 33–4, 36, 40, 98, 133
sense organs 35, 127, 177
sessions 3–8, 20, 28–30, 37–8, 46–7, 51–3, 60, 67–8, 84–5, 87–9, 93–4, 98, 100, 114–15, 117–19, 152–3; analytic 145, 147, 159; clinical 176; evening 66; first 65
sex 67, 79, 118
sexual activity 12, 66, 164
sexual intercourse 67
sexuality 61, 67, 132
Shakespeare, William 10, 122, 146, 152
Sheehan, Paul 128, 133
Sistine Chapel 30
skills 71, 161
skin 20, 24, 48
sleep 33, 79
socialism 101, 179
Sociedade Brasileira de Psicanálise de São Paulo 82–3
sociopathic features 157
Socrates 80–1, 149
"Solomon and the Witch" 136
Sophists 149
Sophocles 60
space 3, 14, 31, 38, 43, 48, 54, 93–4, 142, 151; clinical 179; external 48; interior 131; mental 62; mythical 57; time of participants 38, 150
splits 20, 44, 57, 114, 124, 129, 146, 149, 152, 158–9, 164; as described by Freud in "Fetishism" 20; as described by Melanie Klein 101; Kleinian theory of 107; theoretical 19

St. John's Gospel 10
St. Paul 149
state 8–9, 11, 29–30, 36, 38–9, 42, 46–8, 64, 70, 73–8, 98, 116–17, 130–1, 136, 177–8; disturbed 110; extreme 126; patient's 116; triumphant 147
stem cells 103
stimuli 24, 56, 76, 105, 161, 177; first initial 145; inner 33; sensory 34
Strachey, James 12n2
stresses 28, 72, 92, 121, 123, 172
superego 31, 34, 40, 71, 114; ego-destructive 28, 31; murderous 145, 157
superiority 159, 161–3, 165; of the method of hallucinosis over the analytic method 155; moral 154–5, 159; of patients to the analysts 154
support 28, 54, 109, 153; body 54; mental nutrition 31; moral 70; psychotherapy 78
symptoms 73, 75, 94–5, 136, 171; mental 130; physical 94
synthesis 14, 126, 142, 148–9; aesthetic 126; creative 142; transcendent 149

tachycardia 121
Talamo, Parthenope Bion 151
Taming Wild Thoughts 10, 38, 44
Tavistock Clinic 121, 133n7
Texts for Nothing 128
Thales of Miletus 98
Thebes 35, 61, 63–4, 69
theory 20, 33, 35–6, 38, 40–1, 91–2, 96–8, 100, 103–4, 107–10, 115–17, 140–1, 149–51, 171, 176–8; classic dream 36; interlinked 144; of observation 92, 94, 106, 177; observational 48, 105, 176; psychoanalytical 106, 110; psychotic 41; quantum 109; scientific 39, 43; structural 107; and techniques of contemporary psychoanalysis 17; of thinking 109, 151, 172, 176
thinking 9, 11–12, 28, 40, 42, 47, 92, 103–4, 106–10, 116, 118, 130–1, 151–2; capacity 177; logical 105; mechanics of 144; processes 151; psychoanalytical 103; scientific 108; a theory of 176
Thompson, Geoffrey 121
threats 29, 31, 33, 36, 48–9, 54, 128
tolerance 23, 101, 104–6, 148, 166; binocular 157; of paradoxes 156
Tower of Babel 35, 61, 68

transcendent synthesis 149
transference 5, 7–8, 12, 17, 22–3, 91–4, 107, 112–14, 159–60, 171–5, 177, 179–80; classical 172; Freudian 171, 178; mechanism 17; negative 112; notion of 171–2; positive 113; theory of 6, 91–4, 107; unanalyzed 175
transferential relationships 91, 113
transformations 1, 5–9, 23, 25, 36, 38, 44, 47–50, 53–4, 68, 91–4, 103–11, 115, 129–30, 176–9; autistic 48; Bionian 109; final 108; Freudian 109; groups of 48, 92, 108–9, 111; in hallucinosis 7–8, 30, 42, 48, 53, 62, 64, 104, 107, 109, 155; Kleinian 109; non-integrated 54; notion of 50, 176; ongoing 6, 12; permeating psychoanalytic thinking 104; phenomenal 151; possible 7; process 177, 179; psychic 110; psychoanalytic theory of 109–10; rigid motion 6–7, 44, 48, 92, 94, 107, 109, 178; theory of 48, 94, 103–6, 108–10, 115, 171, 177; from transference to emotional experience in 173; transference to emotional experience in 175, 177, 179; unintegrated 48–9, 54; vicissitudes of 103, 105, 107, 109
transvestites 66–7
traumatic events 112
traumatic fracture between prenatal and postnatal life 17
traumatic suffering 29, 97
trust 94–5, 103–4, 122
Trustin, F. 18, 48
truth 7–8, 20–3, 37, 43–4, 77–9, 81, 129–30, 135, 141–2, 151, 153–6, 165; absolute 21–2, 49, 147, 165, 178; human 157, 166; language of 148; possible 17, 21, 23, 25; psychic 58, 63, 78; real 23; sense of 157, 165; ultimate 18, 124, 149

ultimate reality 23, 25, 49, 110, 129, 132, 145–6, 177–8
uncertainties 3, 19–20, 22, 50, 55, 97, 100, 102, 104, 109, 126; outer cosmic 49; principles 22, 97, 166
unconscious conflicts 6
unconscious dimensions 8
unconscious fantasies 18
unconscious feelings 173, 175
unconscious system 151–2, 166
untruth carriers 145, 153

values 2–3, 15, 17, 30, 74–5, 81–2, 85, 89, 139, 154; counterpunctual 151; culture's 59; judgmental 145; moral 74, 164; old-fashioned 74; potential 66; pre-established 81
Velázquez, Diego 87–9
vertex 7, 58, 63, 72, 75, 78, 80, 106, 109, 155–6, 158, 177, 179–80; analytical function's 177; biological 148, 164; didactic 80; individual 156; musical 148; observational 107; pedagogical 80; psychoanalytic 73, 75, 82, 147–8, 152
vignettes 17, 37, 161
violence 23, 29, 35, 81, 130, 156–8, 165; degenerate stuporous 164; of love overwhelming hate 157; moralistic 28; primitive 29; reactions to 52, 82
vision 24, 42, 104, 106, 122–3, 125, 127, 132–3, 135; binocular 19, 124–5, 127, 130, 132–3, 152; external 122; internal 122; monocular 124–5, 132; patient's 99; skeptical 128; stereoscopic 127

Williams, Meg Harris 28, 31
wives 2–7, 63, 65–6, 74, 88, 161–2
womb 25, 136
women 42, 57, 64, 67, 71, 90, 124–5; disturbed 90; young 125
words 2–3, 10, 40, 42–3, 50, 52–4, 69, 85–7, 89, 110, 112, 126–8, 141, 150, 175–6; analyst's 42–3, 53; binocular 126; client's 41; dying 125; first 5; hate 145; manipulating 85; monocular 126; patient's 42; proffering 141; spoken 141; synthetic 126
World War II 172

Yãnomam Indians 56–8

Zeus 58, 64

Printed in the United States
by Baker & Taylor Publisher Services